WRITING

JAVA

APPLETS

WRITING JAVA APPLETS

John Rodley

CORIOLIS GROUP BOOKS

Publisher	*Keith Weiskamp*
Editor	*Scott Palmer*
Proofreader	*Diane Green Cook*
Cover Design	*Gary Smith*
Interior Design	*Bradley O. Grannis*
Layout Production	*Kim Eoff*
Indexer	*Caroline Parks*

The Coriolis Group
7339 E. Acoma Drive, Suite 7
Scottsdale, AZ 85260
Phone: (602) 483-0192
Fax: (602) 483-0193
Web address: www.coriolis.com

ISBN 1-883577-78-0 : $39.99

Printed in the United States of America

10 9 8 7 6 5 4 3 2 1

This book is dedicated to Miss Beggi, who made me promise.

Contents

Introduction

I've worked in software for a long time now, long enough to know that today's software sensation is tomorrow's trivia question. Thus, I don't change tools very often. When Java first came on the scene, I took a look at it, but only as an academic exercise. As I became more familiar with it (the hard way, by writing code), it quickly became clear that this was not a flash in the pan. Though I've always been neutral in the compu-linguistic holy wars, I found myself telling people "this thing is going to be big." I began writing seriously with it, and eventually developed the idea for the Agent system that forms the core example of this book.

The title of this book—*Writing Java Applets*—is technically correct, but a little misleading. The fact is that everything you'll learn about applets applies equally well to creating stand alone Java applications. The focus here is on learning to write applets, but stand alone application designers can learn a lot from it too.

In the first two chapters, we cover why Java was produced, and how the language is structured. In Chapter 3, we introduce our example application, the Agent system, which harnesses Java's unique power to create a new type of application. In Chapter 4, we talk about the **Applet** class and the **AppletContext** interface, the two sides of the conversation between our running applet, and the browser it runs in. Chapter 5, perhaps the key chapter in the whole book, details how to create compelling applet user interfaces with Java's Abstract Window Toolkit. Chapter 6 takes you through the details of Java's multithreading. Chapter 7 covers Internet communication with Java by creating a number of interesting network-aware applets. Chapter 8 deals with exceptions. Chapter 9 shows you how to implement a class loader, the same mechanism a browser uses to load an applet. And finally, in Chapter 10, we deal with the sticky subject of security—the underlying mechanism and how it's implemented in current browsers.

When you're finished with this book, not only will you know how to create compelling applets, but you'll also have an idea of how to create standalone applications, and you'll understand just where applets fit in the world of computing objects.

Throughout the book, I make a number of observations that assume the reader has some familiarity with C and C++. These observations are attempts to relate

Java to the languages that have preceded it, and from which it has sprung. To get the full benefit of this book, I strongly recommend that you have a basic knowledge of Java—or at least, a little background in C/C++ — is strongly recommended. If you need more tutorial information about the Java language and development tools, take a look at the books *Java Programming EXplorer* (Coriolis Group Books, 1996) or *The Java Programming Language* (Coriolis Group Books, 1996).

I wrote all the examples in this book using an Ether net/TCP-IP network of Windows NT machines: 486DX-33s and 75 MHz Pentiums with 16 MB RAM and one-gigabyte hard disks. To use the examples in this book, you need:

1. At least one Java-capable machine (currently that would mean a computer running under Solaris, Windows 95, Windows NT, the Macintosh operating system, or IBM's OS/2). You also need a CD-ROM drive. The list of Java-capable machines expands every day.

2. A Java-capable browser (Netscape 2.0 or HotJava). In a pinch, the AppleTviewer that comes with the JDK will also do for some of the examples.

3. The Java Development Kit (JDK) from Sun Microsystems.

4. Optionally, you could use An Internet connection. Although not a requirement, an Internet connection that would enable you to connect to Agent Servers out on the Net.

Most of the examples have been tested with NT and Solaris, but trying to test with all operating systems was not possible, and, in theory, Java's platfor m independence should make it unnecessary. (In theory, anyway.) Ther e will undoubtedly be cases wher e a particular example will not run corr ectly in a particular configuration. If you have a pr oblem with any example code, don't hesitate to email me.

I'm committed to supporting this book and its r eaders. I'm always available at my email addr ess john.rodley@channel1.com, as well as thr ough my Web site (: http://www.channel1.com/users/ajrodley), and thr ough the Coriolis Gr oup Web site: (http://www.coriolis.com). Heaven forbid that ther e should be any bugs in the example code, but if any do sur face, the fixes will be posted on both Web pages for easy downloading.

Acknowledgments

This book would not have been possible without the support and encouragement of a number of people. My thanks go out to:

Dennis Foley of BBN, who turned me on to Java.

Keith Weiskamp and Scott Palmer of The Coriolis Group, who made me finish what I started.

Arthur van Hoff and all the people on the Java development team. The volume, timeliness, and enthusiasm of the support they've given Java developers via the mailing lists has been a major factor in Java's success. Without that support, this book would not exist.

Jon Erickson, who published my earliest Java ravings in *Doctor Dobb's Journal* and hooked me up with The Coriolis Group. *DDJ*, as current and useful as ever, was an early and enthusiastic adopter of Java.

Katie and Dudley and the people of newf-l, who reminded me that this book isn't nearly as important as eating, sleeping, shedding, playing in the snow, and going for walks.

My wife—the lovely, and talented, Heather Clark.

Chapter 1

The Java Revolution

The Java Revolution

Java is cool, but why? Take a look at the key features, and judge for yourself.

In its short existence, Java has generated more excitement and more wild speculation than all the other programming languages put together. Some of that is simple hype, a result of the fact that the software industry is now a very big business, but much of it is quite real. Java is a revolutionary force.

Over the course of this book, we'll develop a large application called the *Agent system*. The Agent system will consist of a small, standalone Java program and a bunch of Java applets. The application will also include a number of smaller Java applets to demonstrate particular features of the language. Through the Agent system, I'll try not only to illustrate Java programming techniques, but also to provide you with a glimpse of the new classes of applets and applications that you can write using Java.

Our Agent system will allow Web users to dispatch a program (called an *agent*) to run on each machine in a network of Internet-connected machines and then return its results via the Web. This agent is a Java class. We'll develop a couple of basic agents to do things like finding files, but the power of the system, like the power of Java, is that by using the base **Agent** class, users can write their own agents to do things limited only by their imagination. The base **Agent** class and the standalone agent server deal entirely with the problem of distributing the agent throughout the network.

The Agent system provides a good introduction to Java programming because it utilizes three varieties of Java classes: applets, standalone applications, and classes that can function in either applet or standalone mode. Over the course of developing these classes, we'll get to see the possibilities and limitations of each.

that can function in either applet or standalone mode. Over the course of developing these classes, we'll get to see the possibilities and limitations of each.

But first, let's define what we mean by the term *applet*. An applet is a small program that runs within another, larger, host program, whose purpose is usually to enhance the functionality of the host program and which could not exist without the host program. In Java's case, a Java applet enhances the functionality of a Web browser. A browser can display text, but add an applet and you can make that text bounce around the screen like a ping-pong ball. That's all we really mean when we talk about an applet—a program that runs within a Web browser.

And so, without any further ado, let's look at an applet. Listing 1.1 shows a simple example.

Listing 1.1   hello.java Applet

```
package chap1;

import java.awt.Graphics;
import java.awt.*;
import java.applet.Applet;

public class ch1_fig1 extends Applet {

public void paint(Graphics g) {
   g.drawString( "Hello world", 20, 50 );
   }
}
```

Pretty exciting, eh? We'll get into more details about specific programming techniques later in the book, but the power of that simple nine-line program shows

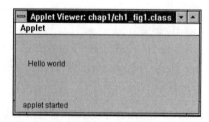

Figure 1.1
hello.Java running in Sun's appletviewer.

you what's possible. For now, let's take a quick look at what makes Java useful in the first place.

We're Talking Applet Programming

One reminder: This book is about Java applet programming, *not* about Java programming in general. If you don't have at least a basic grasp of the Java language, development tools, and their associated techniques, it will be hard for you to follow the discussion in this book.

If you need a good introduction to Java, you (really) can't do better than *The Java Programming EXplorer* by Neil Bartlett, Steve Simkin, and Alex Leslie (Coriolis Group Books, 1996), all of whom are leaders in the Java programming community. For a good Java language reference, see *The Java Programming Language* by Anthony Potts and David Friedel (Coriolis Group Books, 1996).

The Power of the Concept

When people talk about Java, it's not always clear what they're talking about, because Java is not just a language. Java is both a language and a set of class libraries. Much, if not most, of the power of Java comes from these class libraries which, in Java, are known as packages. In that sense, Java is comparable to something like Microsoft Visual C++ with Foundation Classes or Borland C++ with its ObjectWindows Library (OWL). Figure 1.2 shows the package hierarchy for Java.

Java's revolutionary potential is not due to a single feature of the language but to a combination of four features: *network awareness*, *portability*, *security*, and *object orientation*. Some of these features are inherent in the language, while others are derived from the class libraries. These features make possible a whole range of applications that we could only dream of before Java. Let's examine these features in more detail.

Network Awareness

Java's tight integration with the Internet in general—and with the World Wide Web in particular—is the main force driving its explosive growth. Network awareness, as we use the term here, simply means that every provision has been made

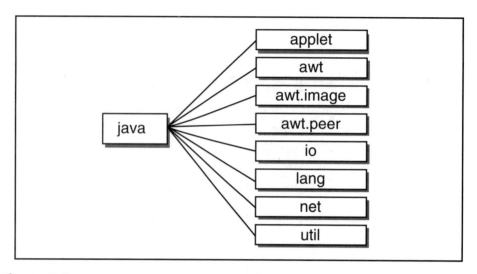

Figure 1.2

The Java package hierarchy.

to allow Java applications to incorporate network capability. For the Internet, this amounts to providing a low-level socket interface.

The Internet is populated by a bunch of servers, each of which performs a particular function, such as Telnet, FTP, or handling operations on the Web. Each of these servers runs on a machine, listening to a port and waiting for a client to connect. Both client and server connect to the network at the lowest level via a socket interface. In Java, for instance, a server program running on mymachine.com can open a socket and accept calls on it with two lines of code, as shown in the following snippet:

```
ServerSocket MyServerSock = new ServerSocket( 1037 );
Socket s = MyServerSock.accept();
```

A client can then connect to mymachine.com with the one line of code shown here:

```
Socket MyClientSocket = new Socket( "mymachine.com", 1037 );
```

When those two calls return, the two machines are connected and can read and/or write to that connection.

Dealing with network I/O at the socket level, while necessary for some applications, can be very tedious, requiring implementation of whatever protocol you intend to use. Fortunately, you can often bypass this step because Java provides higher-level classes for such cases. The example in Listing 1.2 manages to download an HTML file, while avoiding the explicit use of sockets entirely.

Listing 1.2 Downloading an HTML File

```
public class DLHTMLFile extends Applet {
public void start() {
    try {
    URL u = new URL("http://www.channel1.com/users/ajrodley/index.html");
    System.out.println( "u="+u );
        try {
        URLConnection uc = u.openConnection();
        InputStream is = uc.getInputStream();
        byte b[] = new byte[is.available()];
        is.read( b );
        System.out.println( "received byte array "+new String(b,0));
        } catch( IOException e ) {System.out.println( "ioex "+e);}
    } catch( MalformedURLException e1 ) {System.out.println( "mfuex "+e1);}
}
}
```

In this example, Java's **URLConnection** class handles connecting to the http daemon, which serves HTML files at www.channel1.com. The class finds the file we want at that server and creates a byte stream that we can read from that file.

The **InputStream** handles the rest. What you see when you run this applet is the text of my home page printing to the standard output device (or Java console in Netscape).

The messages that the client and server exchange once they connect via sockets is what Java refers to as *content*. Examples of content include the GIF and JPG graphics formats and the HTML document format. The Java class that deals with a particular type of content is known as a *content handler*.

Suppose that we want to display a GIF file on the screen. What we want to end up with in memory is a Java **Image** object. The process of getting that image in memory has three levels:

- The socket connection
- A stream of GIF-formatted bytes (content) flowing over that connection
- An **Image** object created from that GIF-formatted byte stream (by a content handler)

We've seen how Java gives you easy control over the first two levels, but it's the last step that is the payoff. For business reasons, Sun has decided *not* to give coders direct access to their image, FTP, and HTML content handlers, although the image handlers are useable via the **Applet** class. This means that content handlers will be one area where Netscape and other browsers can provide extra value, for which, presumably, users will be willing to pay.

Even with that caveat, Java has taken us a long way toward complete network connectivity. And even though its content handlers are inaccessible, Java does provide a platform on which to build your own content handlers.

Java's Net-centricity is embodied in the java.net and java.applet packages (class libraries). The java.net package supplies the basic classes for dealing with URLs and TCP/IP sockets, and java.applet provides Java's link to the Web, via the **Applet** class—a class that allows an application to appear in the middle of an HTML document when that document is viewed with a Web browser.

The URLs and sockets of java.net are fine building blocks, but it is the concept of embedding programs (applets) within HTML documents that makes Java a revolutionary force. A browsed Web document is a fairly static item. The text just sits there while the user browses through it. Java applets, on the other hand, are active items. A Web page with applets can change according to any of a wide variety of stimuli. These stimuli can come directly from the user, from other applets or processes on the same workstation, or from some process out on the Net. They can come from anywhere, and in a manner that is invisible and/or indecipherable to the user.

Thus, with applets, you can create a Web page that behaves more like the user interface of a traditional application rather than like a regular old HTML page. And if you can get the functionality of a traditional application via a Web page, why buy traditional applications?

The Internet has physically connected a huge number of machines. Yet, in many cases, their only connection to each other are the happy faces they display via HTML. With Java, these machines can work together rather than just smiling stupidly at one another. Net-connected machines now have a language by which they can both request and *provide* services.

Java Compared to HTML

HTML is a language and Web browsers are essentially HTML interpreters. HTML's sole purpose, however, is to describe static text documents. A browser is an intelligent "book," with each HTML document serving as an intelligent page. That is HTML's limitation: Its central metaphor is "a book of pages," and there are only so many things you can make a book do. Java uses an entirely different metaphor: the abstract CPU known as the *Java Virtual Machine* (JVM).

The JVM is a specification that describes the instruction set for an abstract CPU. Every CPU—80486, Pentium, PowerPC—has such a specification. An actual CPU implements that specification in hardware, so you end up with a chip that understands instructions from that instruction set.

There is no physical CPU that understands the JVM instruction set. Instead, Java relies on an interpreter to translate the JVM instructions into instructions that the local CPU understands. Thus, for every different CPU and operating system, there is a different Java interpreter.

Portability

Java is a portable language. It achieves this portability by taking a different approach from that taken by current C and C++ development packages. In C, under DOS, you might write a source file called hello.c that looks like this:

```
int main()
    {
    printf( "hello world\n" );
    }
```

The C compiler turns that file into another file, "hello.exe" that is essentially a stream of instructions from the 80386 instruction set. In fact, if you disassemble hello.exe, you see a stream of 386 instructions like those shown in the following code snippet:

```
PUSH SP
MOV BP, SP
...
RET
```

If you compile the same program on a computer that uses a Motorola 68000 chip as its CPU, hello.exe would contain a different stream of instructions— ones that correspond to the 68000's instruction set. When you want to run hello.exe, the operating system simply feeds the instruction stream directly to the CPU. (I realize that this example is simplified, but it makes the point.)

This approach is very efficient, but it has one drawback: Because different computers use different instruction sets, a compiled program usually will run only on the machine for which it was compiled.

The Internet, however, connects computers of many different types. Therefore, a Java program must be able to run on all (or at least most) of those computer types. The traditional approach of compiling directly to machine code doesn't get the job done.

Java takes a different approach. Instead of translating the Java source code directly into the instruction set of a particular hardware CPU, the Java compiler translates it into a *bytecode file*. This bytecode file contains a stream of instructions from the instruction set of an imaginary CPU known as the JVM (for more information on the JVM, see the Java Note on page 11. These bytecodes *cannot* be fed directly to any real CPU, because no real CPU understands them. Instead, a Java interpreter translates those bytecodes into instructions that the real CPU understands.

The Java equivalent of hello.c, hello.java, goes through the steps shown in Listings 1.3 through 1.5. Listing 1.3 shows the Java source code file. Listing 1.4 shows the "compiled" Java file, which consists of bytecodes—machine instructions for the Java virtual machine. Finally, Listing 1.5 shows how the Java interpreter translates the code from Listing 1.4 into instructions for an actual, physical CPU. (Listings 1.4 and 1.5, by the way, are illustrative and aren't meant to be taken literally. The actual instructions you use might be different.)

Listing 1.3   hello.java Source File

```
public class Hello {
    public static void main() {
        System.out.println( "Hello Java world" );
        }
    }
```

Listing 1.4 Disassembled Bytecode File hello.class

```
PUSH STACK
...
RETURN
```

When you run hello.class, the Java interpreter turns the bytecodes into a stream that looks like the instructions from our compiled hello.exe file, as shown in Listing 1.5.

Listing 1.5 Bytecodes Translated into Machine Code

```
PUSH SP
MOV BP, SP
...
RET
```

Running the bytecodes through the Java interpreter *is* an extra step through which traditional compiled programs don't go. It is this extra step, however, that gives Java its portability, because bytecodes mean the same thing no matter what computer they run on. Our hello.class program will, therefore, run on any machine for which a Java interpreter has been written.

A running Java program thus consists of three pieces: the source file, the bytecode file, and the Java interpreter. As I mentioned earlier, the bytecode file is very similar to the traditional executable in that it contains a stream of machine instructions. The difference is that those machine instructions don't work on any particular physical CPU; they only make sense to the Java interpreter.

This approach to portability is not new. UCSD Pascal enjoyed a brief moment in the sun back in the late 1970s with its implementation of a bytecode interpreter. Unfortunately, it was ahead of its time. The market demand for portable applications was overwhelmed by the demand for the kind of high-performance applications that C could provide.

Java's portability is not especially cheap, however. In order to achieve it, someone has to "port" the Java interpreter to each of the platforms on which Java runs. Unfortunately, a huge portion, if not a majority, of the functionality of Java is contained in native methods—dynamic link libraries that are compiled to native machine code. Many of these native methods use native C++ class libraries that have been built up over the years, such as Microsoft Foundation classes. So when you hear Java enthusiasts, myself included, opining as to how Java will replace C++, just remember that for the current generation of hardware, Java rests on a foundation of C++ code. This will change only when machines that support the JVM instruction set begin to appear.

Security

Up to now, we've talked mainly about the rewards of Javability, the gold-paved streets of Java world. As with every potential reward, there is also an element of risk, and in Java world, much of that risk involves security.

How secure is Java? The short answer is "pretty secure." For many of us, that answer is just not good enough. What does security mean to Java and why should we worry about it? It's probably better to start with what *isn't* secure under Java. Java's network awareness, for example, is simply a product of existing network protocols: http, ftp, and gopher. Java's network communications are no more or less secure than these underlying protocols. Java does not encrypt, although that doesn't mean you can't do it yourself. It's just not part of the language. What this means is that if someone breaks one of these protocols, any Java application using those protocols is also broken.

Running Java applets via the Web does open a *huge* security hole for a whole class of machines that never had to worry about security before. In the bad old days of dial-up bulletin boards (pre-1993), a pretty reliable rule of safe computing was "never run anything downloaded from a bulletin board." Especially in the Mac world, computer viruses were as common as the cold virus is among humans, and the easiest way to catch one was to run something you found on the Net. Now, Java postulates a world where running downloaded executables is *the* basic computing activity.

The question is one of risk/reward. For a single user running a Web browser for education and entertainment, the risks of unsecure network computing are fairly small. Even in the worst case, a downloaded virus wipes out the user's machine; it's only one machine, the work-product of one person. A painful loss, but in absolute terms, fairly small.

The risks multiply exponentially when you start talking about corporate computing. Large-scale corporate computing lurks somewhere in the background of almost every human activity. When the machines that make up this underlying base of computing power start running executables that have been passed, unverified, from one machine to another, the public danger posed by a malignant executable is limited only by the imagination of its inventor.

Thus, for many security-conscious applications, the migration to Java world requires a leap of faith equivalent to the one the Pilgrims took when they left England for North America. What kind of protection can Java offer the security conscious?

Memory Segmentation

Internally, Java maintains two separate memory sections: one section that the Java interpreter uses for itself, and one section that it uses to satisfy the needs of Java applets. An applet cannot, via Java itself, access memory from the Java segment. This is a product both of internal security measures *and* Java's pointer-less design. It would be nearly impossible to get this kind of protection in a language that supported pointers.

Java relies on the native operating system to protect it from malicious external applications. All of the operating systems that Java runs on enforce some system whereby the memory of one application, in this case, the Java applet, is automatically protected from the code of any other application. Java's immunity to this kind of malicious external attack is largely dependent on the native OS.

Native Methods

Some large proportion of Java's security risk is embodied in the ability of applets to get "outside" of Java via native methods and native executable calls. Java allows applets to call out to dynamic link libraries and executables that are assumed already to exist on the workstation. As far as Java is concerned, these native methods and executables are completely unsecure—they can be written in any language, by anyone, for any purpose, malicious or otherwise. This may sound like a fatal weakness, but it really isn't. While Java does not protect you from malicious native methods, it doesn't offer native method virus writers any help, either.

While Java classes are downloaded over the Net as a basic operating procedure, native methods and executables are not. A native method must already exist on a computer in order for a Java applet to execute it. It does not get downloaded. This means that it is as difficult to distribute a native-method virus as it has always been to distribute regular viruses. Native methods, malignant or not, do not appear automatically on a user's workstation in the way that Java classes do. Individual users must be convinced to load them on their workstations, one at a time. Thus, distributed attack via a native method is unworkable. The risk of a successful, large-scale attack via the Java distributed computing mechanism is entirely contained within Java itself.

Access to System Resources via Java

System resources—the network, the file system, and so on—are the ultimate target of spies and virus writers. Programmatic access to them is dangerous, but to completely eliminate that access would be a crippling burden on any language. Java deals with this security/functionality tradeoff by funnelling all potentially dangerous system resource access requests through the Java **SecurityManager** class.

The **SecurityManager** class allows the browser to manage applets' access to system resources. The **SecurityManager** is like a moat between the system resources and the horde of barbarian applets. The browser can choose to fill that moat with obstacles and barbed wire, or it can pave over the moat, allowing applets "the run of the castle." We'll discuss the **SecurityManager** class in more detail in Chapter 10.

The first crop of browsers have mostly chosen to cop out on the security question by putting the burden on the user. HotJava, for instance, allows the user to configure network and file I/O access through an options dialog box.

There is no "solution" to this part of the security problem. You must provide access to system resources to allow applets to get anything done, but providing that access opens the system to attack. The **SecurityManager** provides a workable solution by allowing browsers to validate that access before granting or denying it.

Java is neither secure nor unsecure. Security, like the common cold, is actually a number of problems, some of which are solvable, some of which are not. Java's overall approach to security is to deal with the solvable security issues automatically, and provide the user/browser with a way, via the **SecurityManager**, to gain protection from the rest. This strategy is the only reasonable one. Only time will tell if Java's execution of the strategy has been successful.

Object Orientation

The term *object orientation* has been applied so indiscriminately that only managers still think it means anything. This is unfortunate because Java, combined with the Internet, has the potential to start fulfilling some of the dreams that have long driven object-oriented designers.

There are two basic concepts behind all definitions of object orientation: *inheritance* and *encapsulation*. Inheritance is based on the notion that many objects will be modified versions of existing objects. Inheritance says that if one object inherits another, it gets all the functionality of that object. So, in Java, if we say something like:

```
class convertible extends car { ...
```

we're saying that the new **convertible** class will inherit all the functionality of the existing **car** class. **convertible** becomes a subclass of **car**, and conversely, **car** is **convertible**'s superclass.

Encapsulation is an equally simple idea. All it means is that every element of a program (methods, variables, etc.) must exist within a class, and only those elements that an object needs to see should be visible to that object. Thus, a class must explicitly specify whether a method or variable is "visible" to other classes. For instance, consider the code in Listing 1.6.

Listing 1.6   Encapsulating Vehicle ID Number

```
class car {
protected int VehicleID;
public Scratch scratches[];
}
class AutoFactory {
public void makeACar() {
     car TheAudi = new car();
     }
}
```

In this example, an object of class **AutoFactory** can change **TheAudi**'s array of **scratches**, but it can't change the **VehicleID**. This is encapsulation.

Where C programs are divided into modules, a Java program is divided into classes. Classes are simply a way of dividing the functionality of the program into discrete chunks. The theory of classes is that they "model" the items in the real world that they're supposed to describe. Thus, a program that showed a car moving across the screen would probably have a class named Car that had variables like speed, color, and bumper stickers. Every method (function) and variable in a Java program exists within a class. For example, in our hello.java program (shown previously in Listing 1.3), we had to create a class that contained the main method instead of simply defining a main function as in hello.c.

A running Java program is made up entirely of objects. An object is simply an instance of a class. Take our car example. We can describe a car with the class shown in Listing 1.7.

Listing 1.7 Creating an Object Class

```
class car {
int speed;
Color color;
String bumper_stickers[];
    public car() {
        color = new Color(Color.black);
        speed = 100;
        bumper_sticker = new String("Code happens");
    }
    public speed_up() {
        speed++;
        }
}
```

All this means, however, is that we know *how* to create a car—not that we've actually created one. In order to create one, we'd need to call **new**, as shown in Listing 1.8.

Listing 1.8 Creating an Instance of a Class

```
public void MakeACar() {
    car TheAudi = new Car();
    while( !speedTrap ) {
        TheAudi.speed_up();
        }
    }
```

When you create an instance of a class, it is known as *instantiating* the class. When you instantiate the class, you get back an object. In our example, **car** is a class, while **TheAudi** is an object.

Interfaces, described in more detail shortly, are an object-oriented feature that Java does not inherit from C++. In simple terms, an *interface* is a description of a class. For instance, our car example would translate to an interface, as shown in the following code snippet:

```
interface car {
    public speed_up();
}
```

But an interface is *only* a description. You can't instantiate an interface. In order to get a car object, you have to instantiate a class that implements the car interface, as in Listing 1.9.

Listing 1.9 Instantiating a Class with an Interface

```
class convertible implements car {
    int speed;
    Color color;
    Scratch scratches[];
    public convertible() {
        }
    public speed_up() {
        speed += 10;
        }
    }
```

Now we have a class that can be instantiated via **new**.

Cooperating Objects

The old computing world is made up of millions of islands of computing power, where huge, traditional applications toil away in splendid isolation from one another. Through various torturous mechanisms, these applications can some-times exchange data, but for the most part they treat each other like obnoxious relatives—with tolerance, but not much respect.

The new computing world, according to Java, is populated by teams of objects working cooperatively over the Internet. These Java teams are similar to human work teams. As anyone who's ever worked for a living knows, in order to work together, the members of a team need to know what to expect from one another. The knowledge you use to deal with a co-worker can be split into three general areas: that he or she's a human being, who has a particular job description, and who fulfills that job description in a particular way. These three levels of under-standing have exact analogs in the Java system. Any object is an instance of the class **Object** (the human being), it has a particular interface (the job descrip-tion), and it presents a particular implementation of that interface (the way that person does that job).

The **Object** class is *the* base class for every class in a Java program. This class provides a basic level at which objects that know absolutely nothing about one another can deal with each other. In C or C++, an unknown object would be passed as a **void** * and accessed either as a lump of bytes or by a dangerous type cast. In Java, an unknown object is passed as an instance of class **Object** and accessed via **Object**'s methods. Dangerous type casts can be avoided by querying the object's type; illegal type casts are caught by the interpreter.

As I mentioned earlier, Java gives programmers two ways to use objects: classes and interfaces. By subclassing one of the supplied Java classes, the new class inherits all the functionality of that Java class. Any other object that knows how to use that Java class can also use the new subclass.

Subclassing is akin to adding a musician to a band. Consider the rock band Rodley's Racketeers, which consists of guitarist, a bassist, and a drummer. The band tours, playing a short set of instrumental songs. Now add a singer to the group and call it Rodley's New Racketeers. The new group can still play the old instrumental set, but it can also play a new set of vocal music, too. That's subclassing.

Subclassing has one drawback. It ties you to a particular implementation of the functionality in the superclass (the ancestor class). If, for instance, you subclassed a class that implemented a sorted list, you would be stuck with whatever sort routine that superclass used. To use our band example, if you subclass Rodley's Racketeers, you're stuck with our drummer Keith. If you don't like Keith, you have to "override" him by replacing him with your own drummer. If you don't like the guitarist, or the bassist either, you can replace them too, but then you've ended up replacing the whole band.

That's where interfaces come in (see, I promised we'd get to interfaces). Interfaces are a newer feature that really complement classes. An interface is simply a *description* of one way that a class knows how to interact with the world. Unlike a class, there's no implementation behind an interface. Practically speaking, an interface is merely a set of method definitions (in C this is akin to a set of function prototypes). In that sense, an interface is like a class where all the methods are overridden.

Computer language theorists talk about classes being made up of interface (the set of method definitions) and implementation (the actual code that implements the methods). In our band example, the "definition" of a rock band—guitar, bass, drum, and vocals—is the interface. The actual people, Keith et al, are the implementation of that interface. Splitting the definition of a rock band from the people who implement it allows us to hire bands other than Rodley's

Racketeers. Because they're rock bands—objects that implement the rock band interface—we know that we can ask them to play "Stairway to Heaven" and it will come out right.

It's important to think of any particular class as the methods it implements *plus* all the methods its superclasses implement. Throughout this book, I've provided class inheritance diagrams that show which superclasses make up each Java class. Occasionally, for important classes, I also provide cumulative class desciptions, where all the class and superclass methods are collapsed into one class description.

Conclusion

Java's power comes from four features. Its network awareness allows Java objects to connect to each other. Its portability allows Java objects to run on any machine to which they can connect. Its security features give users the confidence to allow Java objects to run on their workstations. And finally, its approach to object orientation makes it possible to design objects that understand each other just enough to be able to work together, while avoiding the unneccessary dependencies that complicate the design and maintenance of similar objects in other languages.

Chapter 2

The Java Language

The Java Language

Java is unique, but also quite familiar.
Survey the language here with us.

Although Java is new (not to mention being cool), even novice programmers will notice a lot of familiar elements in the language. In this chapter, we'll look at all the elements included in Java—control flow, data types, operators, interfaces, and classes—and we'll see how they work together. We'll contrast Java's elements with their C and C++ analogs and point out the pieces that are unique to Java. Finally, we'll look at Java documentation style using the javadoc tool.

The first step in becoming proficient in a language is to use the language. Java is no exception. Let's write a simple applet and then compile it. Listing 2.1 shows our simple applet.

Listing 2.1   A Simple Applet

```
package chap2;

import java.awt.Graphics;
import java.applet.Applet;

public class ch2_fig1 extends Applet {
String TheString;

public void init() {
   TheString = new String( "Hello Java" );
   resize( 200, 150 );
   show();
    }

public void paint(Graphics g) {
```

```
   g.drawString( TheString, 20, 50 );
      }
}
```

Like all the "hello world" programs that have preceded it, the entire point of this one is to display the string "Hello Java" on the user's screen. To do that, we create a class named **ch2_fig1**. (Everything—methods and variables—in a Java program *must* exist within a class. If you don't have a class, you don't have a Java program.) **ch2_fig1** subclasses the **Applet** class, which allows it to be loaded by a browser. (We talk more about the Applet class in Chapter 4). Within our class, we have one variable, **TheString**, and two methods (functions for you C people)— **init** and **paint**. These methods are all overloads of methods in the **Applet** class. The **init** method is called automatically when the applet is loaded, and it sets our String variable, and resizes and shows the applet. The **paint** method is called automatically whenever the browser thinks the applet needs to repaint its screen— for instance, when the browser is resized.

To compile the applet, you enter the following command at the operating system prompt:

```
javac -classpath \jdk\java\lib\classes.zip ch2_fig1.java
```

Let's take a closer look at this code. **javac** is the compiler (the tool that turns source files into bytecode files). **classpath** is the location of the supplied Java class files *and* the top-level directory for any other Java packages you're trying to use. Later, when we start developing pieces of the Agent system, we'll add our top-level directory, agent, to the classpath. Finally, ch2_fig1.java is our source file.

Executing the compilation command produces a file named ch2_fig1.class, which contains the intermediate code. In order to run the simple applet, we need an HTML file that references the applet. Listing 2.2 shows an HTML file that uses our simple applet.

Listing 2.2   HTML Code That Runs the Simple Applet

```
<title>Chapter 2 - figure 1 - A Simple Applet</title>
<body>
<applet code="chap2/ch2_fig1.class" width=200 height=150>
</applet>
</body>
```

When the users point their browser at this HTML page, the browser reads the **<applet>** tag and passes the class file "chap2/ch2_fig1.class" to the Java interpreter. The applet referenced by the **<applet>** tag must be a Java .class file. Now that we have a compiled class file and an HTML wrapper, we can see the applet in action. There are currently two ways to do this. You can enter the command "appletviewer ch2_fig1.html," which runs the applet within Sun's appletviewer utility. The appletviewer is a shortcut to view applets in action without cranking up a browser. It displays *only* the applet in the HTML file, and none of the other HTML. The other way to view this applet is to open the HTML file in Netscape. Figure 2.1 shows our applet running in Netscape.

Notice how our "Hello Java" text is indistinguishable from the HTML text around it. This is one of the beauties of the Java/HTML combination: seamless integration.

The world of Java consists of millions of small applets from thousands of independent developers. Because of this distributed development environment, Java has to provide a very large namespace for applets. Limiting applet names to the DOS file name convention of eight characters, for instance, would give us approximately 30 to the 8th power (because there are 26 letters plus four allowed punctuation characters) for over two hundred billion possible unique applet names. This limitation would be fine if you don't mind naming your applets

Figure 2.1

The simple applet running in Netscape.

RRRRXXHY or FRTYZZVC. The real problem is that of those two hundred billion possible names, only a very few are descriptive. There are only so many meaningful English (or Chinese or Russian) words that fit in eight characters.

The Net, the world in which Java applets are developed and run, is divided into sites, directories, and files. This is reflected in the URL, which has the format:

```
protocol://site/directory/subdirectory_a/subdirectory_b/filename
```

In order to provide a large namespace—enough so that names can be descriptive—Java package names use a subset of the URL namespace, the directory/filename section. The only two entities in the Java world, packages and classes, correspond exactly to directories and files. The top-level entity in the Java world is a package. For all intents and purposes, a package is a directory. A package contains from 1 to n classes. The physical entity "package" is actually just a directory.

All packages are named according to a hierarchical naming scheme of unlimited depth. The full name of a class has the form "package_name.class_name." Take, for example, Java's predefined **Graphics** class. This is part of the awt package, which is a subpackage of the java package. Thus, the full name of the **Graphics** class is **java.awt.Graphics**. Within an applet, we can refer to a **Graphics** object as either **Graphics** or **java.awt.Graphics**. As an example, consider the class definition in our simple applet, shown in the following code line:

```
public class ch4_fig4 extends Applet {
```

We could rewrite this line as:

```
public class figure ch4_fig4 extends java.applet.Applet {
```

Or, for another example, consider the **paint** method from our simple applet, which is shown in the following code line:

```
public void paint( Graphics g ) {
```

We could rewrite this line as:

```
public void paint( java.awt.Graphics g ) {
```

Packages are reflected in at least two spots in a class file: in the **package** statement that begins the file and in the **import** statements. The **package** statement indicates to which package the class belongs. It must be the first line in the file, and it should give the full package name. The **package** statement for the **Graphics** class reads:

```
package java.awt;
```

The package name must also reflect the directory structure of the compiled class files. Thus, a class named **java.awt.Graphics** must exist in a file named java/awt/graphics.class. A single package can contain any number of classes and subpackages.

Attaching a class to a package also has the effect of making the class public, meaning that it can be imported by other classes. Classes that are not part of a package cannot be imported by other classes. You can define classes that are not part of a package by omitting the **package** statement, which essentially makes them private classes. Because they have no use to anyone else, many classes will fall into this category.

The source file name and the class name must match exactly. This might sound like a stupid restriction, until you hark back to the new world order according to Java. Many, if not most, of the classes used by a particular Java application will exist out on the network. If the compiler had not only to find the file on the network but also load it and search its contents for a particular class, it would increase the network traffic, and slow down the compile—exponentially.

The **import** statement is similar to the **#include** directive in a C or C++ program. It's used to get the class definition for external classes so that the compiler can perform proper type checking, among other things. Every class that is referenced in a Java program file must either exist within that file or be imported via an **import** statement. Thus, because our simple applet subclasses **Applet**, we have to import java.applet. Notice that we use the wildcard operator * to indicate that we want to import all the classes in the java.applet subpackage. You can use the **import** statement to import a single class file, or to import all the classes in a directory. You can use the * operator to import only all the *classes* of a package, not to import all the *subpackages* of a package. In our simple applet, we can get the definition of the **Applet** class by importing **java.applet.***, but not by importing **java.***. Importing **java.*** literally means to "import java/*.class."

In order actually to load a class imported via the 'import package.filename' statement, Java must turn the package.filename statement into a fully qualified path. With package and filename, we have the relative part of the file name. All we need to finish our fully qualified path is a path from the root directory to our class directories—the directory that has our packages as subdirectories. The java compiler gets this from the classpath environment variable. For the simple applet to compile, we need to supply a base directory for the imported java packages. In the current case, this is /jdk/java/classes. If we append an import statement to the classpath, it should give us the absolute file name of the class file we're trying to import. For example, the Graphics class is imported by appending java.awt.graphics to /jdk/java/classes. Here are some examples of classpaths:

- -classpath /jdk/java/classes
- -classpath /agent/classes/rel

You can combine these classpaths in one statement separated by semi-colons, like so:

```
-classpath /jdk/java/classes;/agent/classes/rel
```

Using the Sample Applets

Th Java naming system allows us to use a logical structure for the classes in this book. We create a package for each chapter, as well as packages for each piece of the finished Agent system. In the event of any naming conflicts, we create subpackages to distinguish between similar classes. Figure 2.2 shows the entire package hierarchy for the examples in the book.

The top-level directory, book, is not a package of its own; however, each subdirectory is a package. \book is the directory we supply in classpath, so that, for example, the class name chap2.ch2_fig1 actually resolves to the file \book\chap2\ch2_fig1.class.

Each sample applet gets its own HTML page. Each chapter gets its own page that lists its examples. The entry point to the book is the table of contents page, which, of course, contains links to all the chapter pages.

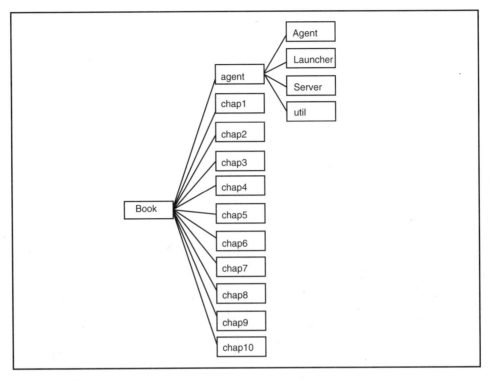

Figure 2.2

Directory structure and Java package hierarchy for this book.

Language Basics: A Quick Tour

Java allows two types of classes: public and private. Public classes are denoted by the keyword **public**. Classes without the **public** keyword are private. Each Java source file can contain only one public class, but any number of private classes. Each class ends up with its own .class file. Take a look at the source file shown next:

```
package MyPackage;

public class Pub {
    }
class Private1 {
    }
class Private2 {
    }
class Private3 {
    }
```

What you will end up with after compiling is four compiled bytecode files: Pub.class, Private1.class, Private2.class, and Private3.class. Thus, in the same package/directory you cannot have both a public and a private class with the same name.

The **class** statement must declare which class this one is subclassing, and what interfaces it implements. A class can subclass *one* class, but it can implement any number of interfaces. For example, the following code line declares a class that extends the **Applet** class and implements the **Runnable** and **ImageObserver** interfaces:

```
class MyClass extends Applet implements Runnable, ImageObserver{ ...
```

A class that does not specify a superclass (that is, does not include an **extends** clause) extends the **Object** class by default.

Methods always occur within a class. They are declared and used the same way you do in C++, so I won't waste a lot of verbiage on it. The one thing to look out for in method declarations is that a method must declare all exceptions that it either throws or passes through. See Chapter 8 for complete coverage of exceptions. Methods can be overloaded, and, unless they are declared as **final**, can also be overridden. Methods have a return type, but (C programmers beware) experience has shown that most methods should return a **void**. Error conditions should never go back to the caller through the return value; use exceptions instead (again, see Chapter 8).

Variables and Scope

There are two basic classes of variable: instance and local. Instance variables are accessible to any method in the class. Local variables are, obviously, local to the method or block within which they are declared. By and large, the scoping rules of C++ apply. Both variable types are illustrated in Listing 2.3.

Listing 2.3   Instance and Local Variables

```
class X {
  int AnInstanceVariable;
  public void MyMethod() {
    int ALocalVariable;
    AnInstanceVariable = 2;
  }
  public void MyMethod1() {
```

```
      int AnotherLocalVariable;
      AnInstanceVariable = 1;
   }
}
```

You can create a scope (area) simply by bracketing a block of code with curly braces, and any variable declared within a scope will be visible only within that scope. Listing 2.4 illustrates a correct use of this technique.

Listing 2.4   Correct Creation of a Scope

```
public void MyMethod() {
   int i,j;
   for( i = 0; i < 100; i++ ) {
     j = i;
   }
   System.out.println( "j="+j );
   }
```

On the other hand, Listing 2.5 fails to compile because **j** is an undefined variable in the scope in which **println** is invoked.

Listing 2.5   Scope Trips on an Undefined Variable

```
public void MyMethod() {
   int i;
   for( i=0; i<100; i++ ) {
     int j = i;
   }
   System.out.println( "j="+j );
   }
```

Like classes, instance variables can also be public or private. The default is private. Therefore, in Listing 2.6, **j** is public, but **i** is private.

Listing 2.6   Private and Public Instance Variables

```
public class MyClass {
   int i;
   public int j;
   ...
```

Static variables and methods apply to the whole class rather than an instance of the class. You can still use a static variable or method even when there isn't one instance of the class in existence. Listing 2.7 illustrates this point.

Listing 2.7 Using a Static Variable in a Class without Instantiating the Class

```
class MyMainClass {
    public MyMainClass() {
        MyClass.TheStaticInt = 1;
        MyClass.TheStaticMethod();
    }
}
class MyClass {
    static int TheStaticInt;
    static void TheStaticMethod() {
        TheStaticInt=2;
    }
}
```

In this case, we have not explicitly instantiated **MyClass**, yet we've used its static methods and variables anyway. Perhaps the most pervasive example of static variable/method use is the method **System.out.println()**. **out** is a static variable of type **PrintStream** in the class **System**, and **println** is a static method within the class **PrintStream**. **System.out** is actually a bit of an anomaly. Public instance variables are extremely rare in the supplied Java packages. Sun prefers to provide access to instance variables through a method with the prefix **get**, like **Component.getGraphics**, which gets a graphics context for drawing.

Java also allows static initialization. That is, you can declare a block of code (surrounded by curly braces) as **static**. It will run once and be applied to the class as a whole rather than instances of the class. This is very useful for, say, initializing a static array of composite types, as shown in Listing 2.8.

Listing 2.8 Initializing a Static Array

```
class MyClass {
    static Integer j[] = new Integer[100];
    static {
        for( int k = 0; k < j.length; k++ )
            j[k] = new Integer(k);
    }
    ...
```

You can have as many static initializers as you want. Initializations are executed in the order in which they are encountered in the file. Unfortunately, multiple initializations can lead to subtle bugs, especially when you have statements that combine type declaration and initialization. For instance, consider the class shown in Listing 2.9.

Listing 2.9   Problems from Multiple Initializers

```
class MyClass {
   int j = 2;
   int k = 1;
   static {
      x = j+k;
      }
   int x = 4;
   ...
```

Here's what happens in the order in which it occurs:

- An **int** named j is created.
- j is set to 2.
- An **int** named k is created.
- k is set to 1.
- The forward reference to **x** causes an **int** named x to be created.
- **x** is set to (2+1).
- **x** is set to 4.

Essentially, the declaration of **x** is "split off" from the initialization of **x**. It is important to remember that declaration and initialization may happen at different times, even though they can be combined in one statement.

Finality

The last modifier we need to think about is **final. final** means different things in different contexts. When applied to a (public or private) static instance variable, you get the effect of a global constant. Consider Listing 2.10.

Listing 2.10   Using the final Modifier

```
public class MyClass {
   public static final int GlobalInt = 10;
}
```

Listing 2.10 is only a code snippet, of course. But if this is the code you use to declare the **GlobalInt** variable, any class, anywhere can reference **GlobalInt** simply as **MyClass.GlobalInt**. As a result, the code line:

```
int x = MyClass.GlobalInt;
```

will set **x** to 10, no matter where it's called, *even if there is not an instance of MyClass.*

Declaring a method as **final** guarantees that it will not be overridden. Many of the methods in the supplied packages are declared **final**, a fact guaranteed to irritate those who might like to "optimize" some of Sun's methods. Declaring a class as **final** guarantees that it cannot be subclassed. Again, many of the supplied classes, the composite types for instance, are declared **final**. Trying to override a **final** method or subclass a **final** class will generate a compiler error.

C++ Compatibility

C++ compatibility is one of the features that has led to Java's rapid acceptance. That syntax compatibility can be summed up in these four categories: keywords, control flow, simple types, and operators.

Keywords

Keywords are the vocabulary of a programming language. For example, **for**, **if**, **while**, **int**, and **char** are all keywords in C/C++ and Java. The vast majority of Java keywords come directly from C and C++. Java keywords are summarized in Appendix A.

Control Flow

Controlling which statements are executed, and in what order, is the most basic task of a programmer, and every language provides flow-control structures to make that easier. In the beginning there was **if** and **goto**. Now things are a little more sophisticated.

Java provides a set of flow-control structures, listed in Table 2.1, that are identical to those of C and C++.

The control structures **if-else**, **while**, **do-while**, **for**, and **return** all work the same as they do in C++. Most of these are familiar to users of any programming language, so we won't waste any time on them. Conspicuous by its absence from this list is the infamous **goto**, one of C++'s C holdovers. The exception-handling structures, **try-catch** and **throw**, are covered in detail in Chapter 8.

Table 2.1 Java Control Structures	
Control Structures	**Description**
for	Loop on a condition—with initialization—increment, and top-exit
do while	Loop on a condition, then bottom-exit
while	Loop on a condition, then top-exit
if else	Branch on condition
try catch	Try a block of expressions, and catch any exceptions; see Chapter 8
throw	Throw an exception; see Chapter 8

Simple and Composite Types

Everything in a Java program is either a simple or composite type. Understanding the difference between them is one of the first hurdles you need to overcome when first learning Java. Java supports a set of simple types similar to that of many C++ compilers. int, char, byte, long, float, double are all here. Note that each simple type has a size that is the same for every platform. A Java int is 32 bits whether its running on an Intel 8086 or a DEC Alpha. Table 2.2 shows the list of simple types and their sizes.

Note that a char is 16-bit Unicode. Unicode is a form of 16-bit character that works for international characters (like Kanji), as well as the English alphabet. IEEE 754 is a specification (from the Institute of Electrical and Electronics Engineers) for the format and precision of floating-point numbers.

Table 2.2 Simple Types and Their Sizes	
Type	**Size in ~~Bytes~~ Bits**
byte	8
short	16
int	32
long	64
char	16 (Unicode)
float	32 (IEEE 754 subset)
double	64 (IEEE 754 subset)
boolean	The size of a boolean isn't useful because you cannot convert back and forth from boolean to any of the numeric types

In C and C++, knowing the size of a variable was often neccessary for doing pointer arithmetic. Because there are no pointers in Java, type sizes are really useful only for determining variable minima/maxima.

Composite types, such as classes, arrays, and interfaces, can be constructed from simple types and from other composite types. As an example, consider the class shown in Listing 2.11. Type **SimpleClass** consists of the simple types class, char, int, and void (**oneFunction**).

Listing 2.11 A Composite Type

```
class SimpleClass {
char oneChar;
int oneInt;
public void oneFunction() {
   oneInt = 2;
   }
}
```

One of the most confusing things about Java is that it comes with a set of composite types (in the java.lang package) that look a lot like the set of simple types. These types are:

- Boolean
- Character
- Double
- Float
- Integer
- Long
- Number
- String

These types exist to encapsulate basic type functionality often found in the C runtime library. For instance, C gives you an integer type, int. In the C runtime library, the **atoi()** function converts a string to integer, and the **itoa()** function converts a C int to a string. Java lumps this functionality into the composite **Integer** type. **Itoa()**'s Java equivalent would be the method **Integer.toString()**, while **atoi()**'s Java equivalent would be the constructor **Integer(String stringNum)**.

Remember too, that some of the casting tricks that used to work in C++ aren't supported in Java. Java is very strictly typed. You cannot cast an object to any other type except one of its superclasses. So these composite versions of the simple types have to provide you with that ability to turn one type (particularly strings) into another type.

TYPES AND INITIALIZATION

Simple and composite types have very different initialization requirements. The following code snippet will compile and run:

```
int j;
j = 1;
```

But change that simple int to a composite Integer, as in the following code snippet, and you get a compiler error complaining about incompatible types.

```
Integer j;
j = 1;
```

In general, composite types don't support assignment via the = operator; instead, you need to pass the desired value as a parameter to the object's constructor. In order to get the same effect as our valid simple type assignment then, we need to modify our code as follows:

```
Integer j = new Integer(1);
```

This code also brings up another crucial difference between simple and composite types. An object of simple type exists the instant you declare it. So when we say "int j" there is a space in memory reserved for an int value. Not so when we say "Integer j." No Integer object exists until we instantiate it via the **new** operator. If you try to reference j before instantiating it with **new**, you'll probably end up throwing a **NullPointerException**.

Composite Objects Must Be Instantiated

It bears repeating: Although objects of simple types are created as soon as they are declared (for example, *int j*), objects of composite types are *not* created automatically when declared (for example, *Integer j*); The latter must be instantiated with the **new** operator.

ARRAYS

Java arrays are composite types, making them very different from arrays in C and C++. For one thing, as composite types, they have to be instantiated via **new**. All you can say about an array in the declaration is "this is an array," as in the following code line:

```
Integer Jarray[];
```

In Java, you can't "size" the array in the declaration the way you do in C and C++, which allow you to write the following code:

```
int jarray[25];
```

This code, while perfectly legal in C and C++, will give you a compiler error in Java. To re-create that construction in Java you'd use this code line:

```
int jarray[] = new int[25];
```

This approach gets you an array of 25 ints that are all initialized to 0. When you're creating an array of simple types, such as int, that's all you need to do. When you're working with composite types, though, instantiating the array is only half the job. Consider the following code line:

```
Integer jarray[] = new Integer[25];
```

This statement only gets you an array full of null objects, which would throw a **NullPointerException** if you tried to use them. In order to populate the array with initialized Integers, you need to run through it instantiating Integers with **new**, as in:

```
Integer jarray[] = new Integer[25];
for( int j = 0; j < jarray.length; j++ )
   jarray[j] = new Integer(0);
```

Like C and C++, Java arrays are 0-based. The first item in a Java array will always be at array index 0.

MULTI-DIMENSIONAL ARRAYS

Java doesn't believe in multi-dimensional arrays, but does allow arrays of arrays, which achieves the same effect. To create an 8-by-16 integer array in C, you'd use a code line such as:

```
int x[8][16];
```

The equivalent statement in Java would read:

```
int x[][] = new int[8][16];
```

Literally translated, this statement says that **x** is an array of eight 16-int arrays. Remember that the array members are simple types, so we don't have to instantiate them individually. The array x has eight elements, each of which is an array. Thus, you can say:

```
int y = x[3].length;
```

which queries the length of the fourth int array in the x array of arrays. This technique has another implication, too. Your array doesn't have to be symmetrical. For instance, the following code is perfectly acceptable in Java:

```
int x[][] = new int[8][16];
x[1] = new int[25];
x[6] = new int[4];
```

This code creates an array of arrays, with each element of the array consisting of an array of 16 ints. Then it replaces the second 16-int array with a 25-int array and the seventh 16-int array with a four-int array. You can still reference these arrays just like C-style multi-dimensional arrays. The code in Listing 2.12, for example, runs through this array, printing every element to standard out.

Listing 2.12 Traversing an Array of Arrays

```
for( int j = 0; j < x.length; j++ )
  for( int k = 0; k < x[j].length; k++ )
    System.out.println( "x["+j+"]["+k+"] = "+x[j][k] );
```

The code in Listing 2.13, however, will throw an **ArrayIndexOutOfBounds-Exception** when **j** equals 6 and **k** equals 4, because we've replaced the original 16-int array with a four-int array.

Listing 2.13   Overrunning an Array

```
for( int j = 0; j < x.length; j++ )
    for( int k = 0; k < 16; k++ )
        System.out.println( "x["+j+"]["+k+"] = "+x[j][k] );
```

Operators

Java supports the usual complement of C++-style operators. The order of precedence of the operators is shown here.

.[]()

++ — ! ~ instanceof

* / %

+ -

<< >> >>>

< <= > >=

== !=

&

^

|

&&

||

?:

= op= (where op is +, -, * ...)

Most of these operators will be familiar, so I won't explain them in detail. Operator order of precedence is identical to that of C/C++. The only unfamiliar operator in the list is **instanceof**, which we'll later use extensively to pull the frame window from an unordered chain of **Component** objects.

Interfaces

In Chapter 1, we talked a little about the theory of interfaces. An interface is basically a description of the input to, and output from a class, with nothing said about *how* the class creates the output from the input. Interfaces are declared exactly the same way as classes (substituting **interface** for **class**).

A class that implements an interface must provide all the methods specified by that interface, and each method must match the interface's definition exactly. If the interface calls for the ABC method, as shown in the following code snippet, any implementation of ABC must have a method xyz that takes an int argument and returns an int, but it can implement xyz in any way it wants:

```
interface ABC {
public int xyz( int a );
}
```

Listing 2.17 declares the **Sortable** interface. Listings 2.15 and 2.16 present two implementations of the **Sortable** interface. And the applet in Listing 2.14 creates one of each of our **Sortable** objects and sorts it using the **Sortable** interface method, **sort**.

Listing 2.14 The Applet That Uses Our Sortable Objects

```
package chap2;

import chap2.*;
import java.lang.*;
import java.util.*;
import java.applet.*;

public class ch2_fig14 extends Applet {

public void start() {
  AlphaList al = new AlphaList();
  al.addElement("abcd");
  al.addElement( "laksdjfdf" );
  al.addElement( "sdsdfdlfkj");
  al.addElement( "ouwet");
  al.addElement( "basdf");

  System.out.println( "AlphaList before the insertion sort" );
  for( int i = 0; i < al.size(); i++ )
    System.out.println( "al["+i+"] = "+(String)al.elementAt(i));
  SortTheSortableThing(al);
  System.out.println( "AlphaList after the insertion sort" );
  for( int i = 0; i < al.size(); i++ )
    System.out.println( "al["+i+"] = "+(String)al.elementAt(i));

  OtherList ol = new OtherList();
  ol.addElement("abcd");
  ol.addElement( "laksdjfdf" );
  ol.addElement( "sdsdfdlfkj");
  ol.addElement( "ouwet");
  ol.addElement( "basdf");
```

```
  System.out.println( "OtherList before the insertion sort" );
  for( int i = 0; i < ol.size(); i++ )
    System.out.println( "ol["+i+"] = "+(String)ol.elementAt(i));
  SortTheSortableThing(ol);
  System.out.println( "OtherList after the insertion sort" );
  for( int i = 0; i < ol.size(); i++ )
    System.out.println( "ol["+i+"] = "+(String)ol.elementAt(i));
  }
public void SortTheSortableThing( Sortable sortableThing ) {
  sortableThing.sort();
  }
}
```

Listing 2.15   The AlphaList Implementation of Our Sortable Interface

```
package chap2;

import chap2.*;
import java.lang.*;
import java.util.*;

/** A class that implements a sortable vector of Strings.
@see Sortable
@author John Rodley
@version 1.0
*/
public class AlphaList extends Vector implements Sortable {

  public AlphaList() {
    super(1);
    }

/** Bubble sort the Vector as Strings.  If they aren't strings, this'll
crash with an illegal cast exception.
*/
  public void sort() {
    int i, j;
    for( i = size()-1; i >= 1; i- ) {
      for( j = 2; j <= i; j++ ) {
        String s = (String)elementAt(j);
        String sp = (String)elementAt(j-1);
        if( sp.compareTo(s) > 0 ) {
          setElementAt(s, j-1);
          setElementAt(sp,j);
          }
        }
      }
    }
```

Listing 2.16   The OtherList Implementation of Our Sortable Interface

```
package chap2;

import chap2.*;
import java.lang.*;
import java.util.*;
import java.lang.*;

/** A class that implements a sortable vector of Strings.
@see Sortable
@author John Rodley
@version 1.0
*/
public class OtherList extends Vector implements Sortable {

    public OtherList() {
        super(1);
        }

/** Insertion sort the Vector as Strings.  If they aren't strings, this'll
crash with an illegal cast exception.
*/
    public void sort() {
        int i, j;
        for( i = 2; i < size(); i++ ) {
            String v = (String)elementAt(i);
            j = i;
            String s = (String)elementAt(j-1);
            while( s.compareTo(v) > 0 ) {
                setElementAt(s, j );
                j--;
                s = (String)elementAt(j-1);
                }
            setElementAt(v, j);
            }
        }

    }
```

Listing 2.17   The Definition of the Sortable Interface

```
package chap2;

/** An interface that defines this object as sortable.  Many different
types of collections will implement this interface, using different
algorithms for the actual sort method.
@author John Rodley
@version 1.0
*/
public interface Sortable {
```

```
// Tells the implementor to sort itself
public void sort();
}
```

The key point to look at here is the **SortTheSortableThing** method in Listing 2.14. This method takes a **Sortable** object as its argument. The **Sortable** interface specifies only one thing, that any implementor provide a method named **sort**. Thus, **SortTheSortableThing** knows only one thing about the **sortableThing** argument—that it will sort itself when we call **sortableThing.sort**.

Notice, in Listings 2.15 and 2.16, that each of our Sortable implementors, **AlphaList** and **OtherList**, provides a **sort** method, but the **sort** methods themselves are quite different. Our applet—ch2_fig14 creates one of each of these classes—then has it sort itself, printing the Vector before and after each sort.

C/C++ Incompatability

Java is not C/C++. It supports a great deal of C/C+ syntax, but has some incompatibilities. The most important of these are operator overloading, pointers, and multiple inheritance. Operator overloading, and to some extent, multiple inheritance are fairly advanced techniques that some C++ coders never use. Pointers, on the other hand, are right at the heart of any C/C++ program, and Java's lack of pointers will probably seem a little scary to C/C++ converts.

Operator Overloading

No issue generated as much heat in the early days of Java as the issue of whether or not to allow operator overloading. Personally, I never used it in my own classes, so I don't miss it at all. The thinking behind omitting it was that it made programs very difficult to maintain. This is easy enough to see. An operator, usually a single character, is simply shorthand for something that could be described in much more detail. a+b could just as easily be written a.Plus(b). When a and b are integers, a+b is completely descriptive. When a and b are complex derived types, the meaning of a+b is crystal clear *only* to whoever wrote the overload.

Thus, most operators are only implemented for the simple types to which they apply, not the composite types. It's important to keep this in mind when dealing with the look-alike composite types, such as Integer. The perfectly innocent code in Listing 2.18 doesn't even compile.

Listing 2.18   Creating Three Integers and Adding Two Together: The Wrong Way

```
Integer i = new Integer(0);
Integer j = new Integer(1);
Integer k = new Integer(0);
k = i+j;
```

What we're trying to do is create three numbers, then set the value of the third to be the sum of the other two. Listing 2.18 doesn't exactly cut the mustard. To get the desired effect, you'd write code such as that in Listing 2.19.

Listing 2.19   Creating Three Integers and Adding Two Together: The Right Way

```
Integer = new Integer(0);
Integer j = new Integer(1);
Integer k = new Integer( i.intValue()+j.intValue());
```

Integer.intValue returns an int. We can use the + operator on ints, so we call **intValue** against our two Integers, add those int values together, and initialize our third Integer with that new int value.

There is one exception to the no operator-overloading rule: the use of + and += on a String concatenates to that String. Outside the world of programming, nobody thinks of "adding" sentences together as in *"this is a test"* + *" of the PA"*. However, Java Strings support the + and += operators. Thus, you can get code like this:

```
String s = new String("abdefg");
String t = new String("hijklmnop");
String u = new String( s+t );
```

In this example, the value of **u** is the concatenation of **s** and **t**. This technique is extremely useful in debugging code, and we'll be using it throughout the Agent system. If we catch an unexpected exception, you'll see a block like this:

```
catch( Exception e ) {System.out.println("Exception "+e); }
```

which concatenates the string "Exception" to the String value of the Exception e using the + operator.

Pointers

There are no pointers in Java. End of story. If you want to walk through something as if it were an array, use an array. Much of what we used **char** pointers for in C/C++ is handled in the constructors for **String**. Perhaps the best example of a place in the Agent system where C-style pointers would have been useful—but instead we go through serious contortions to use Java arrays—is the message handling code in Chapter 7 (Listing 7.11).

Multiple Class Inheritance

There is no multiple class inheritance in Java. That is, a class can have only one superclass. This might seem a severe limitation, but it is mitigated by the ability to use multiply inherited interfaces.

Multiply inherited interfaces are not the same as multiply inherited classes. We talked earlier about how an interface splits the definition of a class from its implementation. A C++ class that inherits multiple classes inherits both the definition and the implementation of those classes. A Java class that implements multiple interfaces inherits only the definition of those classes, not the implementation. Thus, our Java class has to re-write the implementation of the class. This is a limitation, but not as restricting as it might seem. We'll see this as we move through the chapters.

Java Style

Having talked about the language, and built and run a simple applet, now is a good time to talk about programming style. Java World is a totally new place, where the traditional documentation models don't apply.

It used to be that there were three levels of code documentation:

- **Inline doc:** The minimal, inline documentation you always place in code to keep yourself sane when you're maintaining it. This is the most accurate of all the doc forms, but a real pain in the neck to read. It also can't be distributed among people who couldn't be trusted with the source code. It is not very pretty and often contains snide remarks.

- **Readme style doc:** The syntax and return value for most of the functions in the library. This is the kind of doc you got when there is no professional technical writer involved in the process. It is a real pain in the neck to create and nearly impossible to maintain, since the person writing it is also usually writing the product.

- **Commercial quality doc:** The description, syntax, return value, and error conditions for each function in the class library, as well as theory of use and tutorials—suitable for use in a shrink-wrapped class library. This is the kind of documentation we all love to use, and hate to write. It is also very expensive to maintain. Once this kind of doc is in place, it takes an act of Congress just to change a return value.

Readme and commercial doc both have two problems: You have to print them, and because they were created from scratch, it is very expensive to keep them current.

Java operates on a different theory, namely that all documentation is inline, contained within the source code. To this end, Java provides a tool, javadoc, to help create automated package documentation using inline commentary. Because Java's focus is to facilitate interoperability of classes (classes working together), javadoc creates HTML documentation only for the public parts of a class—interfaces implemented, public methods, and variables.

Without requiring you to add anything to your source, javadoc can generate a complete set of linked HTML documents that list your classes, methods, and variables. This "tree" of HTML documents is an outline of your class API. In order to fill in this outline, you need to add inline docmentation that conforms to certain standards.

javadoc expects to encounter the documentation for an item directly before that item appears in the source. That documentation must be enclosed in a /** */ pair, as in the following code snippet:

```
/**
this is my documentation for this class
*/
class MyClass {
...
```

All commentary intended to float through to javadoc documentation must be enclosed within /** */ pairs. Within a javadoc comment, you can also embed javadoc tags, similar to HTML tags, that will make javadoc format the comments in particular ways—adding hyperlinks and emphasizing or de-emphasizing items.

The three classes of javadoc commentary—class, method, and variable—all support different sets of tags. Remember to keep all the tags of the same type together. Also take care when adding HTML tags of your own inside the javadoc commentary, because even if it works for this version, there's no guarantee that future versions of javadoc won't do things a little differently.

Table 2.3 shows javadoc class tags, Table 2.4 shows javadoc method tags, and Table 2.5 shows javadoc variable tags.

Figures 2.3 and 2.4 show how javadoc displays documentation.

Table 2.3 javadoc Class Tags

Tagname	Arguments	Description
@see	item-name	Adds a "see also" entry to the class documentation, which serves as a hyperlink to the item named in the see tag; the item-name can be a local class (@see classname), a fully qualified class (@see fully-qualified classname), or a method (@see classname#methodname)
@version	version description	Adds a version entry to the class doc
@author	author name	Adds an author entry to the class doc

Table 2.4 javadoc Method Tags

Tagname	Arguments	Description
@see	item-name	Adds a "see also" entry to the class documentation. This is a hyperlink to the item named in the see tag. The item-name can be a local class (@see classname), a fully-qualified class (@see fully-qualified classname) or a method (@see classname#methodname)
@param	parameter-name	Adds an entry to the parameter section of the method doc
@return	description of return value	Adds a Returns section to the method doc, which describes this method as returning the described value
@exception	fully qualified class-name	Adds an entry stating that this method throws the named exception

Table 2.5   javadoc Variable Tags

Tagname	Arguments	Description
@see	item to see	Adds a "see also" entry to the class documentation, which serves as a hyperlink to the item named in the see tag; the item-name can be a local class (@see classname), a fully-qualified class (@see fully qualified classname), or a method (@see classname#methodname)

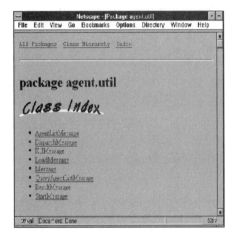

Figure 2.3

javadoc output for our agent.util package viewed in Netscape.

Figure 2.4

javadoc output for ResultMessage class within agent.util package.

Conclusion

Java is brand new, yet surprisingly familiar, especially to those steeped in the C/C++ programming tradition. Attention to a few small but important variations from C++ can make a C++ programmer productive in Java very quickly. And those who aren't already C++ coders should be able to pick up Java very quickly, largely due to its lack of pointers.

Java also supplies a tool, javadoc, that allows coders to generate useable, hyperlinked class documentation directly from the inline documentation that they are already accustomed to writing. This is a new style of documentation generation and it turns doc that used to be decipherable, and available only to the coder, into readable, end-user doc.

Chapter **3**

The Sample Application

The Sample Application

Agents, schmagents. Here's an application that dispatches agents on important, real-life missions.

The idea of intelligent computing agents has been around for so long that, like object orientation, it now means different things to different people. For the purposes of this book, an agent is an intelligent computing entity that propagates itself across the network with little or no assistance from the user who dispatched it, executing its function on every machine it encounters and reporting its results back to the user.

The original implementation of online computing was a wildly exaggerated client-server model: a dumb terminal logged onto a multiuser server. All the meaningful computing activity took place on the server. It had to be that way, since dumb terminals were incapable of doing any computing for themselves. If we compare that model with what happens on the Web today, they're not all that different. You log on to a server, and your "terminal" displays whatever the site tells it to. We can switch servers very easily via hyperlinks, and occasionally the static text will be livened up by a form, an audio clip, or even a cgi-bin script, but the meaningful computing activity still occurs almost exclusively on the server. If we were still using dumb terminals, this limitation is all we could hope for, but in reality, this model vastly underutilizes the computing resources available on any Web-capable PC.

The first crop of Java applets hasn't improved much on that model. The central server sends a Java class to the workstation, where it then executes. At that point, out of all the interconnected machines on the Net, you have two of them working efficiently together, in parallel, to satisfy the needs of a single user. An improvement to be sure, but not much.

What about the hundreds of thousands of other machines that are connected to the Net? Why aren't they helping with the task? In truth, there's only one reason: lack of a viable distributed operating system. While it would be a gross overstatement to call the Agent system we'll be creating a distributed operating system, it does aim to accomplish some of the same goals: to replicate a task across multiple CPUs, in parallel, in order to gain better performance. In our case, the better performance is not better speed (the goal of most distributed operating systems) but *more* results, for example, more hits on a file search.

Searching for a file is actually a perfect example of the limitations of the one-to-one multiprocessing available on the Web today. Many sites that serve files using FTP allow you to search for a file. If you have some idea which site serves the file, you're very likely to find it without much ado: You just hit that server and do a one-to-one query there. But what if you hit server A and the file is really on server B? A and B are physically and logically connected on the Net, but the query on server A will not find the file on server B because there is no mechanism to move the query from A to B.

That is the basic premise behind the Agent system: to get that query from server A to server B. The user, uses a Web browser to pick an agent from a list of available agents, configure it with some set of arguments, and dispatche it to do its work on each machine in a limitless network of interconnected machines. The work that the agent does isn't really important to us. It could be anything from a simple file search to a complicated and expensive commercial database query. We don't really care. The point of the Agent system is to provide a mechanism through which agents of unlimited complexity can traverse the Net doing their jobs.

As an analogy, think of a landlord with a number of buildings. This landlord keeps a list of tradespeople—electricians, carpenters—that she uses regularly. This would be her agent list. When the landlord wants something done to her buildings, she picks the proper agent, such as a plumber, from her list of agents. She tells the plumber what she wants done (configures him) and then sends him out to do the job. This is basically what we propose to do: Pick an agent from a list, configure it, and dispatch it to get the job done.

Given that functional description, our system splits easily into three components, or classes: the user interface (class **AgentLauncher**), which runs on the user's Web browser allowing an agent to be choosen; the server (class **AgentServer**), which enables the agent to run on a particular machine; and the agent itself (class **Agent**), which must travel over the network and execute on all the different servers.

The AgentLauncher

The AgentLauncher, an applet that runs within a user's Web browser, is the user interface to the Agent system. The AgentLauncher has the following tasks to perform:

- Choose an agent from the list of agents.
- Dispatch that agent onto the network.
- Display the results of that agent's work.

Let's start at the beginning and look at how the AgentLauncher is designed to perform these tasks. Figure 3.1 shows an AgentLauncher that has just started.

We supply buttons that correspond roughly to these tasks: Pick, Dispatch, Stop, Kill, and Results. We'll talk more about Stop and Kill later. For now, let's concentrate on the other three.

Choosing an Agent

To select an agent to dispatch, the user clicks on the Pick button, which displays a dialog box like the one in Figure 3.2.

For each agent, we display the class name of the agent, plus a descriptive comment. The user picks an agent from the list box, and clicks on OK. We'll talk

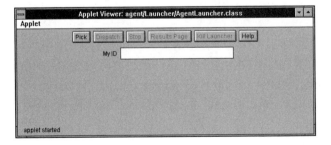

Figure 3.1

An AgentLauncher with no running agents.

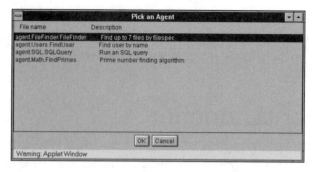

Figure 3.2

The AgentLauncher displaying the list of available agents.

more about how to build and use dialog boxes in Chapter 5. For now, all you need to know is that displaying a dialog box is a fairly straightforward task for an applet. From a design viewpoint, the really interesting question is "Where does this list of agents come from?"

Because the AgentLauncher must run within a Web browser, it suffers from two key limitations that shape its design: lack of file I/O and severely limited network communication. First, some browsers, such as Netscape, do not allow file I/O from applets. Currently, there is no way around this restriction. Second, some browsers only allow applets to open socket connections to the server from which the applet was originally loaded.

At first, this prohibition of file I/O might not seem to be that big a deal. That's because file I/O is so pervasive in standalone applications that we don't even recall using it. Where this becomes problematic for the Agent system is in dispatching agents and viewing results.

In order to dispatch the agent, we need to pick one from an existing, persistent list of agents, and dispatch it to each AgentServer in an existing, persistent list of AgentServers.

Though we'd like to keep the list of agents locally where they ultimately belong, it can't be done because of the file I/O restriction. Thus, we need to keep the agent list (and the agents themselves) on a server, and have the server send us the list in a message.

The AgentLauncher requests the message with a **QueryAgentListMessage** (see Chapter 7) and the dispatching AgentServer responds with an **AgentListMessage** (see Chapter 7), which contains all the information about the agents that can be dispatched from this server. This is the only instance of a query/response message algorithm in the Agent system. All the other messages in the system are "thrown out there" with no requirement that anyone respond to them.

Having picked the agent, the next step is to configure the agent. In order to keep things simple, we'll save configuration for a little later, and jump straight to dispatching.

Dispatching an Agent

Once we've picked and configured the agent, the next step is to dispatch it onto the network with the Dispatch button. From the AgentLauncher's standpoint, all dispatching amounts to is sending a message to the AgentServer that contains the agent name and some configuration information. The **Agent** class file itself resides on the AgentServer, again because of the applet restriction on file I/O. The AgentServer that provides the list of available agents and receives the DispatchMessage is designated as the dispatching AgentServer. Dispatching from the AgentServer's perspective is discussed in more detail later on.

Viewing Results

Our preferred communication solution would be to have all the agents dispatched by a user communicate their results directly back to that user's machine, as in Figure 3.3.

Unfortunately, browsers often restrict an applet's network I/O in such a way that they can only open socket connections back to the server they were loaded from,

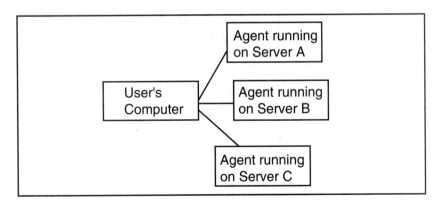

Figure 3.3

Three instances of an agent communicating directly with the user.

forcing us to run all the agent-to-AgentLauncher messages back through a server (the dispatching AgentServer), as in Figure 3.4. This restriction is inconvenient, to say the least, but not fatal.

The AgentLauncher opens only one socket connection, to the AgentServer running on the same machine the applet was served from (the dispatching AgentServer). This is the only connection the browser allows us. We'll talk about agent results in more detail later. For now, all we need to know is that agents report their results in messages back to the AgentLauncher through the dispatching AgentServer.

Stopping an Agent

At some point, our dispatched agent is no longer needed. While we will insert some simple, automatic mechanisms to prevent agents from running forever, we also let the user stop an agent run manually by hitting the Stop button. This action sends a message (see KillMessage in Chapter 7) onto the network that says "Kill any instance of this agent."

Killing the AgentLauncher

For reasons we'll discuss at more length in Chapters 4 and 6, once you start the AgentLauncher, it runs in the background forever, or until you exit the browser. For this reason, we provide a Kill button that terminates any AgentLauncher threads that may be running.

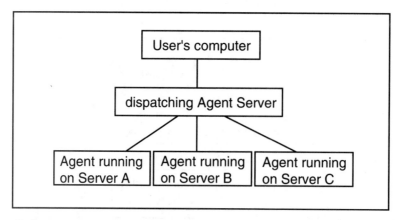

Figure 3.4

Three instances of an agent communicating with the user through a server.

The AgentServer

The agents we dispatch onto the Net need a platform to run on. You can't just connect to a random socket on the Net, dump a Java class into it, and expect it to run. This is where the AgentServer comes in. The AgentServer has one purpose in life—to run agents. What this amounts to is receiving Java class files and configuration information over a network socket connection, instantiating the class, and providing various "services" to the new object (the instance of the received class). Because of the AgentLauncher file I/O restrictions we discussed earlier, the dispatching AgentServer has another small task to perform—serving the list of agents to interested AgentLaunchers. Thus, we can summarize the AgentServer's responsibilities as:

- Dispatching agents
- Running agents
- Serving the list of dispatchable agents to the AgentLauncher

We'll talk in detail about how AgentServers perform these tasks, but first let's look briefly at what kind of program an AgentServer is.

Applications and Applets

The AgentServer is a standalone application. While standalone applications are not the focus of this book, we'll talk about the AgentServer enough that writing standalone apps should be fairly easy to pick up. For design purposes, the main difference between standalone application development and applet development is the unrestricted access to network and file I/O.

We already know that applets must run within a browser. Standalone applications (as the name implies) can run without a browser. All a Java application needs is a Java interpreter. That interpreter is a program named *java*. The following command runs our standalone AgentServer application. Figure 3.5 shows an AgentServer running.

```
java -classpath \agent\classees\rel;\jdk\java\lib\classes.zip agent/
Server/AgentServer
```

Notice how similar the AgentServer is to Sun's appletviewer. Notice also how limited a user interface the AgentServer has. In fact, the only user interaction it allows (besides the load-test function from Chapter 9) is the Exit function. We'll

Figure 3.5

An AgentServer running.

look a little more closely at the unique requirements of standalone applications as we go along.

Dispatching Agents: The Agent Network

A key part of dispatching an agent is knowing where to dispatch it to. We need to maintain a list of AgentServers to which agents may be dispatched. The effect we want to achieve is to have an agent started anywhere on the network eventually cover the whole network. What we come up with is a simple command the agent can give an AgentServer that says, "Redispatch me to all the AgentServers on your list."

Thus, we can define an agent network as any set of AgentServers that have each other in their server lists. There is no system as to how AgentServers link to each other via their server lists. One AgentServer may appear in many different lists. While this makes list maintenance fairly easy, it also means AgentServers must take special precautions to make sure that they don't run the same agent instance twice. Figure 3.6 shows the interlocking server lists of a simple agent network.

We have four AgentServers each with different, occasionally overlapping, server lists. Figure 3.7 shows how an agent started at one of these servers would traverse the network.

The Agent starts at Katie and dispatches to Ginger and Rafi. From Ginger, it redispatches to Rafi, but Rafi recognizes it as one that's already run and dumps it. From Rafi, the agent dispatched from Katie redispatches to Dudley. Once on Dudley, it redispatches back to Katie, which recognizes it as a duplicate and dumps it.

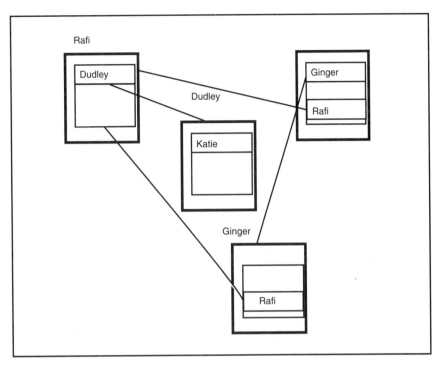

Figure 3.6

A simple agent network.

Notice that the agent tries to load twice on both Katie and Rafi—an inefficency that a more sophisticated propagation strategy would eliminate. Ours is a very

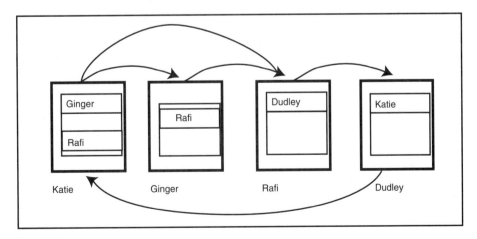

Figure 3.7

An agent traversing the network.

simplistic agent propagation strategy that requires hand-building and maintenance of the server lists. For our purposes, though, it will suffice.

Running Agents: The AgentContext Interface

The AgentServer has two pieces: the tasks it needs to perform simply to exist
and the environment it provides for agents to run in. In this way, the AgentServer
is very much like a Web browser. The browser does many tasks on its own, such
as displaying HTML text, but it also provides an environment for applets to run
in, a way for applets to talk to the browser using the **AppletContext** interface
(which we discuss at length in the next chapter). The AgentServer provides agents
with similar context through the AgentContext interface, as shown in Listing 3.1.

Listing 3.1 The AgentContext Interface

```
package agent.Server;

import agent.*;
import java.lang.*;
import java.net.*;

/** The agent's interface into the environment in which it is
running. This is implemented only by the AgentServer. An agent should
never run any server side functions unless it has a valid AgentContext.
@see agent.Agent
@version 1.0
@author John Rodley 12/1/1995
*/
public interface AgentContext {

/** This is called by the agent to redispatch this agent to all the
servers in the Servers list. The agent can call this method ONLY ONCE! The
server has the option of whether or not to do anything. For security
reasons,
some servers may not dispatch at all. The agent can call dispatch at
any time. Some agents may want to dispatch first, then run; others may
want to run first and then decide whether or not to dispatch based on
results.
@return true if the Agent was dispatched to ANY servers, false otherwise
*/
   public boolean dispatch();

/** This is called by the agent to write a String of result text to the
results HTML file. The agent is responsible for creating syntactically
```

correct HTML. The server may or may not choose to actually write the
string to the file. Servers will be expected to implement checks on
result file size, and agent runtime that will affect whether or not
they actually write the string.
@param HTMLString This is a string of text in HTML that will appear in
the results page for this Agent run.
@return true if the string was written to the output file, false
otherwise.
*/
    public boolean writeOutput(String HTMLString);
/** This is called by the agent to write a String of result text to the
results HTML file. The agent is responsible for creating syntactically
correct HTML. The server may or may not choose to actually write the
string to the file. Servers will be expected to implement checks on
result file size, and agent runtime that will affect whether or not
they actually write the string.
@param HTMLString This is a string of text in HTML that will appear in
the results page for this Agent run.
@return true if the string was written to the output file, false
otherwise.
*/
    public boolean writeOutput(byte b[]);
/** Called by the agent to get the URL of the file that writeOutput has
been writing our result strings to. The agent uses this to pass to
reportFinish.
@see reportFinish
@return the URL of the results file as a String. Result files must have
Web-accessible URLs.
*/
    public String getResultsURL(String AgentID);
/** Called by the agent to make the AgentServer tell the dispatching
AgentServer that this agent has begun working. Receipt of this message
by the AgentLauncher should cause it to create an entry in its agent
list for this agent.
@param AgentID The ID of this agent
@see agent.Launcher
@see agent.Server
*/
    public void reportStart(String AgentID);
/** Called by the agent to make the AgentServer tell the dispatching
AgentServer that this agent has finished work and has created the
following result file. Receipt of this message by the AgentLauncher should
cause it to update this agents entry in the agent list.
@param AgentID The ID of this agent

```
@param url The URL of the results file. If null, there were no results.
@param price The price this AgentServer will charge to view the results
file.
@param comment Any comment the Agent might wish to make about this
result - including its size, running time ...
@see agent.Launcher
@see agent.Server
*/
   public void reportFinish( String AgentID, String url, int price, String
comment );
}
```

Through the **AgentContext** interface, an agent can request the following services from an AgentServer:

- Report that it has started work back to its dispatching AgentServer (which passes it on to the AgentLauncher). This allows the AgentLauncher to maintain the viewable list of working agents. Returns true if successful, false otherwise.

- Report that it has finished work back to its dispatching AgentServer (which passes it on to the AgentLauncher). This message includes the URL of the results file and allows the AgentLauncher to update its viewable list of working Agents. Clicking on this agent will now point the browser at the results file URL.

- Write a string to the results file on the AgentServer host. The supplied string will appear in the results file that the AgentServer has created especially for *this* run of *this* agent. Returns false if the AgentServer chooses *not* to write the string to the results file.

- Get the URL that corresponds to the results file. Returns a URL corresponding to the file where all the strings sent to **writeOutput** were written.

- Redispatch this agent to all the servers in the agent server list. Returns true if the agent was dispatched to any other servers, false otherwise. This is how agents hop across the agent system network—by telling the server they're running on to redispatch them.

Notice that we've eliminated all the communication functions from the agent. All the communications back to the user to report status and give the URL of the results file are handled by calls to the AgentServer through the **AgentContext** interface. This allows, but does not require, us to implement a security system within the AgentServer that restricts agents (whom we might not trust) from making network connections while preserving the ability of AgentServers (whom we do trust) to make those same connections.

Notice also that an agent's access to the file system *can* be severely restricted. The AgentServer is only required to allow the agent write access to a single file into which it can write its results. The agent's only access to that file is through the **writeOutput** calls, which allow the agent to write strings or byte arrays to a file on the AgentServer. The AgentServer, though, retains complete control over that file. The AgentServer can choose whether or not to actually write that string/byte array to the file. If the file is too big, or if the agent's been running too long, or for whatever reason, the AgentServer can simply stop that output. This way, within the AgentServer's **SecurityManager** we can eliminate the agent's file I/O ability entirely without crippling the AgentServer's file I/O ability—something many system administrators are bound to find attractive.

The final call available to agents, dispatch, allows agents to control when and whether they get redispatched to the servers in the current AgentServers list. One place where this control might be useful is in our file-finding example. If an agent finds the file on a particular server, there's no reason to keep dispatching to other servers. After all, how many copies of that file do you need?

The Dispatching AgentServer

Of all the AgentServers in an Agent system, for any particular agent run, there will be one server designated as the dispatching AgentServer. This AgentServer has the only direct connection to the user, and all messages from agents in the field must go through this server. The dispatching AgentServer runs the exact same code as all the other AgentServers.

The reason that we need a special dispatching AgentServer is that an AgentLauncher applet *can only open network connections to the host from which it was loaded.* If you load the HTML page identified by the URL:

```
http://www.channel1.com/users/ajrodley/index.html
```

which contains this **<applet>** tag:

```
<applet code=animator/JohnImage.class height=100 width=200>
```

the AgentLauncher will only be able to make a network connection back to www.channel1.com. Thus, in order to talk to the network of AgentServers, an AgentLauncher loaded from www.channel1.com must funnel all communications through a server running on www.channel1.com. The AgentServer running on www.channel1.com will be the one that starts dispatching any agents chosen from this AgentLauncher. Thus, we designate the server running on www.channel1.com as the dispatching AgentServer.

The dispatching AgentServer deals with two message types (from the AgentLauncher) that other AgentServers do not:

* Dispatch the class named <xxx> configured with <xxx> arguments *from* this dispatching AgentServer to all the AgentServers in the server list.
* Get the list of agents that are available for dispatching *from* this AgentServer.

When an agent is dispatched throughout the network, the address <machine name:port number> of the dispatching AgentServer is included in the message. Other AgentServers then know where to connect when they report results.

The dispatching AgentServer and the AgentLauncher keep an open connection. Should that connection disappear, the dispatching AgentServer knows to cease serving that run of that agent.

Agents

From a user's perspective, the agent is where the real utility of this system is embedded. Say, for instance, a user wishes to search the network for a file with a particular name. What has to happen is that someone needs to write a Java class that runs that search on one machine. The Agent system takes care of getting that class onto all the machines on the network.

Running agents do not communicate with each other. The AgentLauncher configures the agent, the dispatching AgentServer sends it onto the network, and, using the **AgentContext** interface, the running agents all report directly back to the dispatching AgentServer. Inter-agent communication is not prohibited by design. It is simply beyond the scope of what we're trying to accomplish.

Agent: Applet or Application?

An agent is neither an applet nor an application. It is simply a class that embodies all our knowledge about a particular task. In our file-find example, for instance, all the information about searching for files (such as how to deal with directory structures and file name conventions) is embedded in the agent. This also means that the agent, rather than the AgentLauncher, must get its configuration information from the user.

In order to write an agent class, we have to answer the question: What generalizations can we make about agents? Surprisingly few. Any two agents are only guaranteed to have three things in common:

- They subclass **Object**, as all Java classes do.
- They need to be configured.
- They run.

These requirements guide us pretty quickly to the design of a base class for agents shown in Listing 3.2.

Listing 3.2   The Agent Class

```
package agent.Agent;

import java.lang.*;
import java.util.*;
import java.awt.*;
import agent.Agent.*;

// To catch the definition of AgentContext
import agent.Server.AgentContext;

/** The base class for all agents in the agent system. An
almost purely abstract class, with the only bit of
implementation embodied in the setAgentContext method.
@version 1.0 12/1/1995
@author John Rodley
@see agent.AgentContext
@see agent.AgentServer
*/
public abstract class Agent extends Thread {

/** The agent's interface to the AgentServer. If the agent is
loaded on an AgentLauncher, as it will be when it is being
configured, this will be null.
*/
   public AgentContext ac;

/** Called by the AgentServer to set an AgentContext for this
```

```
agent to use when reporting status or creating and reporting
results.

@param agentContext An object implementing the AgentContext
interface. Usually the AgentServer itself.
*/
   public void setAgentContext(AgentContext a) { ac = a; }

/** Called by the AgentLauncher to get the arguments needed
for this run of this agent. Usually creates a dialog box to get
input from the browser user.

@param frame A Frame object, usually the Frame of the browser.
*/
   public abstract void configure( Frame frame );

/** Called by the AgentLauncher to get the arguments that were
set via configure.
@return A Vector of Strings that will be passed back to the
Agent when the AgentServer instantiates it on a server. The
Strings can contain any data that might be meaningful to the
Agent. There is no limit on the number of arguments.
@see awt.Dialog
*/
   public abstract Vector getArguments();

/** Called by the AgentServer to set the arguments this run of
this agent will use. The arguments obtained from the browser
user are stuffed into a portion of the agent load message. The
AgentServer extracts the args from the message, creates a
Vector of Strings and passes that Vector to the agent via this
call.

@param args A Vector of Strings that are exactly what the
AgentLauncher returned to the AgentLauncher from getArguments.
*/
   public abstract void setArguments( Vector args );
}
```

Subclassing **Object** obviously requires no work on our part.

The requirement to be runnable could have been satisfied either of two ways: implementing the **Runnable** interface or subclassing **Thread**. I chose to subclass **Thread**, but could just as easily have done it the other way. The only reason to subclass **Thread** is that we *don't* need to subclass anything else. Remember, Java allows only single class inheritance (no multiple inheritance).

The need to be configured is more difficult to satisfy because it means that we must instantiate the agent within the AgentLauncher. Whenever we load a class in Java, the class loader tries to resolve every class/interface reference in that class. **Agent** references the **AgentContext** interface in the variable **ac**, and the method **setAgentContext**. Thus, the **AgentContext** interface definition (agent/Server/AgentContext.class) must be available to the AgentLauncher, even though an **Agent** instantiated under the AgentLauncher will never use it.

In actuality, an **Agent** instantiated under the AgentLauncher never gets started to run in its own thread because it doesn't need to run asynchronously. We only instantiate **Agent** under AgentLauncher so we can get the list of arguments it needs to run using the **configure** and **getArguments** methods.

Configuring an Agent

Consider a file-find agent that allows you to search for several files in one run. When the user picks this agent from the list, the AgentLauncher calls **Agent.configure**, which can do anything it wants to get the arguments from the user. In most cases, we'd expect it to put up a dialog box that the user can fill out.

Our file-find example (detailed in Chapter 9) displays the dialog box shown in Figure 3.8.

This dialog box, which is constructed, displayed, and processed by an instance of **Agent** created by the AgentLauncher, allows the user to enter seven file names for which to search. It can be as complex or as simple as the particular agent requires. If we did not embed this configuration method within the **Agent** itself, we'd have to do one of the following:

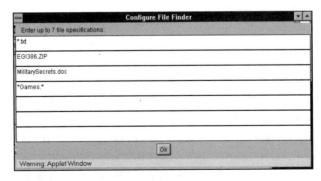

Figure 3.8

The FileFinder agent's configuration dialog box.

- Modify the AgentLauncher to have individualized configuration dialog boxes for each of the available agents.

- Implement a generic configuration dialog box through which all arguments for all agents have to be entered.

The first of these options would make adding new agents a nightmare; the AgentLauncher would have to be modified for each new agent, and then kept in sync with any agent revisions. The second option would severely limit the descriptiveness of the configuration dialog box, making the whole system seem vague and confusing. Encapsulating the knowledge of a task within a single class is one of the goals of object-oriented design. Spreading this knowledge among various classes as those two alternatives propose would amount to object-oriented heresy.

The ultimate result of configuring an agent is a Vector (growable array) of Java Strings. The agent can construct this Vector however it wants. Whatever the Vector looks like when the agent gives it to the AgentLauncher (when the AgentLauncher invokes **Agent.getArguments**) at configuration time is exactly how it will look when the AgentServer passes it into the agent at runtime (with **Agent.setArguments**). The AgentLauncher stores those arguments to be packaged with the agent's class file when the agent is dispatched to the AgentServers.

It might seem that the **Agent** class really doesn't do anything at all. That's true. The **Agent** class is almost purely abstract. An agent writer has to subclass it and add worthwhile content to make the agent useful. The theory is that the Agent system (AgentLauncher, AgentServers, and Agent superclass) will be a medium in which agents can operate. This approach allows coders writing individual agents to concentrate on what the agent needs to accomplish on the target machine, without worrying about how the agent gets onto the target machine, or how to transport the results back to the user.

How Does an Agent Report Results?

Any particular agent will have one job to do—for example, running a database query. But how does the user know what the agent found, what the results of the query were? The agent could send every byte of information it finds back over the network connection to the AgentLauncher, where the AgentLauncher would format it for display to the user. This would work, but it could mean a huge amount of communication between AgentLauncher and agent. We want to restrict that communication as much as possible.

It would also mean a great deal of work on the AgentLauncher to present the information in an attractive manner. In most cases, this would not be feasible, since, by design, the AgentLauncher knows absolutely nothing about the content of the data. The AgentLauncher doesn't know whether the agent is running an SQL query, searching for a file, or querying every system for users named Joe. All the knowledge of the agent's job is contained in the agent itself, including how to best format the results.

The Web provides a perfect solution to this problem. As the agent performs its task, it creates an HTML page describing the results. When it finishes, it sends a single message back to the AgentLauncher giving the URL of the results page. To see those results, the user can merely point the browser at that URL. Figure 3.9 shows the results HTML file created when our sample FileFinder agent searched for *.class on one of the AgentServers in my local network.

The trick of result-reporting is how, within the AgentLauncher, to get the URL of the agent's results file to appear as a hyperlink in the user's current HTML document. We take two approaches to this. One of them is to represent each running agent with an animated icon. Clicking on the icon takes you to the results file for that agent. The AgentServer to which the AgentLauncher is connected also creates its own results file that is simply a list of all the result URLs that have come back from the running agents. Clicking on a "Results" button in the AgentLauncher takes the user to this page. From there the user can also get to the various individual result pages by clicking on one of those links.

One Run of an Agent

Now that we've looked at the system design, we can take a look at how one run, dispatching one agent to do one job, might work from the user's point of view:

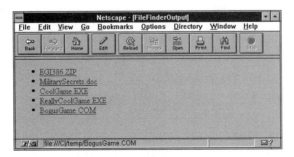

Figure 3.9

A FileFinder agent results file viewed with Netscape.

- The user starts the browser.

- The user points the browser at the HTML page containing the AgentLauncher applet.

- The AgentLauncher connects to the AgentServer and gets the agent list.

- The user chooses an agent from the agent list using the AgentLauncher.

- The user configures the agent using the AgentLauncher.

- The user dispatches the agent using the AgentLauncher.

- The AgentLauncher sends the agent name and configuration info to the dispatching AgentServer, which dispatches it to all the AgentServers that it knows about. Each AgentServer that runs the agent does the same, thus covering the whole network.

- Each of the AgentServers creates an instance of **Agent** and starts it running.

- The user watches the results display as the agent begins to run on all the different servers. As the agents report results, the user clicks on a particular result HTML page to view the result. The user can switch back and forth between result pages and the AgentLauncher, while the AgentLauncher continues to run in the background, collecting new result URLs.

Objects and Classes

The Agent system does not ship objects around the Net. An object is an instance of a class, and the Agent system ships classes. This is an important distinction.

The main reason for this is that there is no practical way to turn a Java object into a lump of bytes that can be pushed across a network connection. In C/C++ this would be trivial. Just cast a pointer to the object to char * and write it to the socket. You can't do that in Java.

More difficult than the problem of how to "package" an object for shipment is the problem of translating context from the machine that the object was instantiated on, to the machine it intends to run on. In order to run an object (rather than a class) that was shipped across the Net, Java would have to replicate the conditions that existed on the machine that instantiated the object. This would be wildly expensive, if possible at all. This is a pretty advanced topic that we're glossing over lightly. Suffice to say that shipping objects rather than classes presents virtually insurmountable problems within Java.

The practical implications of shipping classes rather than objects appear in the communications protocol. Were we shipping objects around the Net, we could configure the agent locally, then dispatch the whole object as one lump of bytes. As it is, we have to ship both the configuration data and the class file as distinct lumps of data and the configuration data has to be applied to the agent every time it starts up on an AgentServer. It's as if, instead of telling our plumber what we want done, and then sending him to the building, we're sending him out to the site with sealed instructions that he can only open once he gets there.

Why Java?

It would not be possible to write an application like this without something like Java. Java's simple network communication package makes it easy to implement our fairly simple protocol (see Chapter 7). Its simple class-loading mechanism allows us to load the classes we've passed over the Net and run them as easily as we run local classes (see Chapter 9). The combination of Java's **Applet** class and a Web browser provides as slick a user interface as you could possibly want.

But most important of all, Java provides portability. With Java we can write *one* AgentServer that will run on any machine. We can write *one* AgentLauncher that will run under any browser. And we can write *one* agent that will run on any AgentServer machine. Once these three pieces are in place, anyone who wants to write a new agent only needs to concentrate on what the agent must do without worrying about how agents traverse the Net, or how they get their results to the user.

Conclusion

In this chapter, we've seen how the Agent system splits into three logical pieces—the user interface, server, and agent. We saw how those three pieces each correspond to a different type of Java class:

- A standalone Java application: the AgentServer.
- A Java applet: the AgentLauncher.
- A Java class that can operate as part of either an applet or application: the agent.

We looked at the strengths and weaknesses of each piece and saw how the security restrictions imposed on applets complicate the design of the system. We saw how to take advantage of the Web by storing our results in hyperlinked HTML documents. Along the way, we saw some of the risks involved with such a system, and how the agent system tries to mitigate them. Some of the risks are:

- Cancerous agent multiplication
- Malicious agents attacking system resources
- Buggy agents eating CPU cycles

We explored the difference between object and classes, and why the Agent system transports classes, rather than objects, over the network. Finally, we discussed the unique combination of features in Java–Web access, network communication, easy class-loading, and portability that makes this type of system possible.

Chapter **4**

A Look into the Applet Class

A Look into the Applet Class

The Applet class is your applets doorway into the browser. Check here as we cross the threshold.

Back in Chapter 1, we wrote a simple applet. In Chapter 3, we designed a system that presents itself on the Web by using an applet, the AgentLauncher, as its user interface. We have an idea of what an applet is, and a reason to use it. Now, it's time to get into more of the details.

In this chapter we'll write some applets and talk about where they appear, what they look like, when they run, and how they interact with their environment. When we're done, we should have a good idea of just what happens when a browser plows into that **<applet>** tag in an HTML document.

Positioning Applets on the Screen

As we've seen, the only way to get an applet to appear on the browser screen is by embedding an **<applet>** tag in an HTML document and then viewing that document. Like every other HTML element, the placement of the **<applet>** tag determines where on the screen the applet appears. Consider the simple example in Listing 4.1. and Listing 4.2, which provides the HTML code to run the applet, contains a number of HTML elements, including text paragraphs and images, our simple applet, then more HTML elements. Figure 4.1 shows how this applet appears running in Netscape.

Listing 4.1   Positioning an Applet

```
package chap4;

import java.awt.Graphics;
import java.applet.Applet;

/** An applet that prints the string ''Hello world'' at absolute
applet-relative coordinates x=20, y=50.
@author John Rodley
@version 1.0
*/
public class ch4_fig1 extends Applet {

/** Actually paint the string on the screen
*/
  public void paint(Graphics g) {
    g.drawString( ''Hello world'', 20, 50 );
  }
}
```

Listing 4.2   HTML Page Referencing Code

```
<!DOCTYPE HTML PUBLIC
''-//SQ//DTD HTML 2.0 HoTMetaL + extensions//EN''>
<HTML><HEAD><TITLE>An Applet in the HTML Milieu</TITLE></HEAD>
<BODY><H1>Some Text</H1>
<P>When you want to place an applet, you simply place it
within the page at the spot you want it to appear.  The
problem of placing applets is the same problem all HTML
elements have - the fact that HTML tags are 'suggestions', not
directives, which browsers are free to interpret
differently.  Now, a pair of goodogs, for your amusement:
<IMG SRC=''chap4/ch4_fig1a.jpg'' ALIGN=''BOTTOM''>
<IMG SRC=''chap4/ch4_fig1b.jpg'' ALIGN=''BOTTOM''>
<P>Below is the applet.  Can you tell the difference between
the applet text, and the HTML?</P>
<applet code=chap4/ch4_fig1.class width=100 height=100>
</applet>
The applet is above us.  Notice that as long as you don't
use non-default backgrounds, it's impossible to tell the
applet from the HTML.</P></BODY></HTML>
```

The two **import** statements used in Listing 4.1 are for the **Applet** class, which all applets subclass, and for the **Graphics** class, which we use in the **paint** method. The code line **extends Applet** tells the compiler that this class should get all the functionality of the **Applet** class. The **paint** method overrides a do-nothing method that is part of the **Applet** class (via its inheritance of **Component**). The line **g.drawString** tells the **Graphics** object to draw a **String** at 20 on the X-axis and 50 on the Y. If you think about it, six lines of code (three of which are boilerplate stuff) have gotten us a functional and useful applet. We'll talk more about the **paint** method later in this chapter, and we'll cover the details of dealing with **Graphics** objects in more detail in Chapter 5. For now, what we're mainly interested in is how the applet fits into the host HTML document.

The rule browsers use when formatting a document is to stretch or compress the document vertically such that a line of text never rolls off the horizontal edge of the screen. If you resize the screen, Netscape will reformat the text *and* reposition the applet. As we resize the document in Figure 4.1 to make it narrower (smaller horizontally), our applet will eventually be pushed out the bottom of the window and we'll have to scroll vertically to get it back on the screen.

If you've played with browsers much, you've probably seen that browsers treat text and images differently. For instance, if you shrink the document in Figure 4.1 to make the window smaller horizontally than the width of our images,

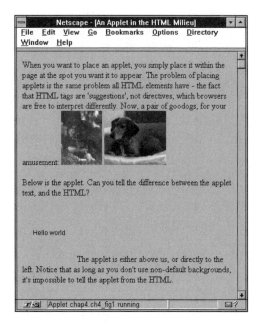

Figure 4.1

Netscape running Listing 4.2.

you'll see the browser add a horizontal scrollbar for scrolling the entire image. Browsers treat applets the same as images—as lumps that always get a rectangular area whose shape can't be changed by the browser.

Breaking down the Applet Class

So far, we've talked about applets in general terms—as small applications. But in Java, **Applet** is an actual class of its own, with very specific capabilities. In fact, the **Applet** class is at the end of a fairly long chain of inheritance consisting of the **Object**, **Component**, **Container**, **Panel**, and **Applet**. In simplistic terms, the first four superclasses give **Applet** the following capabilities:

- **Object** provides the ability to behave as a Java entity.
- **Component** provides the ability to appear as a visual entity on-screen.
- **Container** provides the ability to *encapsulate* other visual entities.
- **Panel** provides the ability to align encapsulated visual entities.

We've already talked a little about the basic Java **Object**. The remaining three classes are part of the windowing system, AWT, which we'll discuss briefly here, and will look at in more detail in Chapter 5. From these superclasses, we can easily infer a lot about what an applet is—it's a space on the screen, a window if you wish, that is a child of the window in which the browser is displaying the HTML text.

Component is the key class in this inheritance chain. Subclassing **Component** makes **Applet** a child window. Visually, a child window is a space on the screen that has the same background color as its parent, the browser main window. It has no border, and no menu, and nothing appears in that window unless we put it there. It can be drawn on at the pixel level (via **Graphics**) and it has the ability to capture events, like mouse clicks and key presses.

However, the **Applet** class is not just the sum of its superclasses. It implements many methods of its own, as shown in Table 4.1.

Over the course of this chapter, we'll use each of these methods, except for **getImage** and the URL grabbing methods, **getDocumentBase** and **getCodeBase**. If you're psyched to start displaying images via **getImage**, you'll have to wait until Chapter 5. We use both **getDocumentBase** and **getCodeBase** extensively in Chapter 7.

Table 4.1 The Applet Class

Method	Argument	Description
getApplet	String	Returns the applet or null if it isn't loaded
getAppletContext		Returns an object implementing the AppletContext interface
getAppletInfo		Returns a String that includes whatever information the applet author chooses; usually author, version, and copyright
getAudioClip	URL or URL,String	Returns an in-memory audio clip that can be played via Applet.play
getCodeBase		Returns the complete URL of this applet
getDocumentBase		Returns the complete URL of the HTML document in which this applet is embedded
getImage	URL or URL, String	Returns an in-memory image that can be drawn via Graphics.drawImage; this call *does not* load the image file over the Net
getParameter	String	Returns the string provided in the value=1portion of the param statement; for example, the argument <param name=GHIJ value=1234> returns returns "1234" after a call to getParameter("GHIJ")
getParameterInfo		Returns a two-dimensional String array explaining the arguments this applet accepts
init		Overload method that gets called whenever the applet is loaded
isActive		Returns true if Applet.start has been called
play	URL or URL,String	
resize	int height, width	
showStatus	String	
start		Overloaded method called each time the user visits the applet's HTML page
stop		Overloaded method called each time the user leaves the applet's HTML page

Resizing an Applet

The size of an applet is set through the **<applet>** tag in the HTML document. In Listing 4.2, we specified a height of 100 pixels and a width of 100 pixels, so the browser made a hole of that size in the document and flowed the text around it.

Unfortunately, some of the current crop of browsers don't deal well with reformatting the HTML document if the applet changes size. Suppose you use **Applet.resize** to make your applet smaller than the size set from the **<applet>** tag with **height** and **width** parameters. The HTML document should reflow to fit exactly around the new, smaller size. If the browser doesn't reflow the HTML document, there'll be an embarassing strip of default background in the spaces around the applet. Listing 4.3 changes our applet to downsize itself, uses a background color other than the default for the applet, and adds a background image to the HTML document. Figure 4.2 shows the improved applet running in Netscape.

Listing 4.3 A "Shriveled" Applet

```
package chap4;

import java.awt.Graphics;
import java.applet.Applet;
import java.awt.Color;

/** An applet that prints the string ''Hello world, again'' at
absolute applet-relative coordinates x=20, y=50 after clearing
the applet workspace to yellow.
@author John Rodley
@version 1.0
*/
public class ch4_fig2 extends Applet {

/** Resize the applet to slightly smaller than the applet
tag sizes us.
*/
  public void init() {
    resize( 90, 90 );
  }

/** Actually paint the string on the screen, first clearing the
workspace to yellow.
*/
  public void paint(Graphics g) {
```

```
    g.setColor(Color.yellow);
    g.fillRect(0,0,size().height, size().width);
    g.setColor(Color.black);
     g.drawString( ''Hello world, again'', 20, 50 );
  }
}
```

Listing 4.4   HTML Code That Runs the Shriveled Applet

```
<!DOCTYPE HTML PUBLIC
''-//SQ//DTD HTML 2.0 HoTMetaL + extensions//EN''>
<HTML><HEAD><TITLE>The Shrivelling Applet</TITLE></HEAD>
<BODY BACKGROUND=''background.jpg''>
<P>A pair of goodogs, to watch your incredible shrinking
applet:
<IMG SRC=''chap4/ch4_fig1a.jpg'' ALIGN=''BOTTOM''>
<IMG SRC=''chap4/ch4_fig1b.jpg'' ALIGN=''BOTTOM''>
Below is the applet, started with an initial size of 100 by
100 pixels:
<applet code=chap4/ch4_fig2.class width=100 height=100>
</applet>
The first word of this sentence should butt right up against
the applets right hand edge even though the applet has shrunk
to 90 by 90 pixels, assuming the browser re-flowed correctly.
</P></BODY></HTML>
```

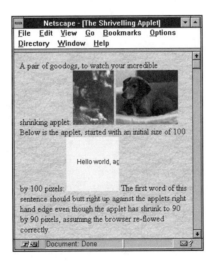

Figure 4.2

The shriveled applet running in Netscape.

84   Chapter 4

So that's what happens if you shrink an applet within its allotted browser space. But what if you want to grow the applet beyond its browser space? It's the same issue in reverse: The HTML document has to be reflowed to provide more space for the growing applet. Listing 4.5 changes the applet in Listing 4.3 to burst out of its allotted space, and Figure 4.3 shows the results.

Listing 4.5   Growing an Applet

```
package chap4;

import java.awt.Graphics;
import java.applet.Applet;
import java.awt.Color;

/** An applet that prints the string ''Hello world, again'' at
absolute applet-relative coordinates x=20, y=50 on a red
background.
@author John Rodley
@version 1.0
*/
public class ch4_fig3 extends Applet {

/** Resize the applet to slightly larger than the applet
tag sizes us.
*/
  public void init() {
    resize( 120, 120 );
  }

/** Actually paint the string on the screen, after clearing the
applet to red first.
*/
  public void paint(Graphics g) {
    g.setColor(Color.red);
    g.fillRect(0,0,size().height, size().width);
    g.setColor(Color.black);
     g.drawString( ''Hello world, again'', 20, 50 );
  }
}
```

Listing 4.6   HTML Code That Runs the Growing Applet

```
<!DOCTYPE HTML PUBLIC
''-//SQ//DTD HTML 2.0 HoTMetaL + extensions//EN''>
<HTML><HEAD><TITLE>The Growing Applet</TITLE></HEAD>
<BODY BACKGROUND=''background.jpg''>
```

```
<P>A pair of goodogs, to watch over your growing applet:
<IMG SRC=''chap4/ch4_fig1a.jpg'' ALIGN=''BOTTOM''>
<IMG SRC=''chap4/ch4_fig1b.jpg'' ALIGN=''BOTTOM''>
Below is the applet, started with an initial size of 100 by
100 pixels:
<applet code=chap4/ch4_fig3.class width=100 height=100>
</applet>
The first word of this sentence should butt right up against
the applets right hand edge even though the applet has grown to
120 by 120 pixels, assuming the browser re-flowed correctly.
</P></BODY></HTML>
```

As you can see, Netscape correctly reflows the document to accommodate whatever applet resizing you might do. Notice also that our text string doesn't completely print out. This is the fate of graphics operations that try to exceed the bounds of the applet: They simply don't happen. In Chapter 5's ticker example, we'll take a closer look at how to fit text into a given area.

When Does an Applet Run?

For traditional computer programs the answer to the question "when does the program run?" is obvious. When the user runs the program, it runs, and when the user closes it, it stops running. The user doesn't have that kind of control over an applet. It is the browser, not the user, that loads, runs, stops, and unloads applets, so the answer becomes a lot more involved. The simplistic answer to the

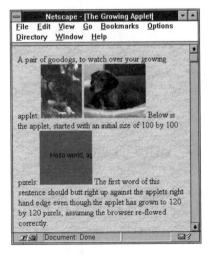

Figure 4.3

The growing applet running in Netscape.

question is this: An applet runs when its space in the HTML document is visible, and stops running when, for whatever reason, that space in the HTML document is not visible.

Unless an applet creates and runs in its own thread, the simple answer holds true. This is because an applet like the simple one shown in Listing 4.1 is running in a thread that the browser has created and controls. When Java applets create their own threads, the answer becomes more complicated. Technically, because these threads are beyond the control of the browser, there is no written-in-stone rule on when an applet runs. In theory, browsers expect well-behaved applets to adhere to the basic rule of run when you're on-screen, and stop running when you're off-screen, but whether or not an applet implements that theory is completely up to the applet writer. We'll discuss threads in more detail in Chapter 6, and eventually write our own multi-threaded and ill-behaved, but wickedly useful, applets.

Whether the applet itself is single or multi-thread, ill or well-behaved, the browser obeys a certain set of rules when trying to run it. In this sense, the browser treats the applet as a peer, where, no matter how the applet behaves, it can expect certain behaviors from the browser. These behaviors, the browser invoking one of four applet methods, are clues as to what is going on in the browser.

Here's a brief rundown of the methods: When the browser first encounters the **<applet>** tag in the HTML doc, it calls **Applet.init**. When a user visits the applet's page, the browser calls **Applet.start**. When the user leaves the applet's page, the browser calls **Applet.stop**, and whenever it decides the applet is not needed anymore and should be expunged from memory, it calls **Applet.destroy**. Thus, **Applet.init** and **Applet.destroy** get called once in the life of an applet, while **Applet.start** and **Applet.stop** can be called any number of times. An applet that cares about whether or not it's loaded or on-screen can override **init**, **start**, **stop** and **destroy**, as shown in Figure 4.4.

Adding Sound to an Applet

Let's improve our simple applet to sing us a little song. Listing 4.7 shows these modifications. Play with the applet. See what happens if you scroll the applet off the screen, or if you hyperlink to another page.

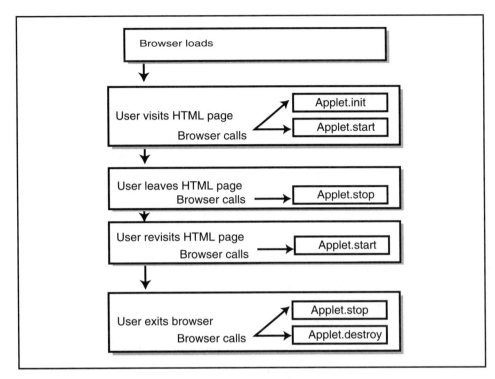

Figure 4.4

Overridden methods along the applet execution trail.

Listing 4.7   The Do-Nothing Applet, with Sound

```
package chap4;

import java.awt.Graphics;
import java.applet.Applet;
import java.applet.AudioClip;
import java.net.*;

/** A simple app that plays a tune, supplied by the applet tag
via the name ''StartClip'' every time Applet.start is called, and
plays another tune, paramater name ''EndClip'' every time
Applet.stop is called. Plays the RunningClip in a loop between
start and stop.
@version 1.0 12/20/1995
@author John Rodley
*/
public class ch4_fig4 extends Applet {
```

```
    String sAppletInfo;
    URL StartClipURL;
    URL EndClipURL;
    AudioClip RunningClip;

    String pinfo[][] = {
       {''StartClip'', ''URL'', ''The URL of an audio clip played at
startup'' },
       {''RunningClip'', ''URL'',
          ''The URL of an audio clip played between start and stop'' },
       {''EndClip'', ''URL'', ''The URL of an audio clip played at stop'' }
       };

/** Whenever a user visits our page, the browser calls this.
This is an override of an Applet method.. */
  public void start() {
     if( RunningClip == null || StartClipURL == null )
       return;
      play( StartClipURL );
     RunningClip.loop();
     System.out.println( ''after loop'' );
   }


/** Whenever the user leaves our page, this gets called.
Another override of an Applet method.
*/
  public void stop() {
     if( RunningClip == null || EndClipURL == null )
       return;
     RunningClip.stop();
    play( EndClipURL );
   }


/** Tell anyone who might inquire what we are.
@return A string describing this applet.
*/
  public String getAppletInfo() {
    return(''JRodley - Java Applets Book - Chapter 4 figure 4'');
     }

/** Tell anyone who might inquire how to use this applet.
@return A 2d string array describing the arguments to this
applet.
*/
  public String[][] getParameterInfo() {
     return pinfo;
   }
```

```
/** Connect to the URLs specified by the StartClip and EndClip
parameters in the applet tag.
*/
  public void init() {
  try {
     StartClipURL = new URL(getParameter(''StartClip''));
     RunningClip = getAudioClip(new URL(getParameter(''RunningClip'')));
     EndClipURL = new URL(getParameter(''EndClip''));
     } catch( MalformedURLException e )
         { System.out.println(''exception''+e );}
  }
}
```

Listing 4.8   HTML That Runs the Do-Nothing Applet

```
<!DOCTYPE HTML PUBLIC
''-//SQ//DTD HTML 2.0 HoTMetaL + extensions//EN''>
<HTML><HEAD><TITLE>The Singing Applet</TITLE></HEAD>
<BODY>
<applet code=chap4/ch4_fig4.class width=100 height=100>
<param name=StartClip value=''http://www.coriolis.com/japp/chap4/
charge.au''>
<param name=RunningClip value=''http://www.coriolis.com/japp/chap4/
charge.au''>
<param name=EndClip value=''http://www.coriolis.com/japp/chap4/
retreat.au''>
</applet>
</P></BODY></HTML>
```

Audio and Parameters

The basis of Java's audio capability is the **AudioClip** class. In order to do any audio, you need to get the actual audio data from a file somewhere on the Net. Where is that file? We could hardwire the file name into the class file, as in the following code snippet:

```
public final static string startClipFile =
new String( ''http://www.channel1.com/users/ajrodley/start.au'' );
```

However, a more flexible way of dealing with data like this is to pass it in as an argument via the **<param name=value=>** construct within the HTML source. In Listing 4.8, we've defined three arguments—**StartClip**, **RunningClip**, and **EndClip**—each of which is the URL of an audio file somewhere out on the Net. In the **init** method, which as we've said is the first override method invoked by the browser, we query these arguments via **Applet.getParameter**. When, in our HTML page, we say:

```
<param name=StartClip value=''http://www.channel1.com/users/ajrodley/
start.au''>
```

the call:

```
String s = getParameter(''StartClip'');
```

returns the **String** http://www.channel1.com/users/ajrodley/start.au.

Applets, as we'll discuss later, operate in a multi-applet environment. This is a good thing, but it imposes some responsibilities on well-behaved applets. The first of these is the responsibility to document the arguments the applet accepts via the **getParameterInfo** method. Listing 4.4 implements both this and the **getAppletInfo** method, which allows users of our applet to find information about the applet's author, its version, and whatever else we want to put in the returned string. These methods are not required, but are courtesies we extend to other applets that may want to know something about us, or to HTML and applet writers who may want to use our applet in their own code.

The singing applet uses two different methods for playing audio clips. The start and end clips only need to play one time through, whenever their method (**start** or **stop**) is invoked, so we can play them simply by passing their URLs to **Applet.play**. We want the running clip to play continuously, though. For that, we need explicitly to create an **AudioClip** object. Thus, in our **init** method, we create three objects: a **URL** for the start clip, a **URL** for the end clip, and an **AudioClip** for the running clip.

The **init** method also contains a new wrinkle for us, an exception handling clause. We deal with exceptions in more detail in Chapter 8. What you need to remember here is that if a method is defined as "throwing" an exception, any method that calls it has to either define itself as *also* throwing that exception, or it has to handle that exception with a **try-catch** statement. Here, we use the latter method. The **URL** constructor throws **MalformedURLException**, so we catch it, and simply make a note of it on standard output. The **URL** constructor throws an exception if the specified URL is not accessible. Thus, if our **init** method runs without throwing an exception, we can be sure that there are accessible files at the URLs we specified.

When **init** is done, we have three objects: two **URLs** and one **AudioClip**. The **URL** constructors only made sure there was a file at the URL but the **AudioClip** constructor actually fetched the data from the URL. To play the start and end clips within the **start** and **stop** methods, we simply invoke the **play** method with the proper audio file's **URL** as the argument. To keep the running clip playing continuously while the applet is on-screen, we simply invoke **AudioClip.loop** in the **start** method. **AudioClip.loop** returns immediately, even though the clip continues to play until **AudioClip.stop** in our applet's **stop** method. Listing 4.9 presents a slightly different version of our do-nothing applet.

Listing 4.9   The Do-Nothing Applet in Its Own Thread

```
package chap4;

import java.util.*;
import java.applet.*;
import java.awt.*;

/* A do-nothing applet that runs in its own thread.

@version x.xx 1.10, 1 August, 1995 xxx
@author John Rodley
*/

public class ch4_fig5 extends Applet implements Runnable {
/** The main thread. */
Thread myThread;
String TheString;
int iteration = 0;

/** Start the main thread for this game. */
  public void start() {
    TheString = new String( ''Applet is on screen now in '' );
    if( myThread == null )
      {
    myThread = new Thread( this );
    myThread.start();
      }
  }

/** Stop this thread. */
  public void stop() {
    TheString =
      new String(''Applet is off screen but still running in '');
  }
```

```
/** The main loop for the main thread. */
  public void run() {
    while( myThread != null )
      {
      try {
      Thread.sleep( 300 );
        } catch( InterruptedException e )
        { System.out.println(''exception'' ); }
      showStatus( TheString+iteration+''th iteration '');
      iteration++;
      }
    myThread = null;
  }
}
```

In this example, we run the applet in its own thread. The key things to note here are the **start** and **run** methods, and the fact that our applet implements the **Runnable** interface. In the **start** method, we push the applet into its own thread by creating a new **Thread** object and passing the applet itself as the only argument to the constructor. This is possible only because our applet implements **Runnable**.

The only requirement of the **Runnable** interface is that you implement a **run** method, as we have here. Sometime after the call to **myThread.start** returns, the **run** method will begin executing asynchronously. Within this **run** method, we simply sit in a loop, sleeping for 300 milliseconds, then incrementing a counter and displaying it in the browser status line. Note that because we only want *one* of these independent threads to run, we check **myThread** within **start**. Otherwise, every visit to this page would create a new thread with the predictable effect on system performance.

Run this applet under Netscape. You'll see the status string changing regularly. Now, hyperlink away to some other HTML page. Notice that the status string keeps changing. We have violated one of the rules of well-behaved applets. Our host HTML document has disappeared, but our applet is still running!

Our new do-nothing applet will continue to run for as long as the browser is up. To kill it, you have to close Netscape. This persistence presents ominous possibilities. In Listing 4.10, a simple change turns the do-nothing applet into a malicious do-nothing applet.

Note: Do not run the applet shown in Listing 4.10 or you will have to kill your browser to get rid of it.

Listing 4.10   Eating CPU Cycles

```
package chap4;

import java.util.*;
import java.applet.*;
import java.awt.*;

/* A malicious do-nothing applet that runs in its own thread,
eating up CPU cycles because it neither sleeps nor exits.

@version x.xx 1.10, 1 August, 1995 xxx
@author John Rodley
*/

public class ch4_fig6 extends Applet implements Runnable {

/** The main thread. */
Thread myThread;
String TheString;
int iteration = 0;

/** Start the main thread for this game. */
  public void start() {
    TheString = new String( ''Applet is on screen now in '' );
    if( myThread == null )
      {
    myThread = new Thread( this );
    myThread.start();
      }
  }

/** Stop this thread. */
  public void stop() {
    TheString =
      new String(''Applet is off screen but still running in '');
  }

/** The main loop for the main thread. */
  public void run() {
    while( myThread != null )
      {
      showStatus( TheString+iteration+''th iteration '');
```

```
      iteration++;
      }
    myThread = null;
  }
}
```

The malicious applet eats up a lot of CPU cycles when it is run. Let's take a close look at the code changes in this listing to see why. We removed the **sleep** call from the **run** method, which results in us simply sit in a loop incrementing a variable. We also removed the call to **showStatus,** which alerts the user that we are still running. If you were to run this applet in Netscape and then hyperlink to another page, you would notice how unresponsive the browser becomes. The key features of this malicious applet are actually omissions, the fact that our **run** method never blocks, and that we didn't implement an **Applet.stop** method that stops our thread. All applets that run in their own thread must take special care to run only when, and only as much as neccessary.

By this point, you've seen the light and want to write well-behaved, threaded applets. But how? Listing 4.11 modifies the threaded do-nothing applet to stop running when the user leaves the page, and then re-start when the user returns.

Listing 4.11   A Well-Behaved Do-Nothing Applet

```
package chap4;

import java.util.*;
import java.applet.*;
import java.awt.*;

/* A do-nothing applet that runs in its own thread.

@version x.xx 1.10, 1 August, 1995 xxx
@author John Rodley
*/

public class ch4_fig7 extends Applet implements Runnable {

/** The main thread. */
Thread myThread;
String TheString;
int iteration = 0;
```

```
/** Start the main thread for this game. */
  public void start() {
    TheString = new String( ''Applet is on screen now in '' );
    if( myThread == null )
      {
    myThread = new Thread( this );
    myThread.start();
      }
  }

/** Stop this thread. */
  public void stop() {
    TheString =
      new String(''Applet is off screen but still running in '');
// This line is the key. If myThread is null, the run method
// returns and the thread disappears.
    myThread = null;
  }

/** The main loop for the main thread. */
  public void run() {
    while( myThread != null )
      {
      try {
      Thread.sleep( 300 );
        } catch( InterruptedException e )
        { System.out.println(''exception'' ); }
      showStatus( TheString+iteration+''th iteration '');
      iteration++;
      }
    }
}
```

With a threaded applet, the thread the applet runs in only exists for as long as the **run** method is running. What we need is code in our **stop** method (which the browser calls whenever the user leaves the page) that will cause the **run** method to break out of its loop. This is what setting **myThread** to **null** does. Then in the **start** method (called whenever the user visits our page) we re-create the thread and set it running. We'll talk more about threads in Chapter 6. In the meantime, the well-behaved, threaded do-nothing applet will serve as a good template for any threaded applets we might need.

Making Our Applets Interact with the Browser

Prior to the beta version of Java, applets existed in a vacuum. They had no way of knowing anything about any other applets. Now, applets can call **Applet.getAppletContext**. This call returns an object that implements the **AppletContext** interface. Usually, this object will be the browser itself, but it might not be. In fact, browsers that wish to protect themselves from rogue applets may create a separate class just to contain the applet context for this call. In any case, it doesn't matter to us because, as with any interface, the definition of the interface is all that you can rely on.

The **AppletContext** class, shown in Table 4.2, provides six methods, which allow an applet to get images and audio clips, learn about other applets active in the browser, and show new HTML documents.

Using **getAppletContext**, we can modify our well-behaved, threaded do-nothing applet to get information about all the other running applets. Listing 4.12 shows our new applet, while Listing 4.13 shows the HTML code used to create four of these applets on one Web page. Figure 4.5 shows the output of our new applet.

Table 4.2	The AppletContext Interface		
Method	**Argument**	**Description**	**Return**
getApplet	String	Returns the applet, or null if It isn't loaded	Applet
getApplets		Returns a list of the applets loaded and casts the members of the Enumeration to Applet to use them	Enumeration
getAudioClip	URL	Returns a playable audio stream	AudioClip
getImage	URL	Returns an in-memory image that can be drawn via Graphics.drawImage	Image
showDocument	URL		
showStatus	String	Returns the message to be displayed in the status bar along the bottom of the browser window	

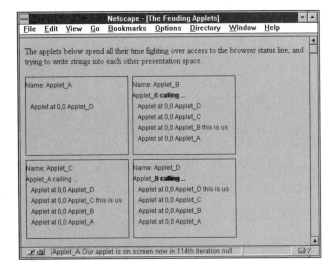

Figure 4.5

The output of the new simple applet.

Listing 4.12 Finding Other Applets

```
package chap4;

import java.util.*;
import java.io.*;
import java.net.*;
import java.applet.*;
import java.awt.*;
/** An applet that finds the other applets that exist within
this AppletContext, fights with them to write a string to the
browser status line, and writes a string directly into the
other applet windows.

@version 1.10, 11/20/95
@author John Rodley
*/

public class ch4_fig8 extends Applet implements Runnable {


/** The main thread. */
Thread myThread = null;
String TheString = null;
```

```
String myName;
String paintString = null;
int iteration = 0;
int paintIteration = 0;

/** Start the main thread for this game. */
  public void start() {
    TheString = new String( ''Our applet is on screen now in '' );
  if( myThread == null )
    {
      myThread = new Thread( this );
    myThread.start();
    }
  }
/** Stop this thread. */
  public void stop() {
    myThread = null;
  }

/** The main loop for the main thread. */
  public void run() {
    while( myThread != null )
      {
      try {
      Thread.sleep( 300 );
        } catch( InterruptedException e )
          { System.out.println(''exception'' ); }
      showStatus( myName+'' ''+TheString+iteration+
                    ''th iteration ''+paintString );
      repaint();
      iteration++;
      }
  }


/** Paint our window.  Display a string in this window for
each applet we find, then display a string in each of the other
applet's windows.
*/
public void paint( Graphics g ) {
  String gString;
  int i = 0;

  // Label this applet with its name
  g.drawString( ''Name: ''+myName, 0, 20 );

  AppletContext ac = getAppletContext();
```

```
    Enumeration e = ac.getApplets();
    Dimension d = size();
    g.drawRect( 0, 0, d.width-5, d.height-5 );
    while( e.hasMoreElements()) {
       Applet a = (Applet)(e.nextElement());
       // If this applet is a ch4_fig8, then it has a name parameter set
       String s = a.getParameter(''Name'');
       if( s == null )
          s = new String( ''not a ch4_fig8 applet'' );
       Point p = a.location();
       gString = new String( ''Applet at ''+p.x+'',''+p.y+'' ''+s );
       // The list will always include ''this'', so check it
       if( a == this )
          gString = new String( gString+'' this is us'' );
       else {
          // Now draw a string into the other applets window
          Graphics g1 = a.getGraphics();
          g1.drawString( myName+'' calling ...'', 0, 40 );
          }
       // Draw the string describing the other applet in our window
       g.drawString( gString, 10, 20*(i+3) );

       i++;
       }
    }

/** If the user clicks on the applet, stop it.
@return false
*/
  public boolean mouseDown(Event e, int x, int y) {
   stop();
      return( false );
   }

/** Initialize the applet. Resize it and give it a name.  Make
sure that the applet is ''named'' via the applet tag.
*/
  public void init() {
  myName = getParameter( ''Name'' );
    if( myName == null )
       myName = new String( ''Set the Name= parameter please!'' );
   resize( 210, 210 );
   }
}
```

The **AppletContext** interface provides the method **getApplets**, which returns an **Enumeration** (basically a vector) containing all the applets running in this **AppletContext**. We retrieve each individual applet via **Enumeration.nextElement**.

The applet returned by **getApplets** is completely capable. We can call any method available in the **Applet** class against that applet. Thus, in our **paint** method, we call **drawString** against our own applet, and against each of the other applets we find. As this page runs, you can see the four applets dueling over the status line and drawing over each other as they draw the intrusive string into each other's graphics context.

In Listing 4.12, we introduce a new class, **Point** and a new interface, **Enumeration**. **Point** simply encapsulates two **ints**, the X and Y coordinates of the point. In C or C++, this would undoubtedly have been implemented as a simple **struct**. **Enumeration** is a far more interesting concept. What does it mean to enumerate something? Here, enumeration means "to walk through a list, using up the elements as you go." Essentially, an **Enumeration** is a list that you can go through once and only once. The interface requires only two methods, **hasMoreElements** and **nextElement**, which force you to use the same flow-control whenever you're dealing with an **Enumeration**. The technique is illustrated in the following code snippet:

```
// assume e is an object that implements the Enumeration interface
while( e.hasMoreElements() ) {
    Object o = e.nextElement();
    ...
    }
// At this point e has been ''used up.''  It cannot be walked through
again.
```

In Listing 4.12's **paint** method, we get an **Enumeration** of **Applets** from the **AppletContext** interface method **getApplets**, then walk through it, dueling with each of the applets it returns. The following code line illustrates one of the powers of Java's object orientation that might not be obvious:

```
Applet a = (Applet )(e.nextElement());
```

This power works like this: **Enumeration.nextElement** always returns an **Object**, but a simple cast of that **Object** to **Applet**, gives us access to the much wider range of capabilities of the **Applet** class. That **Object** was always an **Applet**. It's just that the **Enumeration** doesn't *care* what class its elements are, so it stores them as **Object** and lets the user of the **Enumeration** deal with casting them back to the proper type. What would happen if, by some chance, the call to **e.nextElement** returned an **Object** that was *not* of the **Applet** class? The Java interpreter would throw an **IllegalCastException**. This is something you have to consider very carefully whenever you cast from a base class to a superclass, especially when you're using **Vectors** or **Enumerations** you get from someone else's objects.

With that bit of type-casting wisdom in mind, consider the following code snippet from Listing 4.12:

```
Applet a = (Applet)(e.nextElement());
// If this applet is a ch4_fig8, then it has a name parameter set
String s = a.getParameter(''Name'');
if( s == null )
   s = new String( ''not a ch4_fig8 applet'');
```

This code simply determines whether we're dealing with the proper class of object, a **ch4_fig8**. However, there's a much better way to deal with this, as shown in the following code snippet:

```
Applet a = (Applet)(e.nextElement());
// If a is not a ch4_fig8, move on to the next applet
if( a instanceof ch4_fig8 )
   ...
else
   continue;
```

The **instanceof** operator tells us whether **Object a** is an instance of class **ch4_fig8**. Checking objects with the **instanceof** operator is usually a good idea *before* you try a type cast. In this particular instance, **AppletContext.getApplets** guarantees that it will return an **Enumeration** of **Applets**, so the cast to **Applet** should be safe, but beyond that, we can't be sure, so we use **instanceof**.

AppletContext.getApplets gives us an inter-applet communication mechanism for which there are any number of uses. As another brutally simple example, let's modify the dueling applet of Listing 4.12 so that it kills off all the other applets on a page via **Applet.stop**, ensuring that it's the only running applet on a page.

Listing 4.13 A "Killer" Applet

```
package chap4;

import java.util.*;
import java.applet.*;
import java.awt.*;

/** An applet that finds the other applets that exist within
this AppletContext, and stops them.

@version 1.10, 11/20/95
@author John Rodley
*/

public class ch4_fig9 extends Applet implements Runnable {

/** The main thread. */
Thread myThread = null;
String TheString = null;
int iteration = 0;
int paintIteration = 0;

/** Start the main thread for this game. */
  public void start() {
    TheString = new String( ''Our applet is on screen now in '' );
  if( myThread == null )
    {
      myThread = new Thread( this );
    myThread.start();
    }
  }

/** Resize us to be wide enough for the status string. */
  public void init() {
    resize( 300, 100 );
  }

/** Stop this thread. */
  public void stop() {
    myThread = null;
  }

/** The main loop for the main thread. */
  public void run() {
    while( myThread != null )
      {
```

```
            try {
            Thread.sleep( 300 );
              } catch( InterruptedException e )
                { System.out.println(''exception'' ); }
            showStatus( iteration+''th iteration '' );
            repaint();
            iteration++;
            }
      }
/** Paint our window.  Destroy each applet we find,
then display a string boasting of this achievement.
*/
  public void paint( Graphics g ) {
     String gString;
    int i = 0;

     AppletContext ac = getAppletContext();
   Enumeration e = ac.getApplets();
     while( e.hasMoreElements() ) {
       Applet a = (Applet)(e.nextElement());
      Point p = a.location();
      // The list will always include ''this'', so check it
       if( a instanceof ch4_fig9 )
       gString = new String( ''this is us'' );
      else {
        Container c = a.getParent();
        if( c == null ) // this applet was already removed
          continue;
        // Now destroy the other applet
        a.stop();
        c.remove(a);
       gString = new String( ''Stopped applet at ''+p.x+'',''+p.y+''
''+iteration);
        }
       g.drawString( gString, 10, 20*(i+3) );

       i++;
   }


   }
}
```

Listing 4.14   HTML Code That Runs the Killer Applet

```
<!DOCTYPE HTML PUBLIC
''-//SQ//DTD HTML 2.0 HoTMetaL + extensions//EN''>
<HTML><HEAD><TITLE>The Killer Applet</TITLE>
```

```
</HEAD>
<BODY>
<P>
The applets below spend all their time fighting over access to
the browser status line, and trying to write strings into each
other's presentation space.
</P>
<applet code=chap4/ch4_fig8a.class width=100 height=100>
<param name=Name value=Applet_A>
</applet>
<applet code=chap4/ch4_fig8a.class width=200 height=100>
<param name=Name value=Applet_B>
</applet>
<applet code=chap4/ch4_fig8a.class width=300 height=100>
<param name=Name value=Applet_C>
</applet>
<applet code=chap4/ch4_fig9.class width=400 height=100>
</applet>
</BODY></HTML>
```

Try running this applet and you'll see that only the killer applet remains running. Notice also that, not only do the applets stop running, but their screen output disappears. While we'll talk more about removing **Components** in the next section, it's important to note that even though we've stopped the other applets via the **stop** method, those applets continue to exist, and the **AppletContext** still returns them every time we call **getApplets**. That's why we check the return from **getParent**. Calling **Container.remove** on a **Component** means that the next call to **getParent** will return a null. That's how we know that the **Component** is no longer displayed.

Controlling Stopped Applets

What to do with stopped applets is a more interesting question than it might seem. In Listing 4.12, we added a method, **mouseDown**, that stops the applet if the user clicks on it. This method is shown in the following code snippet:

```
public boolean mouseDown( Event e, int x, int y ) {
   stop();
   return( false );
}
```

Run Listing 4.12 once again and try clicking on one of the applets. What you see is that the applet does stop running, but that its last "state" remains on the screen. In the **AppletContext**'s (browser's) view of the world, the stopped applet still exists, and the allocated section of the browser window should remain uncleared and unused. Try stopping one of the applets, then moving the browser window around. What you'll see is that the applet hasn't really gone away at all. All that's happened is that the **run** method has returned. When the applet window gets covered and then uncovered, Java decides that all the applets need to be repainted and it calls **Applet.paint** for all the applets on the screen. What we need to do is remove the applet from the list of things that get repainted. To do this, we add a single line to **Applet.stop**, as shown in Listing 4.15.

Listing 4.15 Clearing the Applet's Window

```
package chap4;

import java.util.*;
import java.io.*;
import java.net.*;
import java.applet.*;
import java.awt.*;

/** An applet that finds the other applets that exist within
this AppletContext, fights with them to write a string to the
browser status line, and writes a string directly into the
other applet windows.  Modified to stop and 'disappear' from
the screen if the user clicks on the applet.

@version 1.10, 11/20/95
@author John Rodley
*/


public class ch4_fig11 extends Applet implements Runnable {


/** The main thread. */
Thread myThread = null;
String TheString = null;
String myName;
String paintString = null;
int iteration = 0;
int paintIteration = 0;

/** Start the main thread for this game. */
  public void start() {
    TheString = new String( ''Our applet is on screen now in '' );
```

```
  if( myThread == null )
    {
      myThread = new Thread( this );
    myThread.start();
    }
  }


/** Stop this thread. */
  public void stop() {
    myThread = null;
  }

/** The main loop for the main thread. */
  public void run() {
    while( myThread != null )
      {
      try {
      Thread.sleep( 300 );
        } catch( InterruptedException e )
          { System.out.println(''exception'' ); }
      showStatus( myName+'' ''+TheString+iteration+
                  ''th iteration ''+paintString );
      repaint();
      iteration++;
      }
  }


/** Paint our window.  Display a string in this window for
each applet we find, then display a string in each of the other
applet's windows.
*/
public void paint( Graphics g ) {
  String gString;
  int i = 0;

  // Label this applet with its name
  g.drawString( ''Name: ''+myName, 0, 20 );

  AppletContext ac = getAppletContext();
  Enumeration e = ac.getApplets();
  Dimension d = size();
  g.drawRect( 0, 0, d.width-5, d.height-5 );
  while( e.hasMoreElements()) {
    Applet a = (Applet)(e.nextElement());
    // If this applet is a ch4_fig8, it has a name parameter set
    String s = a.getParameter(''Name'');
```

```
     if( s == null )
       s = new String( ''not a ch4_fig8 applet'' );
     Point p = a.location();
     gString = new String( ''Applet at ''+p.x+'',''+p.y+'' ''+s );
     // The list will always include ''this'', so check it
     if( a == this )
       gString = new String( gString+'' this is us'' );
     else {
       // Now draw a string into the other applet's window
       Graphics g1 = a.getGraphics();
      // If this applet's already stopped, g1 will be null
      if( g1 != null )
       g1.drawString( myName+'' calling ...'', 0, 40 );
       }
     // draw the string describing the other applet in our window
     g.drawString( gString, 10, 20*(i+3) );

     i++;
     }
   }

/** If the user clicks on the applet, stop it.
@return false
*/
  public boolean mouseDown(Event e, int x, int y) {
   stop();
    getParent().remove(this);
    return( false );
  }

/** Initialize the applet. Resize it and give it a name.  Make
sure that the applet is ''named'' via the applet tag.
*/
  public void init() {
   myName = getParameter( ''Name'' );
    if( myName == null )
      myName = new String( ''Set the Name= parameter please!'' );
   resize( 210, 210 );
   }
}
```

Our addition to **Applet.stop** clears the space that our **Applet** once occupied, and removes it from the list of **Components**, ensuring that it never gets re-painted. Removing the applet **Component** from the **Container** it resides in re-sults in an applet that has no screen representation. This means that *any* call to that applet's **Component** superclass, such as the **paint** method's call to **a.getGraphics**, will probably fail. We take this into account in **paint** by adding a **null** return check to **a.getGraphics**.

In truth, you can't really get rid of an applet. There's no **delete** operator in Java, so you can't just destroy it, and the garbage collector won't get rid of it automatically until there are no more references to it. The applet was created (via the **new** operation) by the browser, and the applet itself doesn't have write access to the browser's list of applets, so there will always be that one reference to the applet. For now, the best we can do is to remove the applet **Component** from the browser's list of **Components**, and hope that the browser (whichever one it is) will reuse the now-available screen space. We'll talk more about **Components** and **Containers** in Chapter 5.

Applets and Hyperlinks

We can combine our persistent applet with the **AppletContext** to implement a rudimentary Web trolling applet. This applet takes a list of URLs and instructs the **AppletContext** to visit those URLs, in sequence, with a delay of 30 seconds at each document.

Listing 4.16 A Web-Crawling Applet

```
package chap4;

import java.util.*;
import java.io.*;
import java.net.*;
import java.applet.*;
import java.awt.*;

/* A threaded applet that takes a list of URLs as an argument,
then visits each of those URLs, delaying for delay milliseconds
between URL switches.

@version 1.0 12/23/95
@author John Rodley
 */

public class ch4_fig12 extends Applet implements Runnable {

/** The main thread. */
Thread myThread = null;
```

```
int iteration = 0;
Vector docURL;
int delay = 10000;

/** Start the main thread for this game. */
public void start() {
   if( myThread == null )
      {
      myThread = new Thread( this );
   myThread.start();
      }
   }


/** Stop this thread. */
public void stop() {
  myThread = null;
   }

/** The main loop for the main thread. */
public void run() {
   System.out.println( ''Runnable.run'' );
   iteration = 0;
      while( myThread != null )
         {
         AppletContext ac = getAppletContext();
         showStatus( ''Switching to ''+docURL.elementAt(iteration));
         ac.showDocument((URL) docURL.elementAt(iteration ));
         try {
         Thread.sleep( delay );
            } catch( InterruptedException e ) {
System.out.println(''exception'' ); }
         iteration++;
         if( iteration >= docURL.size() )
            iteration = 0;
         }
      myThread = null;
   }

/** Initialize the applet. Resize and load images.
*/
public void init() {
   docURL = new Vector(1);
   int i = 1;
   String sDelay = getParameter(''Delay'');
   if( sDelay != null )
      delay = new Integer( sDelay ).intValue();
```

```
while( true ) {
    String s = getParameter(''Document''+i);
    if( s == null ) break;
    i++;
    try {
    docURL.addElement( new URL(s));
       } catch( Exception e) { break; }
    }
  resize( 210, 210 );
  }
}
```

Java Note

The showDocument Method Is Optional

One serious caveat about this applet: The documentation for **AppletContext** describes **showDocument** as an optional method; browsers are *not* required to implement it. Different browsers implement in different ways, and some don't implement it at all.

The browser makers' reasoning is easy to divine. If you could jump around to various links via Java applets, using the browser simply as a base, the usefulness of the browser's fancy interface is called into question. In fact, the whole design of **showDocument** smells of the kind of corporate politics that often makes programming an exercise in nonsense-control. Why, if **showDocument**'s behavior is undefined, doesn't it at least return a value (instead of a void) or throw an exception to tell you whether it's going to do what you requested?

In Chapter 7, we'll take a more hands-on approach to Web trolling by recursively fetching HTML documents ourselves and searching them for patterns.

Reloading Applets

Most browsers support the notion of "reloading" an HTML page—clearing the browser window, rereading the HTML source from the http server, and redisplaying it in the browser window. This is useful, for example, where pages have cgi scripts embedded (for hit counting, for example) and the page needs to be downloaded for the script to run, or when a page currently in local cache is known to have changed back on the server. Unfortunately, there is no hard and fast rule as to just what it means to reload an applet.

Going strictly by the HTML example, what you might expect is that the applet gets stopped, unloaded (whatever that means), reread from the Web server, reloaded, and restarted. The simple applet in Listing 4.17, a modification of the singing applet shown in Listing 4.7, plays a different audio clip whenever **init**, **start**, **stop**, or **destroy** get called. Try it under your favorite browser and see what happens.

Listing 4.17   Testing the Reload Button

```
package chap4;

import java.awt.Graphics;
import java.applet.Applet;
import java.applet.AudioClip;
import java.net.*;

/** A simple app that plays tunes at the four different stops
along the applet execution trail - init, start, stop, and
destroy.  The parameters?
  StartClip
  StopClip
  DestroyClip
  InitClip

@version 1.0 12/20/1995
@author John Rodley
*/
public class ch4_fig13 extends Applet {
  String sAppletInfo;
  URL StartClipURL;
  URL StopClipURL;
  URL InitClipURL;
  URL DestroyClipURL;

  String pinfo[][] = {
    {''InitClip'', ''URL'',
        ''The URL of an audio clip played at init'' },
    {''StartClip'', ''URL'',
        ''The URL of an audio clip played at start'' },
    {''StopClip'', ''URL'',
        ''The URL of an audio clip played at stop'' },
    {''DestroyClip'', ''URL'',
        ''The URL of an audio clip played at destroy'' }
     };
```

```
/** Whenever a user visits our page, the browser calls this.
This is an override of an Applet method.. */
  public void start() {
    if( StartClipURL == null )
      return;
    play( StartClipURL );
  }

/** Whenever the user leaves our page, this gets called.
Another override of an Applet method.
*/
  public void stop() {
    if( StopClipURL == null )
      return;
    play( StopClipURL );
  }

/** Tell anyone who might inquire what we are.
@return A string describing this applet.
*/
  public String getAppletInfo() {
    return(''JRodley - Java Applets Book - Chapter 4 figure 13'');
    }

/** Tell anyone who might inquire how to use this applet.
@return A 2d string array describing the arguments to this
applet.
*/
  public String[][] getParameterInfo() {
    return pinfo;
    }

/** Play the destroy clip. */
  public void destroy() {
    if( DestroyClipURL != null )
      play( DestroyClipURL );
  }

/** Connect to the URLs specified by the StartClip and EndClip
parameters in the applet tag.
*/
  public void init() {
    try {
      InitClipURL = new URL(getParameter(''InitClip''));
      StartClipURL = new URL(getParameter(''StartClip''));
      StopClipURL = new URL(getParameter(''StopClip''));
```

```
        DestroyClipURL = new URL(getParameter(''DestroyClip''));
      } catch( MalformedURLException e )
         { System.out.println(''exception''+e );}
    if( InitClipURL != null )
      play( InitClipURL );
  }
}
```

For single-threaded applets, this is all very simple, but it gets much more complicated when applets start creating their own threads. It is very difficult, perhaps impossible, for a browser to shut down independent applet threads in an orderly fashion, mostly because there's no way to know what those threads are doing: Only the applet that created the threads knows that. Thus, it is incumbent upon the applet to shut down its own threads in **stop** and/or **destroy**.

Conclusion

Here, we've seen what applets look like, where they appear, and how they behave. We've shown how the interaction between the browser and its applets is strictly defined by the **Applet** class and the **AppletContext** interface. We've also discussed the methods available to an applet, the flow of execution, applet persistence, and the environment in which applets execute. And finally, with the Web-trolling applet, we've seen a little glimpse of how applets can enhance the functionality of browsers to the point of turning them into little more than Java platforms.

Chapter 5

User Interfaces with AWT

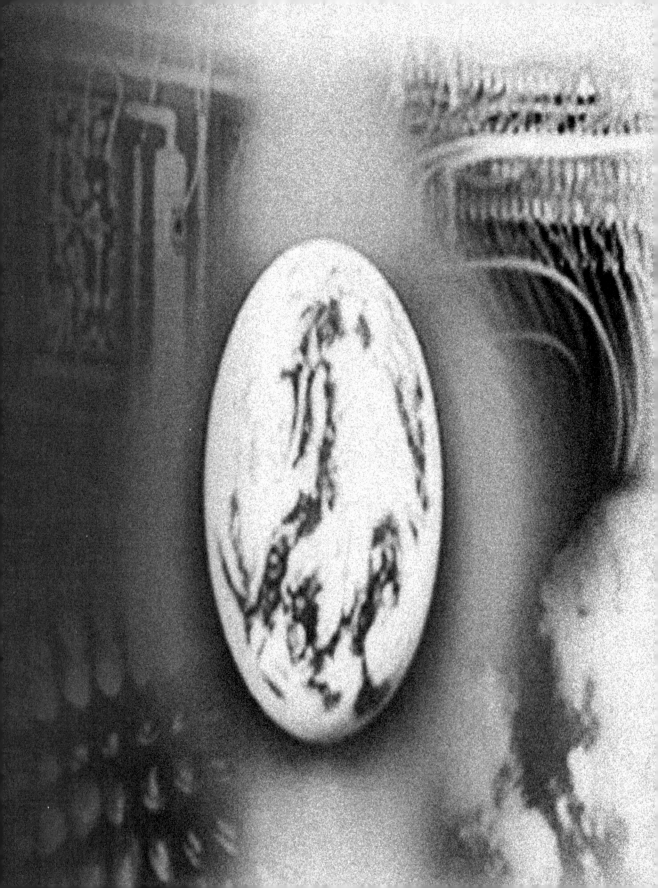

User Interfaces with AWT

Presenting a compelling Web user interface is what brought you to Java. Java's Abstract Window Toolkit gives you the tools you need to make it happen.

The Java AWT (Abstract Window Toolkit) is used to create and maintain an applet's user interface. It attempts to abstract and objectify all the elements provided by the user's native GUI, whether that be Solaris, Windows 95/NT, or Presentation Manager. Within AWT, you'll find button controls, text items, edit fields, dialog boxes, menu items, and a host of other graphical objects that make possible pleasing and efficient user interfaces.

The Graphical Hierarchy

In order to understand the process of writing an applet user interface, we have to look first at the object hierarchy that our applet rests upon. We know already that our applet subclasses the class **Applet**, which subclasses **Panel**, **Container**, **Component**, and **Object**. Between all these lower-level objects there is enough functionality to make our simple applet from Chapter 4 work. Now we'll take a closer look at some of the AWT classes and try to make them do some more interesting work. Figure 5.1 shows the AWT package class hierarchy.

In the native GUI libraries, what typically happens is that a programmer constructs a hierarchy of windows, where the application main window is a child of

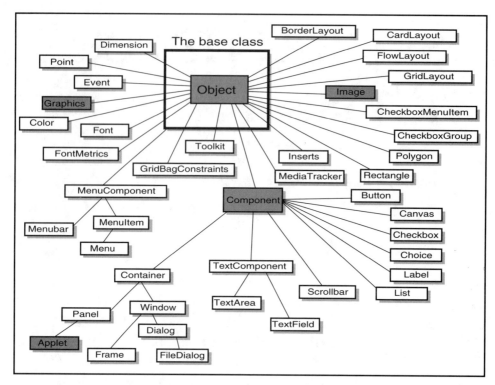

Figure 5.1

The AWT package class hierarchy.

the desktop, and all the other windows within the application are children of the application's main window. In these systems, a window is both something you can draw on, and something that can contain other windows.

AWT splits these two window functions into two descendent classes: **Component** and **Container**. **Container** is simply a **Component** that can contain other **Components**. It keeps a list of the **Components** that belong to it, and through the **LayoutManager** it can arrange its **Components** according to various pre-defined rules. **Component** encapsulates all the rest of the traditional window functionality, including event notification (mouse, keyboard ...), painting, sizing, and font and color management.

If you look again at Figure 5.1, you can see that while **Applet** (which will be our top-level class) subclasses **Container** and by that route, **Component**, it doesn't subclass either **Frame** or **Window**. When you first look Java, you might assume that **Window** and **Frame** are two of the key classes. As it turns out, applet programmers don't have much use for either **Frame** or **Window** objects.

What happens when a browser starts up is that the browser itself is an instance of the class **Frame**. Our applet is instantiated by this **Frame**, but, in true object-oriented fashion, it knows nothing about the **Frame**. This means that anything that's part of the **Frame** or **Window** class is not visible to an applet.

Components and Containers

The **Container** class is a special class created to automatically manage the appearance of, and message handling for, a collection of **Components**. A class like this is absolutely essential for showing HTML documents, where the appearance of the document is generally described in relative, not absolute terms, and often changes with the shape of the window.

The **Component** class is where you find most of the functionality we traditionally associate with GUI windows. Like most base classes, **Component** contains methods that are useful by themselves, and others that must be implemented by the subclass.

The key method for any **Component** is the **paint/update** method. As we saw in Chapter 1 with our basic applet, **paint/update** is where the actual screen drawing happens. The base GUI (Win32, Xwin ...) sends a message indicating the window needs to be repainted, and Java turns that into an invocation of either **paint** or **update**. Remember from Chapter 4 that applets can implement either **paint** or **update**; however, if you implement **paint**, Java clears the screen beforehand, while with **update** it does not. Here I use the term **paint/update** to indicate whichever of these methods you implement.

Within our applet, we can cause **paint/update** to be called by calling **repaint**, but in many cases, **paint/update** will be invoked directly by the system, because the user moved, minimized, or resized the window. Be aware that while a call to **repaint** will eventually result in Java invoking the **paint/update** method, **repaint** itself does not call **paint/update**. **repaint** typically puts a message into the GUIs message queue, which in turn causes **paint/update** to be called. The actual invocation of **paint/update** will occur in a completely separate thread from the one that ran **repaint**.

Layouts and Panels

The **Container** class is designed to keep a collection of **Components** and arrange them neatly on the screen. The basic theory of creating a user interface with AWT is to create a **Container**, create a **Component** for each of your visual elements, and add them all to the **Container**. Each **Container** has a **LayoutManager** attached to it, which arranges the **Components** within the **Container**. Though we've talked only about **Containers**, when we need a **Container**, what we'll actually subclass is **Panel**, which is merely a subclass of **Container** that attaches a default **LayoutManager** (**FlowLayout**) to the **Container**.

The arrangement of **Components** within a **Container** is dictated by the type of **LayoutManager** that's attached to the **Container**. There are five types of layouts: **GridLayout**, **FlowLayout**, **CardLayout**, **BorderLayout**, and **GridBagLayout**, which we can attach to our **Container** via the **Container.setLayout** method. In addition, if we subclass **Panel**, we can use the default **FlowLayout LayoutManager**. Listing 5.1 contains an applet that illustrates the first four layout types. Figure 5.2 show the layout applet running.

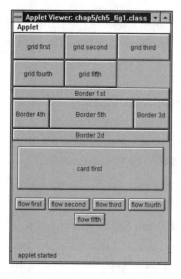

Figure 5.2

The layout applet running.

Listing 5.1   A Simple Applet Illustrating Layout Managers

```
package chap5;

import java.awt.*;
import java.util.*;
import java.io.*;
import java.net.*;
import java.applet.*;
import jvr.animator.*;
import jvr.utils.*;
import java.lang.*;

/** A simple applet demonstrating the characteristics of the
various LayoutManagers. Shows all except GridBagLayout.
@version 1.0 12/15/1995
@author John Rodley
*/
public class ch5_fig1 extends Applet {
Panel cardPanel;

/** Initialize the applet. Create all the panels, set the
appropriate LayoutManagers for each one, and add all
the buttons to the panels. Then resize and show.
*/
public void init() {
  Panel panel;

  // Set up the applet's panel as four rows.
  // This call to setLayout applies to the applet's
  // Panel.
  setLayout( new GridLayout( 4, 1 ));

  // Now create the GridLayout example, a 2 row by 3
  // column panel that should place the buttons as:
  // 1  2 3
  // 4  5
  panel = new Panel();
  panel.setLayout( new GridLayout(2,3));
  panel.add( new Button( "grid first"));
  panel.add( new Button( "grid second" ));
  panel.add( new Button( "grid third" ));
  panel.add( new Button( "grid fourth" ));
  panel.add( new Button( "grid fifth" ));
  // Add this panel to the applet's panel. This will
  // appear as the TOP row of the applet's panel.
  add( panel );

  // Now create a BorderLayout panel with a separate
  // button for each of the BorderLayouts' 5 sections.
  panel = new Panel();
  panel.setLayout( new BorderLayout() );
  panel.add( "North", new Button( "Border 1st" ));
  panel.add( "South", new Button( "Border 2d"  ));
```

```
panel.add( "East", new Button( "Border 3d"  ));
panel.add( "West", new Button( "Border 4th" ));
panel.add( "Center", new Button( "Border 5th" ));
// Add this panel to the applet's panel. This will
// appear as the SECOND row of the applet's panel.
add( panel );

// Now create a CardLayout panel. This will appear as
// a stack with only the button on the top of the stack
// visible.
panel = new Panel();
panel.setLayout( new CardLayout(10,10));
panel.add( new Button( "card first"));
panel.add( new Button( "card second" ));
panel.add( new Button( "card third" ));
panel.add( new Button( "card fourth" ));
panel.add( new Button( "card fifth" ));
cardPanel = panel;
// Now add this panel as the THIRD row of the applet's
// panel.
add( panel );

// Now create a FlowLayout panel and add 5 buttons to
// it. The panel will try to "flow" the buttons into
// the panel as best it can, left to right, top to
// bottom.
panel = new Panel();
panel.setLayout( new FlowLayout());
panel.add( new Button( "flow first"));
panel.add( new Button( "flow second" ));
panel.add( new Button( "flow third" ));
panel.add( new Button( "flow fourth" ));
panel.add( new Button( "flow fifth" ));
// Add this panel to the applet's panel as the bottom
// row.
add( panel );
resize( 300, 400 );
show();
    }

/** Deal with the user click on one of the "card" buttons in
the CardLayout panel. Makes the next button in the button
stack pop to the top.
@return true
*/
public boolean action(Event e, Object o) {
  ((CardLayout)cardPanel.getLayout()).next( cardPanel );
  return true;
  }
}
```

GridLayout takes a number of rows and columns as constructor arguments, and arranges the **Components** along the grid in the order in which they're added to the layout. Notice that **GridLayout** not only manages the location of **Components** but also their size. In fact, only **FlowLayout** does no sizing.

FlowLayout will look more familiar to browser users. It tries to intelligently center **Components** horizontally within the **Panel**. If you play with resizing the applet of Listing 5.1, you'll see that while the **GridLayout Components** change size to maintain the grid, the **FlowLayout Components** keep their original size and change position, even to the point of lining up in a single column if you size the applet thin enough. **FlowLayout** also works well with **Components** that are different sizes, a distinction it shares with **GridBagLayout**.

CardLayout tries to mimic a deck of cards. The only card you see is the one on top of the deck. You can change which card is on top using methods of the **CardLayout** class. In Listing 5.1, we've coded the applet so that clicking any of the buttons causes the card panel to flip to the next card.

BorderLayout postulates a world divided into, at most, five areas: North, South, East, West, and Center. You add each **BorderLayout Component** to its **Panel** with one of these five areas attached to it. Figure 5.3 shows how the five **BorderLayout** areas are aligned on screen.

GridBagLayout

GridBagLayout is the most useful, and most complicated, of the **LayoutManager**s. Basically, it's a form of **GridLayout** that doesn't insist that its **Components** all be a uniform size.

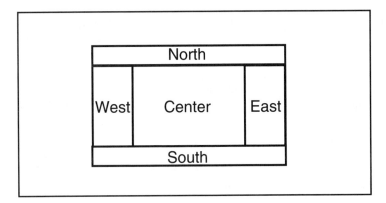

Figure 5.3

Alignment of BorderLayout.

The theory behind a **GridBagLayout** is that every time we add a **Component** to the **Container** (and remember, our applet *is* a **Container**), we describe how it gets sized and positioned. The **GridBagConstraints** class is that description. Each **Component** of the **GridBagLayout** Container is added to that **Container** with a **GridBagConstraints** object attached to it. The **GridBagConstraints** object tells the **LayoutManager** where to place the **Component** and how to size it. Thus, before we look at how to use the **GridBagLayout** itself, we need to know what the **GridBagConstraints** is telling it about the **Components** we're adding.

The one thing to keep in mind when working with a **GridBagLayout**, is that it is a grid, but the size of the grid cells changes as the size of the display space changes. You give the **GridBagLayout** all the **Components**, along with some more or less specific rules about how to position and size them, and it divides the display space into a grid in which all those rules can be satisfied.

POSITIONING A COMPONENT IN GRIDBAGLAYOUT

As we've said, GridBagLayout imposes a grid on the display space. Our intent is to place **Components** within this grid. There are two ways to position items within the grid: We can hardwire them, using **GridBagConstraints. gridx** and **gridy**, or we can let the **GridBagLayout** add them to the grid in the order that we add them to the **Container**. Using **gridx** and **gridy** is very easy. The coordinate 0,0 is the upper left of the grid. If we set **gridx** to 1, **GridBagLayout** positions the **Component** in the second column from the left. If we set **gridy** to 2, **GridBagLayout** puts the **Component** in the third row from the top.

If we choose *not* to use **gridx** and **gridy**, the **LayoutManager** will position them left to right, top to bottom as we add them to the **Container**. We'll see this in operation in the applet shown in Listing 5.2.

Now that we've seen how **GridBagLayout** determines which "cell" to place each **Component** in, let's look at how it positions those cells within the display space.

WORKING WITH WEIGHTS

GridBagLayout builds its grid based on the size of the **Components**. If we have three **Components** that each want to be 20 pixels wide, **GridBagLayout** will use a grid that's 60 pixels wide, giving each cell a width of 20 pixels. What if our **Container** is actually 200 pixels wide though? What does **GridBagLayout** do with that extra 140 pixels? That depends on the value of **GridBagConstraints. weightx** and **GridBagConstraints.weighty**.

If **weightx** is 0.0, the **GridBagLayout** will distribute the extra 140 pixels on each side of the grid, so the grid will be centered horizontally, with 70 pixels on the left and 70 pixels on the right. The same theory applies vertically with **weighty**.

This is actually easier to show than it is to describe. Listing 5.2 shows an applet that creates two rows of three buttons each, and lays them out in a **GridBagLayout**. Listing 5.3 shows HTML code that calls the applet in Listing 5.2.

Listing 5.2 A Java Applet for Testing the Effect of weightx and weighty

```
package chap5;

import java.awt.*;
import java.util.*;
import java.applet.Applet;

/* An applet that shows how the variable
GridBagConstraints.weightx and weighty affect the display of
Components in a GridBagLayout.
*/
public class ch5_fig2 extends Applet {

/** Set up the applet to have three buttons in a row. Use the
parameters FillHeight and FillWidth to determine whether to set
weightx and/or weighty. If either has the value "true", set
its weight to 1.0.
*/
  public void init() {
    GridBagLayout gb = new GridBagLayout();
    GridBagConstraints gbc = new GridBagConstraints();
    setLayout(gb);
    String s = getParameter( "FillWidth" );
    if( s != null ) {
      if( s.compareTo("true") == 0 )
        gbc.weightx = 1.0;
      }
    s = getParameter( "FillHeight" );
    if( s != null ) {
      if( s.compareTo("true") == 0 )
        gbc.weighty = 1.0;
      }
    newButton("First", gb, gbc);
    newButton("Second", gb, gbc);
    // This REMAINDER marks this Component as the
    // end of the row.
    gbc.gridwidth = GridBagConstraints.REMAINDER;
    newButton("Third", gb, gbc);

    gbc.gridwidth = 1;
```

```
    newButton("Fourth", gb, gbc);
    newButton("Fifth", gb, gbc);
    // This REMAINDER marks this Component as the
    // end of the row.
    gbc.gridwidth = GridBagConstraints.REMAINDER;
    newButton("Sixth", gb, gbc);
    resize( 300, 200 );
    }


/** Make a new button with a specified label,
gridbagconstraints, and add it to the specified gridbag.
@param  label The label that will appear in the button.
@param  gbl The GridBagLayout to add this button to.
@param  gbc The GridBagConstraints describing this button.
*/
  void newButton(String label, GridBagLayout gbl, GridBagConstraints gbc) {
    Button button = new Button(label);
    gbl.setConstraints(button, gbc);
    add(button);
    }


}
```

Listing 5.3   The HTML Code That Runs Weight Test Applet

```
<!DOCTYPE HTML PUBLIC "-//SQ//DTD HTML 2.0 HoTMetaL + extensions//EN">
<HTML><HEAD><TITLE>Listing 5-2: Testing
GrigBagConstraints.weightx and weighty.
</TITLE></HEAD>
<BODY>
<applet code="chap5/ch5_fig2.class" height=500 width=400>
<param name="FillHeight" value="false">
<param name="FillWidth" value="false">
</applet>
</BODY></HTML>
```

In the applet's **init** method we set our **Container** (remember, an applet is a **Container**) to use a **GridBagLayout LayoutManager**. Then, we create a **GridBagConstraints**, which we'll use to create our buttons. As we create the buttons, we modify the **GridBagConstraints** as needed.

The only modification we make in this applet is to **gridwidth**. The **GridBagLayout** places our **Components** in the grid in left to right, top to bottom order. Because we're not specifying **gridx** or **gridy** for each item, we have to tell the **GridBagLayout** which **Component** is the last in the row. That is the effect of setting **gridwidth** to REMAINDER. The next **Component** added will go on the next row of the grid. Figures 5.4 through 5.7 show the applet running with various weight settings.

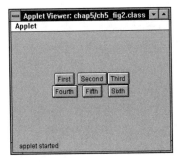

Figure 5.4

weightx and weighty set to 0.0 (default).

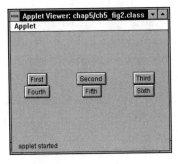

Figure 5.5

weightx set to 1.0, weighty to 0.0 (default).

In Figure 5.4, we leave the weight set at 0.0, the default. The **GridBagLayout** constructed a 2 row by 3 column grid, where the cell height was set to the height of the tallest button, and the cell width was set to the width of the widest button. The cell size in this case has nothing to do with the weights. What setting

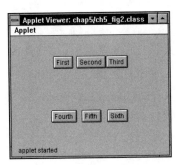

Figure 5.6

weightx set to 0.0 (default) and weighty to 1.0.

the weights to 0 *did* cause was the "extra" space in the display space being distributed around the outside of the grid rather than within the grid. When we set the weight to 0, the buttons appear to huddle together in the middle of the display space.

When we set both weights to 1.0, all the "extra" space in each dimension, x and y, is distributed within the grid. Our **Components** are spread out as the space that used to be piled around the outside is fitted between the cells of the grid instead. Figures 5.5 and 5.6 show what happens when we weight only one of the dimensions. Figure 5.7 shows the result of weighting both.

SIZING A COMPONENT IN GRIDBAGLAYOUT

There are also two forms of padding in **GridBagConstraints**: internal and external. Internal padding, **ipadx** and **ipady**, is "extra" space the **LayoutManager** adds to whatever size the **Component** claims it should be (using **Component.preferredSize** and **Component.minimumSize**). So, say you have an **ipadx** of 5 and an **ipady** of 2 and your **Component.preferredSize** returns a **Dimension** with a height of 10 and a width of 17. The **LayoutManager** will actually try to make the **Component** 20 pixels high and 21 pixels wide, adding **ipadx** to the top and bottom and **ipady** to the right and left. The **Component** itself will be made this big, so the internal padding becomes part of the visual element itself.

External padding specifies the blank space that will appear around the **Component**. To specify external padding, we use a new class, **Insets**, which consists entirely of four public ints:

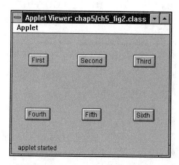

Figure 5.7

weightx and weighty set to 1.0.

- **top:** The space that will appear above the **Component**.
- **bottom:** The space that will appear below the **Component**.
- **left:** The space that will appear to the left of the **Component**.
- **right:** The space that will appear to the right of the **Component**.

Figure 5.8 shows how internal and external padding is distributed in a **GridBagLayout**.

The only members of **GridBagConstraints** that we haven't covered so far are **fill** and **anchor**. **fill** determines how a **Component** is sized within its cell when the **Component.preferredSize** is *smaller* than the cell size. **fill** can have any of four values that are public constants in **GridBagConstraints**, as shown in Table 5.1.

anchor determines how a **Component** is positioned within its cell if the **Component's** preferred size is smaller than the cell size *and* the **Component** is not set to fill the cell. **anchor** can take any of the values shown in Table 5.2, which are all public constants in **GridBagConstraints**.

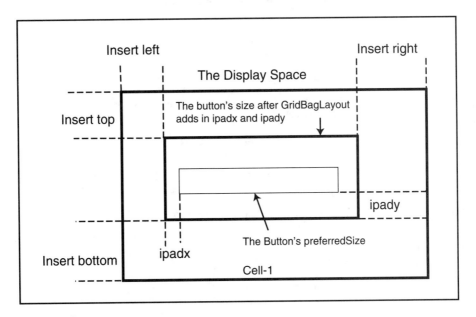

Figure 5.8

Internal and external padding operating on a single button in a GridBagLayout cell.

Table 5.1 Values for GridBagConstraints.fill	
Value	**Explanation**
NONE	The Component retains its preferred size.
HORIZONTAL	The Component retains its preferred vertical size, but is expanded to fill the cell horizontally.
VERTICAL	The Component retains its preferred horizontal size, but is expanded to fill the cell vertically.
BOTH	The Component is expanded to fill the cell both horizontally and vertically.

METHODS IN GRIDBAGLAYOUT

Now that we've seen how **Component** size and position are controlled by the **GridBagConstraints** we attach to them, we can take a closer look at the rest of the methods in **GridBagLayout**. Table 5.3 describes these methods.

Table 5.2 Values for GridBagConstraints.anchor	
Value	**Explanation**
CENTER	The Component is centered within the cell; this value is the default.
NORTH	The Component is placed with its top edge against the top edge of the cell, and centered horizontally.
SOUTH	The Component is placed with its bottom edge against the bottom edge of the cell, and centered horizontally.
EAST	The Component is placed with its left edge against the left edge of the cell, and centered vertically.
WEST	The Component is placed with its right edge against the right edge of the cell, and centered vertically.
NORTHEAST	The Component is placed with its top-left corner against the top-left corner of the cell.
NORTHWEST	The Component is placed with its top-right corner against the top-right corner of the cell.
SOUTHEAST	The Component is placed with its bottom-left corner against the bottom-left corner of the cell.
SOUTHWEST	The Component is placed with its bottom-right corner against the bottom-right corner of the cell.

Table 5.3   GridBagLayout Methods

Return	Method Name	Arguments	Description
void	DumpConstraints	GridBagConstraints	Prints the layout constraints.
void	DumpLayoutInfo	GridBagLayoutInfo	Prints the layout information.
GridBagLayoutInfo	GetLayoutInfo	Container, int	Gets the layout info for the specified Container.
Dimension	GetMinSize	Container, GridBag LayoutInfo	Gets the minimum size of the specified Container.
void	addLayoutComponent	String, Component	Adds the specified component with the specified name to the layout.
GridBagConstraints	getConstraints	Component	Retrieves the constraints for the specified Component.
Dimension	getLayoutDimensions	none	Retrieves the size of the grid.
Point	getLayoutOrigin	none	Retrieves the point of the origin of the grid within the Panel.
double[][]	getLayoutWeights	none	Retrieves weightx and weighty for each of the Components in the layout.
void	layoutContainer	Container	Lays out the Container in the specified Container.
Point	location	int, int	Returns the location of the Component at the specified cell position.
GridBagConstraints	lookupConstraints	Component	Retrieves the GridBagConstraints for the specified Component.
Dimension	minimumLayoutSize	Container	Returns the minimum dimensions needed to lay out the Components contained in the specified Container.
Dimension	preferredLayoutSize	Container	Returns the preferred dimensions for this layout given the components in the specified Container.
void	removeLayout Component	Component	Removes the specified Component from the layout.
void	setConstraints	Component,GridBag Constraints	Attaches the specified GridBagConstraints to the specified Component.
String	toString	none	Returns the String representation of this GridLayout's values.

Using Predefined Controls to Get User Input

Back in Listing 5.1 we used buttons to illustrate the effect of various **LayoutManagers**. In addition, we arranged it so that hitting any of the buttons caused the **CardLayout Panel** to flip over the next card. Well, now that you've seen the buttons in action, we might as well explain them. The AgentLauncher needs five buttons: Pick, Dispatch, Stop, Text-Only, and Configuration. Dispatch, Stop, and Text-Only are used only to call methods within the AgentLauncher. Listing 5.4 shows the source for these buttons.

Listing 5.4   The AgentButton Class and Other Button Classes

```
/** Initialize the applet. Resize and load images.
*/
public void init() {
   int i,j;

     setLayout( new BorderLayout());
     controlsPanel = new Panel();
     controlsPanel.setLayout( new GridLayout( 2, 1 ));
     add( "North", controlsPanel );

     buttonPanel = new Panel();
     pickButton = new PickButton(PICK_STRING);
     dispatchButton = new DispatchButton(DISPATCH_STRING);
     stopButton = new StopButton(STOP_STRING);
     ... Stuff deleted ...
     }

/** A base class for buttons in the AgentLauncher.
*/
class AgentButton extends Button {
   String l;
   Applet applet;

/** constructor - save the Applet, and the label.
@param  ap  The applet.
@param  label The label that appears on the button.
*/
   public AgentButton( Applet ap, String label ) {
     super( label );
     l = new String(label);
     applet = ap;
     }

/** The method called when the button is clicked. Our
subclasses override this to provide their own action
```

```
processing.
*/
  public boolean action(Event e, Object o) {
   return false;
     }


}

/** A class for providing a button that calls up our
Pick-an-agent dialog box.
*/
class PickButton extends AgentButton {
  public boolean action( Event e, Object o ) {
      Frame frame = getFrame();
      PickDialog d = new PickDialog(applet, frame,
                   agentList, alid.header);
      d.ShowAndLayout();
    }
```

We make a Panel to hold the buttons, create the buttons, then add them to the Panel. This results in a more or less reasonable arrangement of buttons, no matter how the user resizes the window.

How we want to deal with the mouse clicks determines how we'll design our buttons. There are a number of places where it looks like you can catch the mouse click for a button. The most obvious choice is to overload **Component.mouseUp/mouseDown**. Another less obvious possibility is to deal with it in the MOUSE_UP/DOWN case of **handleEvent** (we talk more about events later on). Unfortunately, neither of these options really works. Java's **Button** class handles the MOUSE_UP/DOWN events and redispatches them as a single ACTION_EVENT. The MOUSE_UP/DOWN event never reaches any of our **Components**.

The proper way to catch a button click is to overload **action**, as we do in AgentButton (you can also get the same effect by handling ACTION_EVENT in a **handleEvent** case). There is only one type of action that can happen in a **Button** object, so within **action** we simply do whatever that button requires. The event passed as an argument is just an **ACTION_EVENT**, so the **Event.id** is useless, and **Event.x/y** is zeroed out, making them useless, too. The second argument to **action**, an **Object**, is a little more interesting though. This is always the **Component** within which the event occurred.

Our original implementation in Listing 5.4 overloaded **action** within a new **Button** subclass, **AgentButton**, and all our buttons had to subclass **AgentButton**.

Listing 5.5 reworks this to eliminate the **AgentButton** class entirely. What we do is overload **action** within AgentLauncher. Within this new **action**, we figure out which **Button** was clicked by comparing the label of the **Object** to the string labels of our **Buttons**. Once we've figured out which **Button** was clicked, we can easily call the AgentLauncher method that **Button** previously called from its clicked method.

Listing 5.5   Eliminating AgentButton

```
/** Initialize the applet. Resize and load images.
*/
public void init() {
    int i,j;

        setLayout( new BorderLayout());
        controlsPanel = new Panel();
        controlsPanel.setLayout( new GridLayout( 2, 1 ));
        add( "North", controlsPanel );

        buttonPanel = new Panel();
        pickButton = new Button(PICK_STRING);
        dispatchButton = new Button(DISPATCH_STRING);
        stopButton = new Button(STOP_STRING);
        textOnlyButton = new Button( TEXT_ONLY_STRING );
        helpButton = new HelpButton( this );
        resultButton = new Button( RESULT_STRING );
        ... Stuff deleted ...
    }


/** Handle any events that might occur—namely button clicks
from the buttons at the top of the AgentLauncher.
*/
public boolean handleEvent(Event e) {
    if (e.id == Event.ACTION_EVENT) {
        if( e.target instanceof Button ) {
        Button b = (Button)e.target;
            if(b.getLabel().compareTo(PICK_STRING)==0)
                {
                Frame frame = getFrame();
                PickDialog d = new PickDialog(this, frame,
                            agentList, alid.header);
                d.ShowAndLayout();
                }
            if(b.getLabel().compareTo(DISPATCH_STRING) == 0 )
                Dispatch();
            if(b.getLabel().compareTo(STOP_STRING) == 0 )
                StopAgent(currentID);
            if(b.getLabel().compareTo(TEXT_ONLY_STRING) == 0 )
                {
```

```
              DisplayType = TEXT_ONLY;
              textOnlyButton.setLabel(ANIMATED_STRING);
              }
        else {
           if(b.getLabel().compareTo(ANIMATED_STRING) == 0 )
              {
              DisplayType = ANIMATED;
              textOnlyButton.setLabel(TEXT_ONLY_STRING);
              }
           }
        }
     }
   else {
      if( e.id == Event.MOUSE_UP )
         clicked( e.x, e.y );
      }
   return false;
   }
```

This approach has obvious limitations. **Button** labels must be unique. The **Button** label itself also has to appear in two places—in the **Button** constructor and in the **action** handling method—which is a possible source of problems if you try to use literal strings rather than constants. It is, however, more modular in that the **Buttons** have no knowledge of the AgentLauncher applet. Overloading **action** in **AgentButton** forces us to use static methods within the AgentLauncher or pass the AgentLauncher as an argument. Both approaches are valid.

Image Buttons

There is no image button supplied with Java, but creating one is not such a big deal. We've already seen all the pieces we need to implement one. What we need is to create a **Component, ImageButton,** whose **paint/update** method displays one image if the mouse button is down and another if the button is not. The **ImageButton** should also catch the **mouseUp** event and dispatch an ACTION_EVENT. This way, we can use **ImageButtons** exactly the same way we use text buttons. Listing 5.6 shows a simple **ImageButton.** Note that we still pass the label "stop" so that the button can be identified in the applet's **action** method.

Listing 5.6   An ImageButton Class

```
package chap5;

import java.awt.*;
import java.util.*;
import java.io.*;
import java.net.*;
```

```
import java.applet.*;
import jvr.animator.*;
import jvr.utils.*;
import java.lang.*;

/** An applet to demonstrate creating your own button from two images,
an upimage and a downimage.
*/
public class ch5_fig7 extends Applet {

String theURL;
boolean bUpLoaded = false;
boolean bDnLoaded = false;
Image dnImage;
Image upImage;

ImageButton ib = null;

    /**
     * Initialize the applet. Resize and load images.
     */
public void init() {
   theURL = getParameter( "URL" );
   if( theURL == null )
      return;
   try {
      URL upURL = new URL( theURL+"UpImage.gif" );
      URL dnURL = new URL( theURL+"DnImage.gif" );
      System.out.println( upURL+"    "+dnURL );
      Image upImage = getImage(upURL);
      Image dnImage = getImage(dnURL);
      prepareImage( dnImage, this );
      prepareImage( upImage, this );
      while( !bUpLoaded && !bDnLoaded)
         {
         try{ wait(); }
         catch( InterruptedException e )
            {System.out.println( "interrupted" ); }
         }
      ib = new ImageButton( this, upImage, dnImage );
      add( ib );
      add( new Button( "a regular button" ));
   } catch( MalformedURLException e ) { add( new Button("ImageButton Backup")); }
   resize( 400, 200 );
   show();
     }


public synchronized boolean imageUpdate(Image img, int infoflags, int x, int y,
int width, int height)
   {
   System.out.println( "img "+img+" update" );
   boolean bret = true;
```

```
     if( infoflags == ALLBITS || infoflags == ERROR )
       {
       if( img == upImage )
          {
          System.out.println( "upimage" );
          bUpLoaded = true;
          }
       if( img == dnImage )
          {
          System.out.println( "dnimage" );
          bDnLoaded = true;
          }
       bret = false;
       }
     notifyAll();
     return( true );
     }

public boolean action( Event ev, Object o ) {
     switch( ev.id ) {
        case Event.ACTION_EVENT:
           if( ev.target instanceof ImageButton )
              System.out.println( "Got ImageButton click "+ev );
           else
              System.out.println( "Got regular button click"+ev );
           return true;
        default:
           return false;
        }
     }
}

class ImageButton extends Panel {
     Image currImage;
     Image upImage;
     Image downImage;
     Applet applet;
     Rectangle lastBounds;

     public ImageButton( Applet a, Image upI, Image dnI ) {
        lastBounds = bounds();
        applet = a;
        upImage = upI;
        downImage = dnI;
        currImage = upImage;
     }

     public synchronized Dimension preferredSize() {
        return( new Dimension(currImage.getWidth(applet),
             currImage.getHeight(applet)));
     }

     public void paint( Graphics g ) {
```

```
       if( currImage == null )
          return;
       boolean ret = false;
       while( ret == false ) {
          ret = g.drawImage( currImage, 0, 0, applet );
          if( ret == false ) {
             try {
                Thread.sleep( 100 );
             } catch( Exception e ){System.out.println("exception");}
          }
       }
   }

   public boolean handleEvent( Event e ) {
      switch( e.id ) {
         case Event.MOUSE_DOWN:
            currImage = downImage;
            repaint();
            return( true );
         case Event.MOUSE_UP:
            if( currImage == downImage )
               {
               currImage = upImage;
               Event ev = new Event(this, Event.ACTION_EVENT, this);
               getParent().deliverEvent( ev );
               repaint();
               }
            return( true );
         case Event.MOUSE_ENTER:
         case Event.MOUSE_EXIT:
            if( currImage != upImage )
               {
               currImage = upImage;
               repaint();
               }
            return( true );
      }
      return( false );
   }
}
```

Our simple **ImageButton** has a couple of problems that makes it less than completely compatible with the native GUI buttons you get with the **Button** class. Our **ImageButton** should have a third image for use when the **Component** is disabled.

Dialogs/Forms

The AgentLauncher can launch *any* one of a number of agents. In order to provide the user with a choice of available agents, we need to implement a single form that lists all the available agents and allows the user to pick/launch one from the list.

Visually and functionally we have two styles of form. The first is a traditional Windows-style dialog box. This approach places all the controls that make up the form in a separate, moveable window with its own frame that pops up on top of the browser window. The user hits the OK button to accept the values entered into the form, and the window then disappears.

The second style is the inline, Web-style form. This approach displays the components of the form within the browser window, as if they were part of the document. When the document scrolls, the form scrolls, too. Typically, the user accepts the data entered by hitting an Accept button. There is usually no frame around the form's components and the form appears to be just a part of a larger document (though the user is often hyperlinked away when the Accept button is hit). The mailto form is a good example of a Web-style form. Though it consists entirely of buttons, our **ButtonPanel** is another example of an inline form.

Though both styles are equally valid, and equally easy to implement in Java, the dialog box-style has several benefits. The first is that it can be modal. A modal dialog box stays on the screen until the user has filled it in to the satisfaction of the applet writer. Second, when a modal, pop-up dialog box displays on top of the browser window, it is obvious to even the thickest user that the data needs to be filled in. Forms that scroll within the browser window often require extensive inline documentation to ensure that the user fills them out correctly. Third, and perhaps most important to Web page designers, dialog boxes go away when you don't need them. A scrollable form built into a page always takes up screen real estate, even if the user has already filled it out correctly.

The downside of dialog boxes is that the designers of Java really don't want you to be creating your own **Window** objects (of which **Dialog** is one) from within an applet. In fact, the basic theory of applets is that they should be confined to the area within the frame of the browser. When we start creating our own **Window** objects, we escape the boundaries of the browser window, a prospect that browser architects find disturbing.

Most GUIs provide a facility for compiling a static description of a dialog box into an application, such that the source code for the application only has to say "Load the dialog box with ID 100" and a functional dialog box appears with all the components in the right place. You can't do this in Java, at least not yet. Each dialog box must be constructed on-the-fly. This means that you have to go through the following process in the dialog constructor:

- Find the **Frame** window that will be the parent of this dialog box.
- Create the **Window** and **Container** (via the **Dialog** class constructor) for the dialog box.
- Attach a **LayoutManager** to the **Container**.
- Create all the **Components** (Buttons, TextFields ...) of the dialog box.
- Add all the **Components** to the **Container**.
- Show the dialog box.

The one argument you absolutely must provide to any **Window** constructor is the **Frame** object that makes up the main window for the application, in this case, the **Frame** of the browser. In order to prevent applets from creating windows, the **Frame** object is not just lying around, publicly available for you to use, but there is a way to get it. This is the function of the **getFrame** method, which is shown in Listing 5.7.

Listing 5.7   The getFrame Method

```
/** Get the Frame window that is the parent of all the windows
currently on the screen. Every application has ONE Frame that
can be found by trolling through the tree of Containers that
makes up the hierarchy of windows in a Java application.
@return The Frame that is the ultimate parent of the current
Component.
*/
public Frame getFrame() {
   Component c = (Component)this;
   Frame theFrame = null;
   Component parent = (Component)this;
   while( parent != null ) {
     if( parent instanceof Frame ) {
        theFrame = (Frame)parent;
        break;
        }
     parent = parent.getParent();
     }
   return( theFrame );
   }
```

Component.getParent returns the **Container** that holds the **Component**. But every **Container** is also a **Component**, so we can follow the **Container** chain all the way back to the first **Container**. As we go along, we see if the parent **Container** is the one—and only one—instance of a **Frame** because, as you saw back in Figure 5.1, **Frame** subclasses **Container**, and the **Frame Container** must contain all the **Component**s in the system.

Now we have enough information to create an empty dialog box and fill it up with useful controls. In Listing 5.8 we implement a **PickDialog** class that contains the list of available agents, an OK button, and a Cancel button.

Listing 5.8   The PickDialog Class

```
/** A modal dialog box that allows the user to pick one item
from a Vector of Strings.
@version 1.0 1/4/1996
@author John Rodley
*/
class PickDialog extends Dialog {
    List l;
    int selectIndex = -1;
    Frame parent;
    Vector agentList;
    Panel ListPanel;
    Panel ButtonPanel;
    Label label;
    String selectedItem = null;
    public boolean bFinished = false;
    AgentLauncher agentLauncher;

/** Constructor, save the Frame, AgentLauncher, String Vector
and header string for future use. The AgentLauncher is used to
callback when the user hits OK.
@param a  An AgentLauncher to call back to when OK is hit
@param p The parent frame of this dialog, needed for the
Dialog constructor
@param al  The Vector of Strings that will appear in the list
box for the user to choose from.
@param header The String which will appear as a header OVER the
list of possible choices.
*/
  public PickDialog(AgentLauncher a, Frame p, Vector al, String header) {
    super(p, "Pick an Agent", true);
      parent = p;
    agentList = al;
      label = new Label( header );
    agentLauncher = a;

      // Set up all the graphical elements
      // Split the dialog main panel into three elements, top,
      // bottom and middle, via the BorderLayout. The top and
      // bottom size themselves according to the preferred sizes
      // of the text on the top and the buttons on the bottom.
      // The Center panel, which the List fills, uses all the
      // space left in the middle.
      setLayout(new BorderLayout());
```

```
   add( "North", label );
     ButtonPanel = new Panel();
   add( "South", ButtonPanel );
   l = new List( agentList.size(), false );
   for( int i = 0; i < agentList.size(); i++ )
     l.addItem((String) agentList.elementAt(i) );
   if( agentList.size() > 0 )
     l.select( 0 );
   add( "Center", l );

     Button okbutton = new Button("OK");
   ButtonPanel.add( okbutton );
   Button cancelbutton = new Button( "Cancel" );
   ButtonPanel.add( cancelbutton );
   }

/** Return the String item which was selected from the list by
the user.
@return String  The String item that was selected from the
Vector displayed in the dialog.
*/
  public String getSelected() {
     return( selectedItem );
     }

/** Size the dialog box to something appropriate, then make it
non-resizeable so that users don't go resizing it themselves.
*/
  public void ShowAndLayout() {
  show();
  resize( 600, 300 );
  layout();
  setResizable(false);
  }

/** Deal with the user either hitting the OK/Cancel button or
selecting an item from the list. Shows a nag box if the user
hits OK without an item selected. Tells the AgentLauncher to
load the class if the user hits OK.
@return false if the user hasn't selected a proper item, true
otherwise.
*/
public boolean action(Event e, Object o) {

   if( e.target instanceof Button )
     {
   // If this is the OK button, deal with it, else return.
   if(((Button)e.target).getLabel().compareTo("OK") == 0 ) {
     selectIndex = l.getSelectedIndex();
     if( selectIndex == -1 )
       {
         MessageBox m =
         new MessageBox( parent,
```

```
            "You have to pick something, or hit Cancel");
        m.ShowAndLayout();
        return false;
        }
      else
        {
        selectedItem = new String( l.getSelectedItem());
          agentLauncher.LoadAgentClass( parent, selectedItem );
        }
      }
    }
  bFinished = true;
  dispose();
  return true;
  }
}
```

This is a good example of a **BorderLayout**. **Dialog** is a subclass of **Panel**, so we set it up as a **BorderLayout**. In the North region, we place a message that tells the user what to do—pick an agent from the list. In the South, we place a **FlowLayout Panel** that will contain our OK and Cancel buttons. In the Center, we place a list that will contain all the agents from which the user can pick.

Scrolling

HTML pages scroll all by themselves, and if you plunk an applet into the middle of a page, it'll scroll with the page. The AgentLauncher needs scrolling capability so that the user can troll through the potentially huge array of running agents, only a small number of which can fit on the screen at any one time. We could define our applet height as something huge, and let the HTML scrolling take care of it, but we still might spawn more agents than would fit, so defining our own scrolling region is the only way to go.

Creating a Scrollbar is relatively straightforward. Figure 5.9 shows the horizontal scroll bar that results when you use this constructor:

```
Scrollbar( Scrollbar.HORIZONTAL, 50, 10, 0, 100 );
```

There are three ways the user can move the slider, each of which results in a different value change.

- Drag the slider with the mouse, which can leave the slider anywhere.
- Click on one of the arrows at the ends of the scroll bar, which results in the slider value incrementing or decrementing by one.

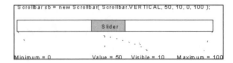

Figure 5.9

The construction of a Scrollbar.

- Click in the empty space on either side of the slider, which results in the slider value changing by "visible" units—in our example, that would be 10.

Just like our **ButtonPanel** buttons, the Scrollbar generates actions that we must catch in the appropriate **action** method. The **action** event doesn't tell us what happened, only that something happened within the Scrollbar. It's up to us to then query the Scrollbar and rebuild our scrolling region appropriately.

Menus

When we enter the AgentLauncher applet, we want AgentLauncher help to be available, yet unobtrusive. The cool way to do this would be to add a menu item to the browser help menu: AgentLauncher help. Unfortunately, menus, like windows, fall into the category of things that you aren't supposed to do with applets. By going through the same **getFrame** nonsense as the dialog boxes, we can get access to the menu bar and all its submenus, adding and removing items at will. What we can't do is get ourselves called when a menu item is selected. All the menu item select events are swallowed up by the **handleEvent** function of the **Frame**. So, unfortunately for us, even though it belongs on the menu bar, our applet help has to be accessed through a button.

Other Controls

There are other controls: Checkbox, Choice, TextField, and TextArea. Of these, Choice and TextField are used later on when we talk about fonts. We also use a pile of Checkboxes in Chapter 10's SecurityDialog. TextAreas are left as an exercise for the you. Just what you needed, right?

Flow Control

We've already seen how Java deals with a mouse click in a button, absorbing the mouse-up and mouse-down messages from the native GUI and turning them into a single ACTION_EVENT. This, in general terms, is how Java abstracts the message-handling mechanism of the native GUIs. With some small amount of processing, Java turns "messages" from the native GUI into **Event** objects, which it directs to the appropriate **Component**s.

By way of background, GUIs like Windows, X11, and Presentation Manager generate a message for all the things that happen outside the application that the application needs to know about. These events include keypresses, hitting the Scrollbar, selecting an item from a list, dragging with the mouse, mouse movements, changing which window has the focus. A C Windows program generally has a single function, the **window** procedure, with a large **switch** statement that catches all the messages the application wants to deal with. The application registers this single message-handling function with Windows; thereafter, Windows calls that function each time a message gets directed to the application. The Java analogue to the **window** procedure is the **handleEvent** method. You can catch any event in the **handleEvent** method, but **Component** provides overloadable methods for most of the likely events. Table 5.4 shows the overloadable event handling methods in **Component**.

Drawing and the Graphics Context

Up to now, we've used the supplied graphical objects, and avoided drawing directly to the screen ourselves. The time has come. Whatever GUI our applet is running under, that GUI's key task is to notify the applet when the window needs to be refreshed. Java delivers this notification to the applet by calling one of two override methods: **Component.paint** or **Component.update**.

With **paint**, the entire **Component** is cleared to the background color before **paint** is invoked. With **update**, the window is not cleared. **update** methods are inherently more difficult to write because you have to clear any areas that need clearing manually rather than relying on the automatic clear in **paint**.

Listings 5.9 and 5.10 show two versions of an applet that displays two strings. One of the strings sits in the upper left corner of the applet, and one marches around the screen. The first applet uses **paint**. As the string marches across the screen, both the marching string and the stationary string flicker. In the applet that uses **update**, not only does the marching string flicker less, the stationary string doesn't flicker at all. The **update** method is slightly more complicated by having to clear the area where the string used to be.

Table 5.4 Overloadable Event Handlers and Corresponding Java Events

Component	Method	Java Event.id Description
action	ACTION_EVENT	Button was clicked.
gotFocus	GOT_FOCUS	Window is now the input focus.
keyDown	KEY_ACTION, KEY_PRESS, F1-F12, LEFT, RIGHT, HOME, END, PGUP, PGDN, ESC	A key was pressed; the key that was pressed is available in Event.key, and the state of Ctrl, Shift, and meta keys is available via the controlDown, shiftDown, and metaDown methods.
keyUp	KEY_ACTION_RELEASE, KEY_RELEASE	
lostFocus	LOST_FOCUS	This window is no longer the input focus.
mouseDown	MOUSE_DOWN	The left mouse button was clicked down. It may still be down.
mouseDrag	MOUSE_DRAG	The user is keeping the left mouse button down and is dragging it across the screen.
mouseEnter	MOUSE_ENTER	The mouse has entered this Component's window.
mouseExit	MOUSE_EXIT	The mouse has left this Component's window.
mouseMove	MOUSE_MOVE	The mouse is moving; it may or may not be dragging.
mouseUp	MOUSE_UP	The left mouse button has been released.

Listing 5.9   The paint Version of the Marching String Applet

```
package chap5;

import java.awt.*;
import java.util.*;
import java.io.*;
import java.net.*;
import java.applet.*;
import jvr.animator.*;
import jvr.utils.*;
import java.lang.*;

/** An applet that displays the same string in two places: one
fixed, the other changing at 50ms intervals. This applet uses the paint
method which is very simple, but which should also produce a
large amount of flicker.

@version 1.0 11/3/1995
@author John Rodley
*/
public class ch5_fig10 extends Applet implements Runnable {
```

```
/** The main thread */
Thread myThread = null;
FontMetrics fm = null;
int width = 0;
int height = 0;
int x = 0;
int y = 0;
String TheString;
```

```
/** start - Whenever a user visits our page, Applet calls
this method, which overrides the Applet method. The method creates a
thread and passes this AgentLauncher into it. It works because
we implement the Runnable method.
*/
  public void start() {
    int i;
    if( myThread == null )
      {
      myThread = new Thread( this );
      myThread.setName( "PaintTest" );
      myThread.start();
      }
  }
```

```
/** Stop this thread. */
  public void stop() {
    System.out.println( "JohnImage stop - user is leaving my page" );
    myThread = null;
  }
```

```
/** The main loop for the main thread. */
  public void run() {
    int i;
    while( myThread != null )
      {
      try {
      Thread.sleep( 50 );
      } catch( Exception e ) {
        System.out.println("Exception" ); }
      moveString();
      repaint();
      }
  myThread = null;
  }
```

```
/**
Initialize the applet. Resize and show.
*/
  public void init() {
    resize( 200, 150 );
    show();
  }
```

```
/** Move the marching string by changing the x and y coords it
will paint at the next time it paints. Should move left to
right, top to bottom.
*/
  void moveString() {
    Rectangle r = bounds();
    if( x + width > r.width )
      {
      x = 0;
      if( y + height > r.height )
        y = height*2;
      else
        y += height;
      }
    else
      x++;
  }


/** Update the window, erasing things from their old positions
and painting them anew at their current positions. */
  public void paint(Graphics g) {
    if( fm == null )
      {
      TheString = new String( "Java is cool" );
      fm = g.getFontMetrics();
      width = fm.stringWidth( TheString );
      height = fm.getHeight();
      x = 0; y = height*2;
      }
    g.drawString( TheString, 0, height );
    g.drawString( TheString, x, y );
  }
}
```

Listing 5.10   The update Version of the Marching String Applet

```
  Image offscreen;
  Dimension offscreensize;
  Graphics offgraphics;


/** Update the window, erasing things from their old positions
and painting them anew at their current positions.
*/
  public void update(Graphics g) {
    if( fm == null )
      {
      TheString = new String( "Java is cool" );
      fm = g.getFontMetrics();
      width = fm.stringWidth( TheString );
      height = fm.getHeight();
      x = 0; y = height;
      }
    // We use the offscreen graphics context to do a total
```

```
    // repaint if the applet has changed size.
    Dimension d = size();
    if ((offscreen == null) ||
        (d.width != offscreensize.width) ||
            (d.height != offscreensize.height)) {
        offscreen = createImage(d.width, d.height);
        offscreensize = d;
        offgraphics = offscreen.getGraphics();
    }
    offgraphics.setColor( g.getColor());
    offgraphics.clearRect( lastx, lasty-height, width, height );
    offgraphics.drawString( TheString, x, y );
    g.drawImage(offscreen, 0, 0, null);
    lastx = x;
    lasty = y;
}
```

Understanding the Coordinate System

One of the immediate advantages of using a multi-platform package is that up and down always mean the same thing. The Java coordinate system puts 0,0 in the upper left of the screen, and that's the way it is (so sayeth Sun). x coordinates increase to the right, y coordinates increase downward. This is okay, as far as it goes, but it leads to something of an inconsistency. If you draw a String with a height of 10 and a width of 5 at (0,0) it occupies a rectangle with corners (0,0) (0,-10) (5,0) (5,-10). However, if you clear (or fill, or draw ...) a rectangle of that same size located at (0,0) the cleared rectangle has corners (0,0) (0,10) (5,0) (5,10). Figure 5.10 shows a call to **drawString**, and **fillRect** with the same origin and dimensions.

The following rules (which account for our inconsistency problem) govern origin and drawing direction for various operations:

- The origin of a **drawText** (or **drawChar**) operation is the left end of the baseline (see Figure 5.10) of the text. The text will appear to draw up and to the right of the origin.

- The origin of GUI controls, like Buttons, Labels, Choices, and so on is the upper left corner of the control. The control will appear to draw *down* and to the right of the origin. Ditto for rectangles (as in **Graphics.drawRect**) and other shapes.

Within the **Graphics** class you get two methods for dealing with the coordinate system, **translate** and **scale**. **translate** moves the origin for the current **Graphics** context so that all future operations on the **Graphics** context are relative to the newly set origin. This is very useful when you have margins, or when you split the screen into distinct sections. This is essentially what happens when Java calls

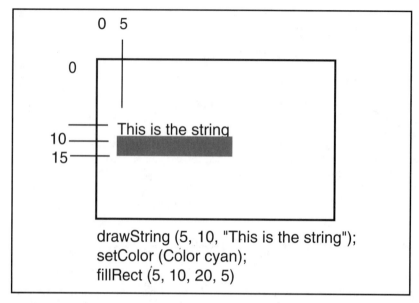

Figure 5.10

Drawing text and rectangle with the same origin.

Component.paint. It gets a **Graphics** object for the entire applet, translates it to the origin of the **Component** and passes the translated **Graphics** object to **Component.paint**.

Using Fonts

Listing 5.11 shows an applet that illustrates some of the basics of font and color management, as well as some of the things we've been saying about using the **update** method. The point of the applet is to display a string on a ticker, passing the string through a rectangular window at a constant speed in an endless loop, like a stock ticker. We want the ticker to be a fixed width and just a little taller than the string itself.

The size and shape of characters drawn on an applet's screen depends entirely on the font attached to that graphics context. There are two classes to think about when dealing with fonts, the **Font** class itself and the **FontMetrics** class. The **Font** class allows us to retrieve/build fonts with the face, point size, and style (bold, italic ...) we need. A **Graphics** object always has a **Font** attached to it, which we can query using **Graphics.getFont**.

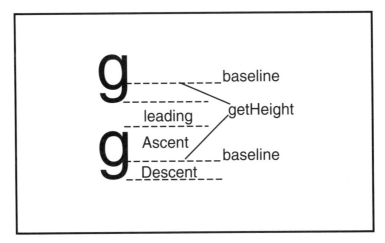

Figure 5.11

FontMetrics of the letter g.

But the **Font** only embodies general information about the font: shape, relative size, weight. We need to know specifically how many pixels wide and tall various characters will be. The **FontMetrics** class, illustrated in Figure 5.11, provides us with a way of determining how text drawn using a particular font will appear in a particular graphics context.

There is nothing tricky about the information in **FontMetrics**. **getHeight** returns the maximum vertical dimension of the largest character in the font, plus the space between lines. In techno-type terms this is *ascent* (height of the character above the baseline), *descent* (height of the character below the baseline) and leading (space between the top of this line and bottom of the next line).

The Ticker **update** method uses **FontMetrics** for two purposes: to decide how tall the ticker should be and to know how much of the string can fit into the ticker. The one thing to notice when we draw text in **update** is that we offset the line upward by **getMaxDescent**. When you say **drawChar(0,0)** what you're saying is draw the character and place its left edge at 0 on the x and its BASELINE at 0 on the y. Many characters, like our g, descend below the baseline and if we don't offset by **MaxDecent**, the descenders will be chopped off.

Listing 5.11   The Ticker Applet

```
package chap5;

import java.util.*;
```

```
import java.io.*;
import java.net.*;
import java.applet.*;
import java.awt.*;

/** A Ticker applet, runs a String through a rectangular box as
if it were a stock-style ticker.
@version 1.0 11/17/1995
@author John Rodley
*/
public class ch5_fig12 extends Applet implements Runnable {
  Thread myThread = null;  // Our thread.

  int width = 300;
  int height = 20; // the height of the grid
  int leftMargin = 1;
  int topMargin = 1;

  Ticker ticker = null;

  public ch5_fig12() {
  }

/** The applet start method. If there's no thread, make one
and pass us in; otherwise, do nothing.
*/
  public void start() {
   if( myThread == null )
     {
       myThread = new Thread( this );
     myThread.start();
     }
  }

/** The applet stop method. If there's a thread, set it to null
and that will break us out of the thread.run method.
*/
  public void stop() {
     if( ticker != null )
        ticker.stopIt();
   myThread = null;
   }

/** The Thread run method. Start the ticker in its own
thread, then sit in a loop sleeping for 1 second until we get
killed.
*/
  public void run() {
     String s = new String( "Welcome to John's Home Page ... home of the latest
in Java applets ... and loads of cool articles ... " );
   ticker = new Ticker( this, s, leftMargin, topMargin, width, 65 );
     ticker.start();
while( myThread != null )
     {
        try {Thread.sleep( 1000 );}
```

```
            catch( Exception e ) { System.out.println( "exception");}
        }
    myThread = null;
    }

/** Initialize the applet. Resize and load images.
*/
  public void init() {
      resize( leftMargin + width + leftMargin, topMargin + height + topMargin);
  }
}

class Ticker extends Thread {
  Applet applet;
  boolean bRun = true;
  int startx, starty;
  int height, width;
  int firstChar = 0;
  int lastChar = 0;
  String s;
  Color PromptColor;
  FontMetrics fm;
  int interiorHeight;
  char ca[] = null;
  int delay = 50;
  int inc = 0;

  public Ticker( Applet a, Vector v, int x, int y, int w, int waittime ) {
    applet = a;
      startx = x;
    starty = y;
      width = w;
    delay = waittime;
      s = new String( (String)v.elementAt(0));
    for( int i = 1; i < v.size(); i++ )
        {
          s = new String( s + "   " );
          s = new String( s + (String)v.elementAt(i));
        }
    }

  public Ticker( Applet a, String inputString, int x, int y, int w, int waittime
) {
      applet = a;
    startx = x;
      starty = y;
    width = w;
      delay = waittime;
    s = new String( inputString );
    }

  public void run() {
      int inc = 0;
    paintFirst( applet.getGraphics());
      while( bRun == true ) {
```

```
      paint1(applet.getGraphics(), inc++);
    try {Thread.sleep( delay );}
    catch( Exception e ) { System.out.println( "exception");}
    }
}

public void stopIt() { bRun = false; }

public void paintFirst( Graphics g ) {
    int i, j;
  int numChars = 0;

    g.translate( startx, starty );
  // Set these here since we're assured of having a valid graphics context
    fm = g.getFontMetrics();
  interiorHeight = fm.getHeight();
    applet.resize( width+30, interiorHeight*2 );
  PromptColor = Color.black;

    g.setColor( Color.cyan );
  g.fill3DRect(-1, -1, width+2, interiorHeight+2, true);
    ca = new char[s.length()];
  s.getChars( 0, s.length(), ca, 0 );
    int stringWidth = 0;
  for( i = 0; i < s.length(); i++ )
    {
      if(( stringWidth+fm.charWidth(ca[i])) >= width )
        {
        numChars = i;
        break;
        }
      stringWidth += fm.charWidth( ca[i] );
      }
  g.setColor( PromptColor );
    g.drawChars( ca, 0, numChars, 0,interiorHeight-fm.getMaxDescent());
  firstChar = 0;
    lastChar = numChars-1;

  String s2;
    s2 = new String( ca, firstChar, numChars );
  }

public void paint( Graphics g ) {
    int i, j;
  int numChars = 0;

    if( ca == null )
      {
    paintFirst( g );
    return;
      }
  System.out.println( "repainting  ticker" );
    g.translate( startx, starty );
  // Set these here since we're assured of having a valid graphics context
    fm = g.getFontMetrics();
```

```
      interiorHeight = fm.getHeight();
        PromptColor = Color.black;

      g.setColor( Color.cyan );
        g.fill3DRect(-1, -1, width+2, interiorHeight+2, true);
      g.setColor( PromptColor );
        if( firstChar < lastChar )
            g.drawChars( ca, firstChar, lastChar-firstChar, 0,interiorHeight-
fm.getMaxDecent());
        else
          {
            g.drawChars( ca, firstChar, s.length()-firstChar,0,interiorHeight-
fm.getMaxDecent());
          String s2 = new String( ca, firstChar, s.length()-firstChar);
          int stringWidth = fm.stringWidth( s2 );
            g.drawChars( ca, 0, lastChar, stringWidth,interiorHeight-
fm.getMaxDecent());
          }
        g.translate( -startx, -starty );
      }

    public void paint1( Graphics g, int inc ) {
        g.translate( startx, starty );

// System.out.println( "paint1 firstChar = "+ca[firstChar]+" lastChar =
"+ca[lastChar] );


      String s2;
      if( lastChar > firstChar )
        s2 = new String( ca, firstChar,(lastChar-firstChar)+1 );
      else
        {
        String s3 = new String( ca,firstChar,(s.length()-firstChar));
        String s4 = new String( ca, 0, lastChar );
        s2 = new String( s3+s4 );
        }

      int i, j, nextChar;
      int stringWidth = 0;
      j = firstChar;
      for( i = 0; i < s.length(); i++ )
        {
        if( j >= s.length() )
          j = 0;
        if(( stringWidth + fm.charWidth( ca[j] )) > width )
          {
          System.out.println( "lastchar doesn't fit!!!!" );
          break;
          }
        stringWidth += fm.charWidth( ca[j] );
        if( j == lastChar )
          break;
        j++;
        }
```

```
   nextChar = lastChar+1;
   if( nextChar == s.length())
      nextChar = 0;
   int charWidth = fm.charWidth(ca[firstChar]);
   // Move the string left by the width of the first char on the ticker
/* We could just move the length of the string, but that would
leave the last char as an artifact on the right until the new last char
overwrote it, so we copy the entire area from firstchar to the right
edge because there should be some amount of blank space on the right and
copying will leave the blank as an artifact, rather than last char.
*/
   int z = width-charWidth;
   g.copyArea( charWidth, 0, (width-charWidth), interiorHeight,-charWidth,0);

   // Clear the space on the right that's being vacated by the last
   // char currently on the ticker.
   g.setColor( Color.cyan );
   g.fillRect( stringWidth-charWidth, 0, width-(stringWidth-charWidth),
interiorHeight);

   z = width-(stringWidth-charWidth);
   int w = stringWidth-charWidth;
   // Determine how many chars will fit
   int currWidth = width-(stringWidth-charWidth);
   int nChar = nextChar;
   int numChars;
   for( numChars = 0; numChars < s.length(); numChars++ )
      {
      currWidth -= fm.charWidth( ca[nChar] );
      if( currWidth < 0 )
         break;
      nChar++;
      if( nChar >= s.length())
         nChar = 0;
      }
   if( numChars > 0 )
      {
      int charIndex = 0;
      int xloc = stringWidth - charWidth;
      g.setColor( Color.black );
      g.drawChars( ca, nextChar, 1, xloc ,interiorHeight-fm.getMaxDecent());
      lastChar = nextChar;
      }
   firstChar++;
   if( firstChar >= s.length())
      firstChar = 0;
   }
}
```

For many applications, the default font suffices. When it doesn't, we have to go
fishing for a font that suits our needs. Listing 5.12 adds font and color choices to
our ticker applet, and Figure 5.12 shows the resulting applet in action.

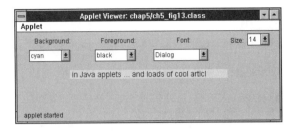

Figure 5.12

The new ticker applet in action.

Listing 5.12 Adding Font and Color Picking to the Ticker Applet

```java
package chap5;
import java.util.*;
import java.io.*;
import java.net.*;
import java.applet.*;
import java.awt.*;

/** A stock-style ticker that runs a one-line string through a
horizontal box. Allows picking the foreground and background
color, the font and size of the string, and sizes the box
appropriately to the chosen font/size.
@version 1.0 10/30/1995
@author John Rodley
*/
public class ch5_fig13 extends Applet implements Runnable {
  /** The thread the applet itself runs in */
 Thread myThread = null;

  int width = 300;
  int height = 200; // the height of the grid
  int leftMargin = 100;
  int topMargin = 1;
  Choice fontChoice;
  public String currentFontChoice;
  String fonts[];
  int pointSize;
  int style;
  Vector sizes;

  Choice foreColorChoice;
  Choice backColorChoice;
  Choice sizeChoice;

  public int currentBkClridx;
  public int currentFrClrIdx;
  public int currentFontIndex;

  MyColor colors[];
```

```
   BackPanel fontPanel;
   BackPanel forePanel;
   BackPanel backPanel;

   Ticker ticker = null;

/** Applet.start override. Starts a new thread for the applet
to run in if one doesn't exist, else does nothing.
*/
   public void start() {
     if( myThread == null )
       {
       myThread = new Thread( this );
       myThread.start();
       }
   }


/** Called when either the font or color has been changed via
the font/color controls. Gets current settings from font/color
controls and sets the font within the ticker Component such
that the next time the string gets painted, it will use the new
font.
*/
   public void changeFontOrColor() {
     currentFrClrIdx = foreColorChoice.getSelectedIndex();
     currentBkClridx = backColorChoice.getSelectedIndex();
     currentFontIndex = fontChoice.getSelectedIndex();
     ticker.foreColor = colors[currentFrClrIdx].color;
     ticker.backColor = colors[currentBkClridx].color;
     pointSize =
       (new Integer( sizeChoice.getSelectedItem())).intValue();
     ticker.currentFont =
       new Font( fonts[currentFontIndex],  style, pointSize );
   }


/** If the ticker is running, make it stop, and set the applet
thread to null so that the applet run loop exits.
*/
   public void stop() {
     if( ticker != null )
       ticker.stopIt();
     myThread = null;
   }


/** The run loop. Does nothing except sit sleeping for 1
second at a time.
*/
   public void run() {
     ticker.start();

     while( myThread != null )
       {
       try {Thread.sleep( 1000 );}
```

```
        catch( Exception e ) { System.out.println( "exception");}
        }
    myThread = null;
    }

/** Initialize the applet. Create and initialize the font/color
choice controls and set the default values for each.
*/
    public void init() {

//  Get the list of fonts available from this GUI
    Toolkit t = Toolkit.getDefaultToolkit();
    fonts = t.getFontList();

//  Set the panel up as a 2row, 1col grid where the font/color
//  choice controls will occupy the first row, and the ticker
//  itself will occupy the second row.
    setLayout( new GridLayout( 2, 1 ));

//  Create the Panel that will hold all the controls.
    Panel p = new Panel();


//  Create the fore color choice
    foreColorChoice = new Choice();
//  Create a list of named colors
    colors = new MyColor[14];
    int i = 0;
    colors[i] = new MyColor( "black", Color.black );
    foreColorChoice.addItem( colors[i].toString() );
    i++;
    colors[i] = new MyColor( "white", Color.white );
    foreColorChoice.addItem( colors[i].toString() );
    i++;
    colors[i] = new MyColor( "red", Color.red );
    foreColorChoice.addItem( colors[i].toString() );
    i++;
    colors[i] = new MyColor( "green", Color.green );
    foreColorChoice.addItem( colors[i].toString() );
    i++;
    colors[i] = new MyColor( "blue", Color.blue );
    foreColorChoice.addItem( colors[i].toString() );
    i++;
    colors[i] = new MyColor( "cyan", Color.cyan );
    foreColorChoice.addItem( colors[i].toString() );
    i++;
    colors[i] = new MyColor( "gray", Color.gray );
    foreColorChoice.addItem( colors[i].toString() );
    i++;
    colors[i] = new MyColor( "dark gray", Color.darkGray );
    foreColorChoice.addItem( colors[i].toString() );
    i++;
    colors[i] = new MyColor( "light gray", Color.lightGray );
```

```
      foreColorChoice.addItem( colors[i].toString() );
      i++;
      colors[i] = new MyColor( "orange", Color.orange );
      foreColorChoice.addItem( colors[i].toString() );
      i++;
      colors[i] = new MyColor( "magenta", Color.magenta );
      foreColorChoice.addItem( colors[i].toString() );
      i++;
      colors[i] = new MyColor( "pink", Color.pink );
      foreColorChoice.addItem( colors[i].toString() );
      i++;
      colors[i] = new MyColor( "yellow", Color.yellow );
      foreColorChoice.addItem( colors[i].toString() );

//    Create the background color choice
      backColorChoice = new Choice();
//    Create a list of named colors
      colors = new MyColor[14];
      i = 0;
      colors[i] = new MyColor( "black", Color.black );
      backColorChoice.addItem( colors[i].toString() );
      i++;
      colors[i] = new MyColor( "white", Color.white );
      backColorChoice.addItem( colors[i].toString() );
      i++;
      colors[i] = new MyColor( "red", Color.red );
      backColorChoice.addItem( colors[i].toString() );
      i++;
      colors[i] = new MyColor( "green", Color.green );
      backColorChoice.addItem( colors[i].toString() );
      i++;
      colors[i] = new MyColor( "blue", Color.blue );
      backColorChoice.addItem( colors[i].toString() );
      i++;
      colors[i] = new MyColor( "cyan", Color.cyan );
      backColorChoice.addItem( colors[i].toString() );
      i++;
      colors[i] = new MyColor( "gray", Color.gray );
      backColorChoice.addItem( colors[i].toString() );
      i++;
      colors[i] = new MyColor( "dark gray", Color.darkGray );
      backColorChoice.addItem( colors[i].toString() );
      i++;
      colors[i] = new MyColor( "light gray", Color.lightGray );
      backColorChoice.addItem( colors[i].toString() );
      i++;
      colors[i] = new MyColor( "orange", Color.orange );
      backColorChoice.addItem( colors[i].toString() );
      i++;
      colors[i] = new MyColor( "magenta", Color.magenta );
      backColorChoice.addItem( colors[i].toString() );
      i++;
      colors[i] = new MyColor( "pink", Color.pink );
```

```
    backColorChoice.addItem( colors[i].toString() );
    i++;
    colors[i] = new MyColor( "yellow", Color.yellow );
    backColorChoice.addItem( colors[i].toString() );
    backColorChoice.select( "cyan" );

//  Set the default point size, font, and font style
    pointSize = 10;
    style = Font.PLAIN;
    currentFontIndex = 0;
    currentFontChoice = new String( fonts[0] );
    fontChoice = new Choice();

//  Add all the possible fonts to the Choice control and put
//  the paddle on the default font.
    for( i = 0; i < fonts.length; i++ )
      fontChoice.addItem( fonts[i] );
    fontChoice.select( currentFontChoice );

/*  Create a panel to hold all the controls. This panel will
occupy the entire top half of the applet and contain all the
controls including font, fore and back color, and point size
This panel will have one row and four cols. Each
Choice/Label combo will get its own panel that will occupy one
fourth of this panel.
*/
    p.setLayout( new GridLayout( 1, 4 ));
    BackPanel p1;
    p1 = new BackPanel( this );
    p1.add( new Label( "Font:" ));
    p1.add( fontChoice );
    fontPanel = p1;

//  Create a panel to hold the choice control and its prompt
    p1 = new BackPanel(this);
    p1.add( new Label( "Background:" ));
    p1.add( backColorChoice );

    forePanel = p1;

    p1 = new BackPanel(this);
    p1.add( new Label( "Foreground:" ));
    foreColorChoice.select( "black" );
    p1.add( foreColorChoice );
    backPanel = p1;
    p.add( backPanel );

    sizeChoice = new Choice();
    int j = 0;
    sizes = new Vector(1);
    for( i = 8; i < 48; i+=2 )
      {
      sizes.addElement( (new Integer( i ).toString()));
```

```
              sizeChoice.addItem( (String)sizes.elementAt(j) );
              j++;
              }
         p1 = new BackPanel(this);
         p1.add( new Label( "Size:" ));
         sizeChoice.select( "12" );
         p1.add( sizeChoice );

//   Add the panel holding the Choice controls and prompts to
//   the panel that makes up the top half of the applet.
         p.add( forePanel );
         p.add( backPanel );
         p.add( fontPanel );
         p.add( p1 );

//   Add the 4-column grid panel holding the choice controls to
//   the main applet panel.
         add( p );

//   Set a default string to use in the ticker
         String s = new String( "Welcome to John's Home Page ... home of the latest
in Java applets ... and loads of cool articles ... " );

//   Create the ticker
         ticker = new Ticker(this,s,leftMargin,topMargin,width,65);

//   Make sure the font and color are set within the ticker.
         changeFontOrColor();

//   Add the ticker to the main applet panel. It will appear as
//   the second row of the grid.
         add( ticker );

//   Size the applet.
         resize( leftMargin + width + leftMargin,
                    topMargin + height + topMargin);
         }
}


/** A Ticker applet, runs a String through a rectangular box as
if it were a stock-style ticker. Extended to make use of
configurable forground and background colors, as well as point
size, and font family.
@version 1.0 11/17/1995
@author John Rodley
*/
class Ticker extends Panel implements Runnable {
  Applet applet;
  boolean bPainted = false;
  boolean bRun = true;
  int startx, starty;
  int height, width;
  int firstChar = 0;
```

```
    int lastChar = 0;
    String s;
    Color PromptColor;
    FontMetrics fm;
    int interiorHeight;
    char ca[] = null;
    int delay = 50;
    int inc = 0;
    Thread myThread = null;
    public Color foreColor;
    public Color backColor;
    public Font currentFont;


/** A constructor that allows us to use a Vector of Strings as
the string that will march across the ticker window.
@param a  The applet this ticker appears in. Used for
callbacks.
@param  v The Vector of Strings. We'll create the string in the
ticker window by appending all the strings in this Vector
together.
@param  x The x coordinate of this ticker within the applet
@param  y The y coordinate of this ticker within the applet
@param  w The width of the ticker window
@param  waittime  The delay between marching the ticker one
char to the left.
*/
  public Ticker( Applet a, Vector v,
            int x, int y, int w, int waittime ) {
    applet = a;
    startx = x;
    starty = y;
    width = w;
    delay = waittime;
    s = new String( (String)v.elementAt(0));
    for( int i = 1; i < v.size(); i++ )
      {
      s = new String( s + " " );
      s = new String( s + (String)v.elementAt(i));
      }
    myThread = new Thread( this );
  }



/** A constructor that allows us to use a Vector of Strings as
the string that will march across the ticker window.
@param a  The applet this ticker appears in. Used for
callbacks.
@param  inputString The string that appears in the ticker window.
@param  x The x coordinate of this ticker within the applet
@param  y The y coordinate of this ticker within the applet
@param  w The width of the ticker window
@param  waittime  The delay between marching the ticker one
char to the left.
```

```
*/
  public Ticker( Applet a, String inputString, int x,
                     int y, int w, int waittime ) {
    applet = a;
    startx = x;
    starty = y;
    width = w;
    delay = waittime;
    s = new String( inputString );
    myThread = new Thread( this );
  }

/** Called to start the thread that this ticker will run in.
*/
  public void start() {
    myThread.start();
  }


/** The run loop for the thread this ticker runs in. Calls
paintFirst to set up the initial state of the ticker, then sits
in a loop invoking repaint. Delays by "delay" milliseconds
between calls to repaint.
*/
  public void run() {
    paintFirst( applet.getGraphics());
    while( myThread != null ) {
      repaint();
      try {Thread.sleep( delay );}
      catch( Exception e ) { System.out.println( "exception");}
      }
  }

/** Called to stop the thread this ticker runs in.
*/
  public void stopIt() { myThread = null; }

/** Called to set up the initial visual state of the ticker.
Erases the ticker window and paints the string across it
starting with the first char in the String.
@param g   A graphics context to paint into.
*/
  public void paintFirst( Graphics g ) {
    int i, j;
    int numChars = 0;

    g.translate( startx, 0 );
    setFont( currentFont );
    g.setFont( currentFont );
//  Set these here since we're assured of having a valid
//  graphics context
    fm = g.getFontMetrics();
    interiorHeight = fm.getHeight();
```

```
      g.setColor( backColor );
      g.fill3DRect(-1, -1, width+2, interiorHeight+2, true);
      ca = new char[s.length()];
      s.getChars( 0, s.length(), ca, 0 );
      int stringWidth = 0;
      for( i = 0; i < s.length(); i++ )
        {
        if(( stringWidth+fm.charWidth(ca[i])) >= width )
          {
          numChars = i;
          break;
          }
        stringWidth += fm.charWidth( ca[i] );
        }
      g.setColor( foreColor );
      g.drawChars( ca, 0, numChars, 0,
            interiorHeight-fm.getMaxDecent());
      firstChar = 0;
      lastChar = numChars-1;

      String s2;
      s2 = new String( ca, firstChar, numChars );
    }

/** Called to update the ticker window.
@param  g The graphics context to paint into.
*/
  public void update( Graphics g ) {
    if( currentFont.equals( g.getFont()) == false )
      bPainted = false;

    if( bPainted == false )
      {
      paintFirst( g );
      bPainted = true;
      return;
      }
    g.translate( startx, 0 );

    String s2;
    if( lastChar > firstChar )
      s2 = new String( ca, firstChar,(lastChar-firstChar)+1 );
    else
      {
      String s3 = new String( ca,firstChar,
            (s.length()-firstChar));
      String s4 = new String( ca, 0, lastChar );
      s2 = new String( s3+s4 );
      }

    int i, j, nextChar;
    int stringWidth = 0;
```

```
    j = firstChar;
    fm = g.getFontMetrics();
    for( i = 0; i < s.length(); i++ )
      {
      if( j >= s.length() )
        j = 0;
      if(( stringWidth + fm.charWidth( ca[j] )) > width )
        {
        System.out.println( "lastchar doesn't fit!!!!" );
        break;
        }
      stringWidth += fm.charWidth( ca[j] );
      if( j == lastChar )
        break;
      j++;
      }
    nextChar = lastChar+1;
    if( nextChar == s.length())
      nextChar = 0;
    int charWidth = fm.charWidth(ca[firstChar]);

  // Move the string left by the width of the first char on the ticker
/* We could just move the length of the string, but that would
leave the last char as an artifact on the right until the new last char
overwrote it, so, we copy the entire area from firstchar to the right
edge because there should be some amount of blank space on the right, and
copying will leave the blank as an artifact, rather than last char.
*/
    int z = width-charWidth;
    g.copyArea( charWidth, 0, (width-charWidth),
        interiorHeight,-charWidth,0);

  // Clear the space on the right that's being vacated by the last
  // char currently on the ticker.
    g.setColor( backColor );
    g.fillRect( stringWidth-charWidth, 0,
        width-(stringWidth-charWidth), interiorHeight);

    z = width-(stringWidth-charWidth);
    int w = stringWidth-charWidth;
  // Determine how many chars will fit
    int currWidth = width-(stringWidth-charWidth);
    int nChar = nextChar;
    int numChars;
    for( numChars = 0; numChars < s.length(); numChars++ )
      {
      currWidth -= fm.charWidth( ca[nChar] );
      if( currWidth < 0 )
        break;
      nChar++;
      if( nChar >= s.length())
        nChar = 0;
      }
```

```
    if( numChars > 0 )
      {
      int charIndex = 0;
      int xloc = stringWidth - charWidth;
      g.setColor( foreColor );
      g.drawChars( ca, nextChar, 1, xloc,
          interiorHeight-fm.getMaxDecent());
      lastChar = nextChar;
      }
    firstChar++;
    if( firstChar >= s.length())
      firstChar = 0;
    inc++;
    }
  }
/** A panel that exists to gather all the controls in one
LayoutManager and funnel all the actions from those controls
through one callback to the applet that the controls are trying
to modify.
*/
class BackPanel extends Panel {
  ch5_fig13 applet;

/** Constructor - just save the applet for later use by
handleEvent.
@param  a The ch5_fig13 that we'll call back to whenever
something happens in the controls.
*/
  public BackPanel( ch5_fig13 a ) {
    applet = a;
    }

/** Called whenever something happens in one of the controls.
Causes a call back to the ch5_fig13 applet, which then reads
the controls to see what the user's desire is.
@return true if the event was an action requiring us to change
the font or color, false otherwise.
*/
  public boolean handleEvent( Event ev ) {
    switch( ev.id ) {
      case ev.ACTION_EVENT:
        applet.changeFontOrColor();
        return( true );
      }
    return( false );
    }
  }

/** A class designed simply to link a string name with a Java
Color. In C, this would have been a simple struct. Note
override of the toString method.
*/
class MyColor extends Object {
```

```
   String name;
   Color color;

/** Create the specified color, then save that Color and the
name.
@param  nname The name we're assigning to this color
@param  c The actual Java Color we're attaching to this name.
*/
   public MyColor( String nname, Color c ) {
     color = new Color( c.getRGB() );
     name = nname;
     }

/** Return the String name we've assigned to this Java Color.
@return The string name that was passed to the constructor.
*/
   public String toString() { return( name ); };
}
```

Notice that both **Component** and **Graphics** have **setFont** methods. The end result of **Component.setFont** is to set the font in the graphics context that gets passed to the **paint/update** method. However, if we call **Component.setFont** within a **paint/update** method, the graphics context that was passed to **paint/update** will still have the old font attached to it. This is why, in **paintFirst**, we call both **Component.setFont** and **Graphics.setFont**.

Another thing to notice is how we get the list of available fonts from the AWT Toolkit. The **Toolkit** is an AWT class that provides a very thin layer around the native GUI API. In most cases, you will not need to deal directly with the **Toolkit**. Most of the methods in the **Toolkit** are used by other Java classes to create native GUI elements. So the **Choice** class, for example, uses **Toolkit.createList**. Use the Java classes, not the **Toolkit** methods. The Java classes are stable, but the **Toolkit** is not. The only three things available in the **Toolkit** that you might need in the normal course of business are the font list, the screen resolution, and the screen size.

Adding Color

Colors are similar to, but even simpler than fonts. A graphics context will always have two **Colors** attached to it, the current color and the background color. All the draw operations (**drawString, drawChars, fillRect** ...) except **clearRect** use the current color. You can query and change the current color via **getColor** and **setColor**. There are 13 basic colors, shown with their RGB values in Table 5.5, embodied in constants in the **Color** class.

Table 5.5   The Basic Colors and their RGB Values

Color	Red	Green	Blue
black	0	0	0
blue	0	0	255
cyan	0	255	255
darkGray	64	64	64
gray	128	128	128
green	0	255	0
lightGray	192	192	192
magenta	255	0	255
orange	255	200	0
pink	255	175	175
red	255	0	0
white	255	255	255
yellow	255	255	0

There are three color constructors that allow you to make a new color based on its RGB values. The first uses the first eight bits of three separate 32-bit integers to make up the basic 24 bits—eight bits each for red, green, and blue. The second uses the first 24 bits of a single 32-bit integer (16-23 for red, 8-15 for green, 0-7 for blue). The third lets you specify the RGB values as floats, allowing for a wider range of values (though the display will probably cut that back to 24 bits max).

Images and the ImageObserver Interface

A huge portion of the network bandwidth consumed by applets involves downloading images. If we try to download images in a sequential fashion, starting the download and then blocking until the complete image arrives, we condemn applet users to long waits where seemingly nothing is happening. This is not only undesirable, but completely unneccessary. Through the use of three things, **Applet.getImage**, **Graphics.drawImage**, and the **ImageObserver** interface, we can download images asynchronously, while still knowing when the complete image has arrived and is ready to be drawn.

The applet shown in Listing 5.13 downloads a gallery of pictures and displays
them in rows.

Listing 5.13   The Display Gallery Applet Using
ImageObserver

```
package chap5;

import java.util.*;
import java.io.*;
import java.net.*;
import java.applet.*;
import java.awt.*;
import java.awt.image.*;

/** A class that displays a grid (via FlowLayout) of images
whose URLs are passed in from the HTML page. While the images
are being loaded, we display expanding circles in the spaces
the images would occupy. Example of ImageObserver use.
@version 1.10, March 1, 1996
@author John Rodley
*/


public final class ch5_fig18 extends Applet implements Runnable {

/** The main thread. */
Thread myThread = null;

public boolean bImageLoadingError = false;
public Vector ImageName;
Panel32 Panels[];
String sBadImage;
public static ch5_fig18 current;


/** start - Whenever a user visits our page, Applet calls this method
which overrides the Applet method. The method creates a thread and passes this
AgentLauncher into it. It works because we implement the Runnable method. */
public void start() {
   if( myThread == null )
     {
     myThread = new Thread( this );
     myThread.setName( "ch5_fig18" );
     myThread.start();
     }
   }

/** Create the Panels that will each hold one of our images.
Each panel gets a hollow Image object created from the string
URL supplied in the HTML page.
*/
```

```
void createPanels() {
  for( int i = 0; i < ImageName.size(); i++ ) {
    // Now make sure the URL is valid.
    URL u;
      try {
    u = new URL( (String)ImageName.elementAt(i) );
      // The URL is valid, get the image.
      Panels[i] = new Panel32(getImage(u));
      add( Panels[i] );
      }
      catch( MalformedURLException me ) {
        bImageLoadingError = true;
        sBadImage = new String((String) ImageName.elementAt(i) );
        break;
        }
      }
  }

/** Stop this thread. */
public void stop() {
  myThread = null;
  }

/** The main loop for this thread. Sleep for 1/3 second, then
repaint all the panels. Only runs for as long as it takes for
the images to load. */
public synchronized void run() {
  int i;
  boolean bLoaded = false;

  current = this;
  createPanels();
  layout();
  show();
  while( myThread != null )
    {
    try {
    Thread.sleep( 300 );
    }
    catch( Exception e ) {
    System.out.println( "exception" );
    break;
      }
    repaint();
    }
  }

/** Create the image name Vector, then fill it with Image<n>
parameters retrieved from the HTML page. Create Panel array.
*/
public void init() {

  current = this;
```

```
    ImageName = new Vector(1);
     for( int i = 0; i < 50; i++ ) {
        String s = getParameter( "Image"+i );
        if( s == null ) {
         Panels = new Panel32[i];
           break;
           }
        ImageName.addElement( s );
        }
     }
```

```
/** Paint the applet's display space. Repaints each of the
Panels. Checks whether all the images have been displayed. If
so, it kills the thread that called this by setting myThread to
null. This method will STILL get called by the browser whenever
it needs to repaint this window.
*/
public void paint( Graphics g ) {
  boolean allLoaded = true;

  if( Panels == null )
    return;
  for( int i = 0; i < Panels.length; i++ ) {
    if( Panels[i].flags != ALLBITS )
      allLoaded = false;
    if( Panels[i] == null )
      return;
    Panels[i].repaint();
    }
  if( allLoaded )
    myThread = null;
  }
}
```

```
/** A class embodying a Panel that displays a 32-by-32 pixel
image. Contains a hollow Image object obtained from
Applet.getImage and passed to the constructor. Also contains
the flags that are passed in to ImageUpdate. When the flags =
ALLBITS, the whole image is here.
*/
class Panel32 extends Panel implements ImageObserver {
  public Image image = null;
  public int flags = 0;
  int iteration = 0;
  boolean firstTime = true;
```

```
/** constructor - store the Image for drawing later.
@param  im  Image to be drawn on this Panel.
*/
  Panel32( Image im ) {
    image = im;
    }
```

```
/** Override of Component.imageUpdate, an implementation of
ImageObserver.imageUpdate. Called by an image producer every
time an interesting point in image loading occurs. When
infoflags = ALLBITS, the image is all here and can be drawn.
@param  img The image that we're talking about.
@param  infoflags The state of the image-load - a constant from
ImageObserver's public variable set.
*/
  public synchronized boolean imageUpdate(Image img,
          int infoflags, int x, int y, int width, int height)
  {
    flags = infoflags;
     return( true );
  }


/** Paint the Image on the screen. If all the bits of the
image aren't available (flags != ALLBITS) draw an expanding
circle on the space. We have to call drawImage at least once
in order to provoke the browser image-loading thread to
actually load the image over the Net.
*/
  public void paint( Graphics g ) {
    boolean ret = false;
    if( flags == ALLBITS || firstTime ) {
      ret = g.drawImage( image, 0, 0, this );
      firstTime = false;
      }

    if( ret == false ) {
      g.setColor( Color.black );
      int start = 16-(iteration/2);
      g.fillOval( start, start, iteration, iteration );
      iteration++;
      if( iteration >= 32 )
        iteration = 0;
      }
    }

/** Tell anyone who's interested (the LayoutManager) that we
always want to be 32-by-32 pixels.
*/
  public Dimension preferredSize() {
    return( new Dimension( 32, 32 ));
    }

/** Tell anyone who's interested (the LayoutManager) that we
always want to be 32-by-32 pixels.
*/
  public Dimension minimumSize() {
    return( new Dimension( 32, 32 ));
    }
  }
```

While the images are being downloaded, the applet tries to entertain the user by drawing an expanding circle in the space to be occupied by the image.

The first class to look at is **Panel32**. This is a subclass of **Panel** that represents the display space the image will be displayed in. There is one **Panel32** for each image we want to display. The **preferredSize** and **minimumSize** methods are overrides of **Component** methods, which tell the **LayoutManager** what size our **Panel** wants to be. These two methods contain an important assumption, namely that our **Panel** will be 32-by-32 pixels. If our image isn't 32 by 32, we're in trouble.

If you look up in ch5_fig18's **createPanels** method, you can see that we create one of these **Panels** for each image URL provided by the HTML file. Then we add the **Panels** to the applet's **Container**, and call **layout**. This call causes the **LayoutManager** (**FlowLayout** in this case) to create the spaces for our images.

Our **Panel32** has two more methods, **paint** and **imageUpdate**. **paint** is an override of **Component.paint**, and is responsible for actually drawing our image on the screen. **paint** splits into two pieces, one block that draws the image, and one block that draws the expanding circle we want to see while the image is being loaded. We don't draw the image unless one of two conditions is true:

- This is the first time **paint** has been called
- All the bits in the image have been loaded over the Net

Why do we need to call **drawImage** the first time **paint** is called? Because Java doesn't actually load the image over the Net until we try to draw it into some graphics context. This call to **drawImage** starts the loading process.

The circle-drawing block is predicated on the boolean ret, which is set by **drawImage**. When **drawImage** fails to draw the image for whatever reason (say because the bits aren't all here yet), it returns false; if the draw fails, we fall into the circle-drawing block.

So now we've created all our **Panels** (via **createPanels**), and the **run** method of our new thread has started running. As yet, nothing has appeared on the screen. In our **run** method loop, we just sleep and call **repaint**. As you might remember from Chapter 4, the call to **repaint** causes a call to the applet's **paint** method. In **paint**, we call **repaint** for each of the **Panels**, which ends up invoking the **Panel's** **paint** method. Now we're finally gonna draw something.

In the first call to **Panel32.paint**, we fall into the **drawImage** block, and call **drawImage,** which starts the image loading. The last argument to **drawImage** (an **ImageObserver**) is the key here. The call to **drawImage** returns immediately. If the bits of the image aren't all available yet, it simply returns false without drawing the image. But it keeps the **ImageObserver** argument for later use.

This is why **Panel32** implements **ImageObserver** and passes itself to **drawImage**. The Java image-loading thread calls back to **ImageObserver.imageUpdate** as the bits of the image are loaded. When all the bits are loaded, **imageUpdate** is called with the **infoflags** parameter set to **ALLBITS**. So as the user waits, two things are happening in this applet: The applet's **run** method is calling **Panel32.paint** to draw the expanding circles, and Java's image loading thread is calling **Panel32.imageUpdate**. When all the bits are in, the **paint** method draws the image rather than the expanding circle.

Conclusion

At this point, we've constructed a basic user interface for our AgentLauncher. The user can set parameters, pick the agent to launch, and view the status of each running agent in either text or image format. The user can also scroll through the list of running agents easily.

Along the way, we've learned how to use all the visual elements that Java provides, from network-loadable image files to native GUI dialog boxes. Our applet has grown fairly complicated, but in very simple increments.

Chapter **6**

Managing
Multitasking

Managing Multitasking

6

With Java's multithreading, your applet can be a veritable three-ring circus of cooperating threads. Check here to start the show.

For years, multiprocessing systems have allowed you to run multiple processes (programs) simultaneously. More recently, many operating systems have begun to support multithreading, allowing programmers to spawn multiple subprocesses, or *threads*, within each process.

Threads differ significantly from processes. In a non-multithreaded system, there are only processes and related processes. Related processes share only open file handles. In a multithreaded system, each process is made up of from *1 to n* threads and all the threads in the process generally share global variables as well as open file handles. This sharing of global variables makes it very easy for threads to share work product, while remaining single-mindedly dedicated to their assigned task.

To get a better handle on the shift from single-threaded to multithreaded programming, picture a company where every employee has his own building (complete with telephone system, bathroom, cafeteria, office supplies, and parking lot). Each employee can do his job as long as everything he needs is in his building, a condition the company goes to great expense to try to ensure. Any job that requires access to another employee's work product is immensely complicated and requires a considerable amount of communication. If the boss wants something done, she has to pick up the phone. This is the single-process/single-thread model. Now, put all those employees into a single building. You immediately get less cumbersome communication and more efficient resource utilization.

This is the single-process/multithread model.

Java is an inherently multithreaded language. As such, it depends on operating system support for threads and multitasking. This is one of the reasons that Java has not, as of this writing, been ported to the immensely popular Windows 3.1 operating environment. In fact, to see just how multithreaded Java is, we need only look at **Object**, the base class for all Java classes. Six of Object's twelve public methods involve thread control and inter-thread communication.

Creating Threads

Java encapsulates the notion of a thread in a class named, appropriately enough, **Thread**. Table 6.1 lists the methods for the **Thread** class. This class incorporates most of the thread attributes and control methods available to programmers who write to the native operating system thread control API.

Table 6.1 Thread Class Methods	
Method	**Description**
public Thread()	Creates a new thread. Underlying operating system thread is not created until Thread.start is called. This applies to all Thread constructors.
public Thread(String *name*)	Creates a new thread with the specified name.
public Thread(ThreadGroup *group*, String *name*)	Creates a new thread with the specified name and adds it to the specified ThreadGroup.
public Thread(Runnable *target*)	Creates a new thread from an object implementing the Runnable interface.
public Thread(ThreadGroup *group*, Runnable *target*)	Creates a new thread from an object implementing the Runnable interface and adds it to the specified ThreadGroup.
public Thread(Runnable *target*, String *name*)	Constructs a new thread from an object implementing the Runnable interface and sets its name to *name*.
public Thread(ThreadGroup *group*, Runnable *target*, String *name*)	Same as previous, but adds the thread to the specified ThreadGroup.
public static int activeCount()	Returns the number of active threads in this thread group; does not include subterannean threads.
public int countStackFrames()	Returns the number of stack frames in this thread. The thread must be suspended for this to work. Throws IllegalStateException if thread is not suspended.

Continued

Table 6.1   Thread Class Methods (Continued)

Method	Description
public static Thread currentThread()	Returns the currently executing Thread object.
public void destroy()	Kills the thread without cleanup. The equivalent of Unix's "kill -9" for Java threads.
public static void dumpStack()	Dumps the stack for the current thread.
public static int enumerate (Thread tarray[])	Copies references to every active thread into the supplied Thread array. Returns the number of threads in the array.
public String getName()	Returns the thread's name; that is, whatever name was assigned by setName. If no name has been set using setName, Java assigns a name of the form "Thread-N" where N indicates that this is the Nth thread to be created in this thread group.
public int getPriority()	Returns the thread's priority. This will be a value between Thread.MIN_PRIORITY and Thread.MAX_PRIORITY.
public boolean isAlive()	Returns true if the underlying operating system thread is executing; that is, if start has been called successfully and stop has not been called yet. Also returns true if a running thread has been suspended. Equivalent to asking if Thread.run is still executing.
public boolean isDaemon()	Returns true if this is a daemon thread, that is, if a successful call to setDaemon(true) has been made.
public synchronized void join	Waits for *num_millisecs* milliseconds for this thread to die. Waits forever(int num_millisecs) if *num_millisecs* is 0.
public synchronized void join()	Waits forever for this thread to die. Do not call join on your own thread. Always use in a construction such as: Thread x = new Thread(); x.start(); x.join().
public void resume()	Resumes execution of a suspended thread. Throws IllegalStateException if thread was not suspended.
public void run()	Overrides this method with the main loop for the new thread. This is the method that runs in the new operating system thread.
public void setDaemon (boolean *bDaemon*)	Sets the threads daemon status to *bDaemon*. If true, Thread becomes a daemon thread. Must be called before the thread becomes active; that is, before any call to Thread.start.
public void setName (String newName)	Sets the thread's name to newName. Can be called at any point in the thread's life.
public void setPriority(int if newPriority)	Sets the threads priority to *newPriority*. Throws IllegalArgumentException newPriority is not within the range Thread.MIN_PRIORITY to Thread.MAX_PRIORITY.

Continued

Table 6.1	Thread Class Methods (Continued)
Method	**Description**
public static void sleep(int *millis*)	Tells the current thread to pause for *millis* milliseconds.
public synchronized void start()	Causes Java to create a new operating system thread and begin running the run method in the new thread. Returns immediately, usually before the thread has begun execution.
public synchronized void stop()	Stops a thread by throwing a ThreadDeath object. If the thread has not started, it will be killed immediately rather than waiting for it to start.
public void suspend()	Suspends the thread. Calls resume to restart the thread.
public String toString()	Returns a String that includes the thread name, priority, and thread group.
public static void yield()	Yields this thread's time slice to the next thread waiting to execute. Has no effect if there are no threads available to execute.

There are two types of **Thread** constructors that correspond to the two different ways of getting an object to run in its own thread. The first, most obvious way, is to subclass the **Thread** class. We use this method with the AgentDispatcher, which subclasses **Thread** and creates its own socket. We could have done it the other way around, subclassing **Socket** and creating a thread, but as the saying goes, "You make your choices and take your chances." Listing 6.1 demonstrates how AgentDispatcher extends the **Thread** class so that it will run in its own thread.

Listing 6.1 Extending the Thread Class

```
/** There is one AgentDispatcher active at any one time. It
maintains a CONSTANT connection from the AgentLauncher to the
Dispatching AgentServer.
@version 1.0
@author John Rodley 12/1/1995
*/
class AgentDispatcher extends Thread {
   Socket s;
   public AgentDispatcher( String ServerName, int port ) {
     setDaemon(true);
     try {
        s = new Socket( InetAddress.getByName(ServerName),port );
        } catch( IOException e )
         {System.out.println("exception "+e ); }
     }

/** Dispatch a kill message to all servers telling them to
terminate the named agent with prejudice.
*/
```

```
   public void StopAgent(String id) {
      KillMessage km = new KillMessage(id);
      try { s.getOutputStream().write( km.getMessageBytes()); }
      catch( IOException e )
         { System.out.println( "stop output exception "+e); }
      try { s.close(); }
      catch( IOException e1 )
         { System.out.println( "stop close exception "+e1); }
      }

/** Tell the dispatching agent server to dispatch this agent.
*/
   public void Dispatch( String Name, String ID, Vector Args ) {
      DispatchMessage dm = new DispatchMessage(Name,ID,Args);
      try { s.getOutputStream().write( dm.getMessageBytes()); }
      catch( IOException e )
        { System.out.println( "dispatch out exception "+e); }
      }

/** The main run loop for this thread. Sits in a loop reading
the socket and processing messages. The only messages that
should come in over this socket are StartMessage and
ResultsMessage.
*/
   public void run() {
      byte buffer[] = new byte[8192];
      while( true ) {
         try {
         int ret;
         if(( ret = s.getInputStream().read( buffer )) != 0 )
           {
           if( ret < 0 ) {
              System.out.println( "connection lost");
              break;
              }
           ClientProcess( buffer, ret );
           }
         } catch( IOException e ) {
           System.out.println( "IOexception "+e );
           break;
           }
        }
      try{s.close();}
      catch(Exception e)
         { System.out.println("run close exception "+e);}
      }
```

```
/** Parse a message from the dispatching agent server. Only
valid message types are Start and Results. Take appropriate
action for each message type, updating the AgentLauncher
display.
*/
  public void ClientProcess( byte b[], int numbytes ) {

  String command;
  int currentOffset = 0;
  String s;
  int messageStart;
  boolean bret = false;

  while( currentOffset != numbytes ) {
  messageStart = currentOffset;
    // Every message starts with 4 bytes of command
  command = new String( b, 0, currentOffset, 4 );
    currentOffset += LoadMessage.PREFIX_SIZE;

  // Followed by 10 bytes ASCII length of the whole message
    // including command
  String sLength = new String( b, 0, currentOffset, 10 );
    currentOffset += LoadMessage.LOADLEN_SIZE;

  if( command.compareTo(ResultMessage.RESULT_PREFIX ) == 0 )
    {
      ResultMessage rm = new ResultMessage();
    rm.parse( b, currentOffset );
    AgentLauncher.currentAgentLauncher.reportResult(
            rm.server, rm.theURL);
    }
  else
    {
      if( command.compareTo(StartMessage.START_PREFIX ) == 0 )
        {
      StartMessage sm = new StartMessage();
      sm.parse( b, currentOffset );
      AgentLauncher.currentAgentLauncher.addAgentFace(sm.server);
        }
    else {
      System.out.println( "Message is BOGUS "+b);
       return;
        }
    }
    Integer il = new Integer( sLength );
```

```
      currentOffset = messageStart + i1.intValue();
    }  // while bytesused
  }
}
```

The theory behind the AgentDispatcher is simple and common to most threaded I/O. The AgentDispatcher needs to handle both sides of the AgentLauncher-dispatching AgentServer conversation. We want messages from the AgentServer to the AgentLauncher to be handled asynchronously as they occur so that, for instance, a Results message from a particular server will cause the AgentLauncher to change the display for that server as soon as it's received.

In order to achieve that, we write a **run** method that is a simple infinite loop that reads the socket and processes whatever it receives by making calls back into the AgentLauncher. We'll talk more about the details of **run** methods later, but the key thing to realize here is that the **run** method is the top-level method of the new operating system thread, and that within the **run** method, the call to **InputStream.read** blocks. That is, the call doesn't return until it has read some data over the socket. Thus, given the sporadic nature of our communications, the new operating system thread spends most of its time sleeping.

There are only two direct references to threads in the AgentDispatcher. The first one is in the declaration itself where we declare that AgentDispatcher **extends Thread**. Then, within the constructor, we set the thread to be a *daemon thread*. We'll discuss daemon threads at more length later in this chapter. Listing 6.2 shows the AgentLauncher creating and starting a new AgentDispatcher.

Listing 6.2 The AgentLauncher Creating and Starting an AgentDispatcher

```
/** Dispatch the current agent. currentAgent is an instance of
the agent we wish to dispatch, and he has already configured
himself via Agent.configure. We need to get his arguments as a
Vector of Strings, create a dispatcher, then tell the
dispatcher to dispatch using the currentAgent with those
arguments.
@see Agent
@see AgentDispatcher
*/
public void Dispatch() {
   Vector v = currentAgent.getArguments();
   currentDispatcher =
      new AgentDispatcher( disServerName, disServerPort );
```

```
currentDispatcher.start();
currentDispatcher.Dispatch( currentClassName, currentID, v );
changeAppState( AGENT_DISPATCHED );
}
```

Remember that AgentLauncher is our top-level object—our applet—and AgentLauncher.Dispatch is invoked when the user clicks on the Dispatch button. Within **Dispatch** we instantiate AgentDispatcher, which gives us, via subclassing, a **Thread** object. Then we call **Thread.start** to get the actual operating system thread running. The invocation of **Thread.start** is the key call in the whole thread creation process. Without it, there will not be a new operating system thread.

Though there are only those two direct references to threads in the AgentDispatcher, it is nonetheless a good example of a threaded object because it encapsulates some functionality that executes within the new operating system thread, and some that does not. In this example, AgentLauncher.Dispatch (the AgentDispatcher constructor), AgentDispatcher.Dispatch, and AgentDispatcher.StopAgent all run in one thread, while AgentDispatcher.run and AgentDispatcher.ClientProcess run in another. Later on, when we discuss the start and run methods, we'll find out how to tell which methods execute in which threads.

Thread Groups

You may have noticed that some of the **Thread** constructors take a **ThreadGroup** argument. In Chapter 5 we saw how Java groups **Components** into **Containers** to facilitate operations on collections of **Component** objects. **ThreadGroup** performs a similar function in thread control—to group threads into one lump where they can be operated on as a group, and to protect threads from each other.

The Runnable Interface

In a multiple-inheritance situation, the subclassing constructor would be all you'd need because all runnable objects could simply inherit **Thread** with all their other superclasses. But Java doesn't allow multiple inheritance, and it doesn't seem reasonable to create a long inheritance branch (with **Thread** up near the root) simply to make something runnable.

Fortunately, there's a second style of **Thread** constructor. This one takes an object that implements the **Runnable** interface as one of its parameters. We use this constructor with our AgentLauncher applet which, in its **start** method, creates a **Thread** and passes itself as the parameter to the **Thread** constructor. This constructor was specifically designed to deal with situations where you don't want to subclass **Thread**.

The **Runnable** interface has only a single method: **run**. The **run** method contains the main loop of a **Runnable** object. Our AgentDispatcher's **run** method, for example, contains a loop that simply reads a socket.

Thus we have two classes, **AgentLauncher** and **AgentConnectionHandler**, that run in their own thread but get there by different routes. **AgentLauncher** is a subclass of **Thread**, while **AgentConnectionHandler** is a subclass of **Object**, which implements the **Runnable** interface. Listing 6.3 shows the parts of the AgentLauncher that relate to its use of threads and the **Runnable** interface.

Listing 6.3   The AgentLauncher Implementing the Runnable Interface

```
public final class AgentLauncher extends Applet implements Runnable {

/** The main thread */
Thread myThread = null;

/** start - Whenever a user visits our page, Applet calls
this function. This is an override of an Applet method. It creates a
thread and passes this AgentLauncher into it. It works because
we implement the Runnable method. */
  public void start() {
  currentAgentLauncher = this;
  if( myThread == null )
    {
    myThread = new Thread( this );
    myThread.setName( "AgentLauncher" );
    myThread.start();
    }
  }
```

In Chapter 4, we discussed that **Applet.start** is called whenever the user "visits" the page containing our applet. When we come into **start** for the first time, we want to get our AgentLauncher's **run** method executing in a new operating system thread. In order to do that, we use a new style of **Thread** constructor, one that takes a **Runnable** object as one of its arguments. In Listing 6.3, the

AgentLauncher itself (in the **start** method) is the **Runnable** object. When, in **AgentLauncher.start**, we call **myThread.start**, we get the same effect as we got in Listing 6.1—the **run** method of our AgentLauncher executes in a new operating system thread.

The start and run Methods

When I think of a **Thread** object, what immediately comes to mind is a thread that begins execution with the constructor of the object, and terminates after the destructor returns. This is most emphatically *not* the case with Java **Thread** objects (or almost any objectified threads). The **Thread** constructor and the **start** method both execute in the thread *from* which they were invoked. Only the **run** method executes in the new thread. Of course, this means that any method invoked from within the **run** method will also execute in the new thread.

No matter which type of **Thread** you create, it's important to realize just what methods execute in which thread. Listing 6.4 shows the creation of an AgentDispatcher and shows in which thread each line of code executes.

Note: The 1, 2, and question mark that begin some lines in the code in Listing 6.4 are only there for your edification; they would not appear in the actual Java code.

Listing 6.4   Using Operating System Threads

```
public void Dispatch() {
1  Vector v = currentAgent.getArguments();
1  currentDispatcher =
       new AgentDispatcher( disServerName, disServerPort );
1  currentDispatcher.start();
1  currentDispatcher.Dispatch( currentClassName, currentID, v );
1  changeAppState( AGENT_DISPATCHED );
   }


class AgentDispatcher extends Thread {
   Socket s;
1  public AgentDispatcher( String ServerName, int port ) {
1     setDaemon(true);
1     try {
1        s = new Socket( InetAddress.getByName(ServerName),port );
1        } catch( IOException e )
1           {System.out.println("exception "+e ); }
1     }
```

```
  public void StopAgent(String id) {
?    KillMessage km = new KillMessage(id);
?    try { s.getOutputStream().write( km.getMessageBytes()); }
?    catch( IOException e )
?       { System.out.println( "stop output exception "+e); }
?    try { s.close(); }
?    catch( IOException e1 )
?       { System.out.println( "stop close exception "+e1); }
    }

  public void Dispatch( String Name, String ID, Vector Args ) {
?    DispatchMessage dm = new DispatchMessage(Name,ID,Args);
?    try { s.getOutputStream().write( dm.getMessageBytes()); }
?    catch( IOException e )
?       { System.out.println( "dispatch out exception "+e); }
    }

  public void run() {
2    byte buffer[] = new byte[8192];
2    while( true ) {
2      try {
2      int ret;
2      if(( ret = s.getInputStream().read( buffer )) != 0 )
         {
2        if( ret < 0 ) {
2          System.out.println( "connection lost");
2          break;
           }
2        ClientProcess( buffer, ret );
         }
2      } catch( IOException e ) {
2        System.out.println( "IOexception "+e );
2        break;
         }
       }
2    try{s.close();}
2    catch(Exception e)
2       { System.out.println("run close exception "+e);}
    }

public void ClientProcess( byte b[], int numbytes ) {
2 All code execcutes in 2
  }
}
```

In this example, **AgentLauncher.Dispatch** starts running in thread 1. It then creates an AgentDispatcher, and starts it running in its own thread via **Thread.start**. **Thread.start** creates the new thread, thread 2, and starts it running our **run** method. All the code in **run** executes in thread 2. In addition, every method invoked from **run** also executes in thread 2, so **ClientProcess** all happens within thread 2. Notice that, in this example, we can't specify which thread **StopAgent** and **Dispatch** run in. If the user presses the Kill or Dispatch buttons, these methods are invoked from thread 1, and thus run in thread 1. They might, however, be invoked in response to a message from the AgentServer. In that case, the message comes over the socket and is read in the **run** method that executes in thread 2. The message is passed to **ClientProcess**, still in thread 2, and anything invoked by **ClientProcess** runs in thread 2.

Though we call the whole class **Thread**, you should really think of the **run** method and the underlying operating system thread as one and the same. The first line of the **run** method is the first line of Java code executed by the new thread, and the return from the **run** method is the last line of Java code executed by the new thread. This is why every **run** method you see will be some sort of loop. In essence, the **run** method is the equivalent of **main**() in a single-threaded C program. Everything that happens in the new thread starts within the **run** method. (Conversely, if you can't trace an instruction back to somewhere within the **run** method, it didn't happen in that thread!) When the **run** method returns, the thread disappears from the system. In fact, **run** never really returns. Because it executes independently, it has nowhere to return to.

The **run** method is never explicitly called. Instead, we invoke the **start** method, which causes Java to create a new operating system thread that executes the **run** method. One of the most frustrating mistakes you can make in Java is to create a **Thread**, then forget to invoke **Thread.start**(). Another mistake (and yes, I've made it) is to invoke **run** rather than **start**. In that case, **run** executes in the invoking thread, and the code you thought would execute in the invoking thread never does, because **run** is running and doesn't return immediately the way **start** would.

Another thing to keep in mind is that **Applet.start** and **Thread.start** are fundamentally different things. **Applet.start** is designed to be overridden to do whatever needs doing when the user leaves a page. **Thread.start** should never be overridden, because it contains the functionality that actually creates the new operating system thread.

Thread Control

We've seen that the **Thread** object and the underlying operating system thread are not the same thing. You can actually have a **Thread** object without an underlying operating system thread. There are two points in a **Thread**'s life when this is the case: before the **start** method is invoked (the thread hasn't been created yet) and after the **run** method returns (the thread has already disappeared).

Thus, the **Thread** class is actually made up of the underlying operating system thread (the **run** method) and a set of thread monitoring and control methods. Some methods can be invoked from outside the thread (outside the **run** method) and some can't. Table 6.2 shows which **Thread** methods can be invoked on the current thread, and which need to be invoked against an external thread.

Table 6.2 Determining Where to Invoke Thread Methods

Method Name	Applies to Current Thread	Applies to Other Thread	Applies to All Threads
activeCount			X
checkAccess	X	X	
countStackFrames	X		
currentThread	X		
destroy	X	X	
dumpStack	X		
enumerate			X
getName	X	X	
getPriority	X	X	
getThreadGroup	X	X	
interrupt		X	
interrupted	X		
isAlive	X	X	
isDaemon	X	X	
isInterrupted		X	
join		X	
resume		X	
run	-	-	-

Continued

Table 6.2   Determining Where to Invoke Thread Methods (Continued)

Method Name	Applies to Current Thread	Applies to Other Thread	Applies to All Threads
setDaemon	X		
setName	X		
setPriority	X	X	
sleep	X		
start		X	
stop		X	X
suspend	X	X	
toString	X	X	
yield	X		

start and **stop** we use to create and destroy the underlying operating system thread. You must invoke **start** to create the thread, but you don't need to use **stop** to get rid of it. Most applets rely on the return from the **run** method to destroy the thread.

We can also pause a thread with the **suspend** method. This method halts thread execution but leaves the thread in memory, allowing us to **resume** execution right where we left off when **suspend** was invoked. Later on, with animation, we create a series of threads, and **suspend** or **resume** them according to the activity of the remote agents.

join is another important thread-control mechanism that we'll use later on in our applet initialization methods. The point of calling **join** is to simply wait for the thread you're calling **join** against to die. For Unix types, it's the equivalent of **waiting** for a child process. **join** is actually an easy concept, made difficult by a stupid label. In real life, if I join you, we both continue to exist. In threads, when one thread **join**s another, the one **join**ed must die before the **join**er can continue. By all rights, this method should have been named "waitForTheDeathOf."

Thread Attributes

Each thread has three attributes that can be set and queried: *name, priority,* and *daemon status.* The thread name is just that, an identifier we can attach to the **Thread.** We set the thread names within the Agent system, but never use them.

I did this mostly for debugging and system monitoring purposes. Java itself doesn't use thread names for anything and there's no requirement for thread names to be unique. Internally to Java, threads are identified by the unique handle the operating system gives them.

Thread priority is also a straightforward concept, exactly analogous to process priority under Unix. Higher priority threads are scheduled (by the operating system) to run more frequently than lower priority threads. Priority can be changed on the fly via **Thread.setPriority**. Different operating systems use different ranges for priority values. Some even flip the precedence, with lower values getting higher priority. Thus, Java defines three constants, **MIN_PRIORITY**, **NORM_PRIORITY**, and **MAX_PRIORITY**. Any time you set the priority of a Java **Thread**, use a number based on these constants.

The concept of daemon status, though common to most multithreaded systems, is a little more difficult to explain. The Java interpreter also will not exit until all non-daemon threads have terminated. In essence, the interpreter **join**s all non-daemon threads before exiting. Giving a thread daemon status essentially frees it from that control, allowing the interpreter to exit without waiting for the thread to terminate. A thread should be made daemon unless it absolutely *must* do some cleanup (other than memory management), like closing open files, before the system exits.

Daemon status is set via **Thread.setDaemon**, which must be invoked *before* the **Thread**'s **start** method gets invoked (that is, before the underlying system thread actually starts executing). I generally put it in the constructor.

When Do Applet Threads Run?

One of the first questions that arises when you start spawning multiple threads is determining when each of these threads will be running. Consider the following scenario: A user enters a page that contains an applet and a single link to another HTML page. The browser reads the **<applet>** tag, loads the applet, and sets it running. The user then clicks on the hyperlink, jumping to another page. The page with your applet in it disappears, but what happens to the thread running on the user's machine that contains your applet code? The short answer, as you might expect, is that it stops running. No surprise there.

Especially for our application though, this presents real problems. For one thing, we want to view partial results—that is, we want to follow a hyperlink to a results page while our agents are still in the field collecting more. The problem there is that if the AgentLauncher stops running, the agents in the field will stop dispatching and eventually die off.

What saves us in this situation is that any threads created by our AgentLauncher can be left running while the user hyperlinks elsewhere. All we have to do is break one of the cardinal rules of applet writing, which says that when the browser invokes **Applet.stop** against your applet, you should stop running. When the browser invokes **Applet.stop** against our AgentLauncher, the only thread we terminate is the one that updates the display window, which of course we don't need when the user is looking at another page. All the other threads continue running.

Shared Resources and Synchronization

One issue that single-threaded programmers never have to deal with is coordinating access to shared resources. By shared resources, we mean anything that more than one thread needs to use. In most cases, this means a file or a block of memory. We need to coordinate access because we're doing a series of operations on the resource. The operations need to happen in one lump so that other threads don't see partial changes.

One of the ways we coordinate access to shared resources is via synchronized methods/blocks. There are many places in our application where synchronized execution might be useful, but the easiest to understand is probably the **reportResults** method in the AgentServer. When an agent finishes his work on an AgentServer, he connects to the dispatching AgentServer and sends a message containing a single URL pointing to his results HTML document. The dispatching AgentServer combines all these URLs into a single results page the user can jump to via the Results button.

Each SocketHandler on the AgentServer runs in a separate thread. When the SocketHandler reads a Results message over that connection, it calls **AgentServer.ReportResults** to add that URL to the list of results URLs. You might think that funneling result reporting through a single function guarantees thread safety but that's not the case, because all the calls to **reportResults** are happening in different threads.

Consider what happens when two agents, 007 and 99, report a result at the same time. 007 reports his results in http://www.info.com/result.html, while agent 99 reports her results in http://www.kaos.com/max.html. What we're hoping to see in the dispatching AgentServer results HTML document are two lines like those shown in the following code snippet:

```
Results from server <A HREF="http://www.info.com/
result.html">www.info.com</A>.
   Time elapsed 3:21 qty 13k - price $2.30
Results from server <A REF="http://www.kaos.com/max.html">www.kaos.com</A>
   Time elapsed 1:15 qty 39k - price FREE
```

What would happen, though, if the two calls to **AgentServer.reportResults** run at exactly the same time? You could end up with an HTML page like that shown here:

```
Results from server <A HREF="http://www.info.com/
result.html">www.info.com</A>
Results from server <A HREF="http://www.kaos.com/max.html">www.kaos.com</
A>
   Time elapsed 1:15 qty 39k - price FREE
   Time elapsed 2:30 qty 13k - price $2.30
```

That, of course, would be incorrect. One way we could remedy this situation would be to synchronize access to **AgentServer.reportResults**, as shown in Listing 6.5 with a synchronized **reportResults** method.

Listing 6.5   A Synchronized Method

```
/** Add this Agent'1s results to the cumulative results page that
we've been amassing for the whole run of this agent.
@param  r The ResultMessage that the agent is sending back to
the AgentLauncher.
*/
public synchronized void reportResults( ResultMessage r ) {
  // If this search has already been cancelled, don't bother
  if( resultFile == null )
    return;
  if( r.theURL == null ) {
    try {
      FileOutputStream fos =
        new FileOutputStream( resultFile );
      PrintStream ps = new PrintStream( fos );
      ps.println( "<P>" );
      ps.println( "Results from server <A HREF=\""+r.theURL+
```

```
        "\">"+r.server+"</A>");
      ps.println( "\tprice "+r.price);
      if( r.comment != null )
        ps.println( "\t"+r.comment );
      }
    catch( IOException ioe ) {
      System.out.println( "reportResults ioexc "+ioe );
      }
    }
  }
```

The purpose of this method is to print a String to the dispatching AgentServer's results file. The content of the String depends on the content of the **ResultMessage** that is supplied as an argument. The **ResultMessage** simply tells us where the agent stored his results and how much they'll cost to view. See Chapter 7 for the details of **ResultMessage**. If the URL is null, there were no results and we display that (via **showNoResults**).

The key feature of this method is the **synchronized** keyword in the declaration. The situation we want to avoid is one where two threads invoke the method at the same time and our calls to **println** get interlaced as we talked about earlier. The **synchronized** keyword in the declaration guarantees that only one copy of the method can be running at one time. Another way to put this is that our **synchronized AgentLauncher.reportResults** can now only run in one thread at a time.

Efficient Serialization

Our synchronized **reportResults** method does what we need, but it actually does more locking than we really need. Synchronizing the method locks the entire method when all we really need to do is lock the block of code containing the two invocations of **println**. So we rewrite **reportResults** to use a **synchronized** block around those two lines, as shown in Listing 6.6.

Listing 6.6 Using a Synchronized Block

```
/** Add this agent's results to the cumulative results page that
we've been amassing for the whole run of this agent.
@param  r The ResultMessage that the agent is sending back to
the AgentLauncher.
*/
public void reportResults( ResultMessage r ) {
```

```
// If this search has already been cancelled, don't bother
if( resultFile == null )
  return;
if( r.theURL == null ) {
  try {
    FileOutputStream fos =
      new FileOutputStream( resultFile );
    PrintStream ps = new PrintStream( fos );
    synchronized( ps ) {
      ps.println( "<P>" );
    ps.println( "Results from server <A HREF=\""+r.theURL+
      "\">"+r.server+"</A>");
    ps.println( "\tprice "+r.price);
    if( r.comment != null )
      ps.println( "\t"+r.comment );
      }
    }
  catch( IOException ioe ) {
    System.out.println( "reportResults ioexc "+ioe );
    }
  }
}
```

The method itself is no longer synchronized. Multiple threads can invoke the method without blocking waiting for another thread to finish with it. What we've added is a synchronized block within the method, which creates the smallest possible window of time where one thread might be waiting for another to finish working.

Each object in the system has a lock associated with it. In most cases, the lock is not used. Various threads can use the object without restriction. However, when thread A invokes a **synchronized** method (or block), it "acquires" the lock for the object associated with that **synchronized** method (or block). If thread B has already acquired the lock, thread A waits until thread B releases the lock before it executes the **synchronized** method. In our final **reportResults** method, we use the lock on our **PrintStream**, ps, to synchronize our block. This locking mechanism is exactly analogous to the more familiar record, table, and file locking that current operating systems and DBMSs provide.

As in DBMS record and table locking, we try never to lock more code than is absolutely necessary. Each time a thread fails to acquire a lock, it (and possibly the user) waits until the lock is released. This is wasted time that should be kept to an absolute minimum.

Our first, unsynchronized **reportResults** had the potential to misorder lines, but not to intermix the characters of one line with another. This is because **println** itself is **synchronized**. The moral: Considerable care has been taken with the multithreading issues in Java, so it's often the case that the level of synchronization you need is already implemented. Don't go around synchronizing blocks and methods until you're sure the synchronization you need isn't already there.

It's often hard for people to grasp the pervasiveness of synchronization situations, especially if they're new to the multithreading world. For a quick indication, flip through the class documentation and see just how many of the methods are synchronized.

Subterranean Threads

You now have the wherewithal to go out and create billions and billions of threads of your very own, but even if your applet never explicitly creates a single thread of its own, there are already multiple threads in any Java applet. These are the four subterranean threads that always exist in a running Java program: the main interpreter thread, the finalizer thread, the idle thread, and the garbage collector. The interpreter thread is the easiest to understand because its sole purpose is to execute the compiled Java byte codes from the .class file. You can think of a traditional, single-threaded interpreter as one in which all the functionality is stuffed into the interpreter thread.

The idle thread, the garbage collector, and the finalizer work together. The idle thread, running at a very low priority, simply maintains a flag that tells whether or not it has run. The idle thread's priority is chosen so that it almost never runs unless all other threads in the Java runtime are blocked. The garbage collector, running at an even lower priority than the idle thread, checks whether the idle thread has run. If the idle thread has been running, that probably means that it's a good time to run a garbage collection. The finalizer thread is a low-priority thread that helps with garbage collection. After the garbage collector identifies an object as inaccessible, the finalizer calls the object's **finalize** method, if it exists, to do any cleanup that might be necessary. The system tries to run garbage collection and finalization only when there is CPU time to spare. This design provides good performance for event-driven applications where the majority of realtime is spent waiting for events.

Other Threads

The subterrannean threads exist in any Java program—applet or application. Applets have another whole class of peer threads—the browser threads. Web browsers are all multithreaded by design. When you see a browser changing the status line, updating the screen, and responding to user input all while downloading a graphics file, that's a result of conscious multithreaded design. In most browsers, applets will not have access to any threads other than those the applet itself creates, but you should be aware that, in any browser, threads are coming and going all the time.

Inter-Process Communication

Java does not really support the notion of inter-process communication (IPC), not much of a surprise since it doesn't really believe in processes either. This has important implications for coders who've written multithreaded or multiprocess applications in C. As language features, DDE, semaphores, mailboxes, queues, OLE, system-wide shared memory, and most other traditional forms of IPC are absent.

There is only one form of IPC that is provided for Java programs—anonymous pipes via the **Process** and **Runtime** classes. In brief, **Runtime.exec** gets you a **Process** object, from which you can get **Stream** objects connected to the process standard in, standard out, and standard error. For security reasons, **Runtime.exec** is usually unavailable to applets. Thus, it's use is beyond the scope of this book.

Inter-Thread Communication

Java provides anonymous pipes for inter-thread communication via the **PipedInputStream** and **PipedOutputStream** classes. These are classic anonymous pipes that function just like the ones we're all familiar with from Unix. The basic theory of PipedStreams is that you create one end, then create the other end, passing it the handle to the first end in the constructor.

Inter-Applet Communication

Using the **AppletContext** interface we talked about in Chapter 4, it is relatively easy to get applets to communicate. In fact, once an applet retrieves an **Applet** object from the **AppletContext**, communication is as easy as invoking a method or setting a public variable. There is no need to use extraordinary mechanisms like sockets or anonymous pipes. Listing 4.12 shows an example of a relatively unfriendly applet-to-applet conversation.

When to Thread

We've seen how useful and necessary threads are, so by now you should be bursting to turn every Integer into its own thread. Hold on and take a deep breath. Threads *are* useful and necessary, but they have limitations that you need to consider, too.

For one thing, context switching involves some amount of overhead, so every thread you create adds some drag to the overall system—the operating system spends cycles switching among threads, and the more threads, the more cycles the OS spends context switching.

Threads are also a system resource and most operating systems have a hard limit on both the total number of threads in the system and the number of threads that one user can create. Think of it this way: If you spend 500 threads making "active" integers for your rotisserie baseball league scoring application, your DBMS may run out of transaction processing threads—a bad tradeoff. For total threads, a number somewhere around one thousand is typical. Per-user threads will be something less than that.

When deciding whether or not to thread an object, I tend to concentrate first on the difference between active and passive objects. A network socket is an active object, an integer is not; keyboard is active, file is not. Most objects that respond to events generated outside the application deserve their own threads.

A final reason to get with the program when it comes to threads: Java provides weak to non-existent support for polling I/O. There is no analogy to the Unix select system call that so many Unix programmers rely on for polling I/O. If you intend to do network I/O, you will probably want to write it as we have here, as blocking I/O in a separate thread.

Animation

So far, we've threaded our **Applet** and **AgentDispatcher** communication classes. That's all well and good, but efficient multitasking and well-structured communication code is not what brought us here, is it? Admit it, you really bought this book just to put cartoons on your home page, didn't you?

Well having gone through the applet, awt, and lang packages, we now have all the tools to do that. What we'll do now, is modify the **AgentFace** class so that while the agent is off doing his work on the remote AgentServer, the corresponding graphic representation on the user's screen will be animated. From a UI standpoint, this is a major advance, as the activity on the screen better represents the activity happening behind the scenes out on the Net.

Wait and Notify

We implement our animation the same way the old cartoonists used to—by flashing a new image on the screen at regular intervals to give the illusion of motion. To do that, we need to load a potentially large series of images into memory over the network. This image loading is not just a lengthy operation, but it is also unpredictably lengthy. For this reason, browsers retrieve images in a separate thread. We cannot tell from a call to **Applet.getImage** whether or not the image we're trying to draw has been loaded over the Net yet. In fact, if we simply call **getImage** for all our images, then try to draw them with **Component.drawImage** many of them will not actually get drawn for a long time. The only indication we ever get that our images have *not* been loaded is a bad return value from **drawImage**.

How do we deal with this situation? We could simply sit in a loop calling **drawImage** until the bad return value changes, but that wastes a lot of CPU cycles. There's a better way. Using the **ImageObserver** interface and the **wait-notify** thread-control mechanism we can have our main **Applet** thread block (sleep) until all the images are loaded. Listing 6.7 shows how the AgentLauncher implements an **ImageObserver/wait-notify** solution to image loading.

Listing 6.7   Image Loading in the AgentLauncher

```
public class AgentLauncher extends Applet implements Runnable {

/** The set of gifs to cycle through after an agent reports no results. */
String notstartedgifs[] = {
  "notstarted7.gif",
  "notstarted6.gif",
  "notstarted5.gif",
  "notstarted4.gif",
  "notstarted3.gif",
  "notstarted2.gif",
  "notstarted1.gif"
```

```
};

/** The set of gifs to cycle through after an agent reports no results. */
String runninggifs[] = {
  "running7.gif",
  "running6.gif",
  "running5.gif",
  "running4.gif",
  "running3.gif",
  "running2.gif",
  "running1.gif"
};

/** The set of gifs to cycle through after an agent reports no results. */
String noresultgifs[] = {
  "noresult7.gif",
  "noresult6.gif",
  "noresult5.gif",
  "noresult4.gif",
  "noresult3.gif",
  "noresult2.gif",
  "noresult1.gif"
};

/** The set of gifs to cycle through after an agent reports no results. */
String resultgifs[] = {
  "result7.gif",
  "result6.gif",
  "result2.gif",
  "result3.gif",
  "result4.gif",
  "result5.gif",
  "result4.gif",
  "result3.gif",
  "result2.gif",
  "result1.gif"
};

/** The set of gifs to cycle through after an agent reports no results. */
String dispatchedgifs[] = {
  "dispatched7.gif",
  "dispatched6.gif",
  "dispatched5.gif",
  "dispatched4.gif",
  "dispatched3.gif",
```

```
    "dispatched2.gif",
    "dispatched1.gif"
};

/** Override of Applet.init
*/
  public void init() {
    ..
    LoadAnimationImages();
  }

/** Load all the images this applet needs for its animation
sequences. Blocks until all the images have been loaded over
the Net OR one of the images reports a load error.
*/
public synchronized void LoadAnimationImages() {
     ImageLoaderThread = new ImageLoader[5];
     prefetchGC = createImage(1, 1).getGraphics();

     runningImages = createAgentImages( runninggifs );
     ImageLoaderThread[0] = new ImageLoader( this,runningImages,
                                             prefetchGC);
     resultImages = createAgentImages( resultgifs );
     ImageLoaderThread[1] = new ImageLoader( this,resultImages,
                                             prefetchGC);
     noResultImages = createAgentImages( noresultgifs );
     ImageLoaderThread[2] = new ImageLoader( this,
                                 noResultImages,prefetchGC);
     dispatchedImages = createAgentImages( dispatchedgifs );
     ImageLoaderThread[3] = new ImageLoader( this,
                                 dispatchedImages,prefetchGC);
     notStartedImages = createAgentImages( notstartedgifs );
     ImageLoaderThread[4] = new ImageLoader( this,
                                 notStartedImages,prefetchGC);
     boolean notloaded = true;
     while( notloaded )
       {
       if( ImageLoaderThread[0].allLoaded())
         if( ImageLoaderThread[1].allLoaded())
           if( ImageLoaderThread[2].allLoaded())
             if( ImageLoaderThread[3].allLoaded())
               if( ImageLoaderThread[4].allLoaded())
                 {
                 notloaded= false;
                 break;
```

```
                    }
      try{
        wait(); }
     catch( InterruptedException e )
       {System.out.println( "interrupted" ); }
         }
  showStatus( "All images loaded!" );
}



/** Take an array of image file names and return
an array of AgentImages corresponding to those image
file names. Creates valid URLs from each image file name using
the URL that the applet was loaded from as the base, and
assuming that all the images are contained in a
subdirectory named "images."
@return An array of AgentImages with each member initialized
with the String URL of an image file, leaving the Image object
uninitialized and the loaded flag set to false.
*/
AgentImage[] createAgentImages( String file[] ) {
  int i;

  URL u = getCodeBase();
  String fn = new String(u.toString());
  StringTokenizer st = new StringTokenizer(fn,"/");
  String s = null;
  int count = st.countTokens();
  for( i = 0; i < count-1; i++ ) {
    if( s == null )
      s = new String( (String)st.nextElement());
    else
      {
      if( i == 1 )
        s = new String(s+"//"+(String)st.nextElement());
      else
        s = new String(s+"/"+(String)st.nextElement());
      }
    }

  String directory = new String( s+"/images/");

  AgentImage ag[] = new AgentImage[file.length];
  for( i = 0; i < file.length; i++ ) {
    System.out.println(directory+file[i]);
    ag[i] = new AgentImage( directory+file[i] );
```

```
    }

  return( ag );
  }
} // End the AgentLauncher class


/** Override of Component.imageUpdate, an implementation of
ImageObserver.imageUpdate. Called by an image producer every
time an interesting point in image loading occurs.
@param  img The image that we're talking about.
@param  infoflags The state of the image-load - a constant from
ImageObserver's public variable set.
*/
public synchronized boolean imageUpdate(Image img,
          int infoflags, int x, int y, int width, int height)
  {
  System.out.println( "img "+img+" update" );
  if( infoflags == ERROR )
    bImageLoadingError = true;
  if( infoflags == ALLBITS || infoflags == ERROR )
    {
    ImageLoaderThread[0].setImageLoaded( img );
    ImageLoaderThread[1].setImageLoaded( img );
    ImageLoaderThread[2].setImageLoaded( img );
    ImageLoaderThread[3].setImageLoaded( img );
    ImageLoaderThread[4].setImageLoaded( img );
    }
  notify();
  return( true );
  }


}


/** A class to consolidate the loading of an array of images
into one place.

@version  1.2
@author John Rodley
*/

class ImageLoader extends Object {
AgentImage ai[];
AgentLauncher agl;
Graphics prefetchGC;
```

```java
public boolean isFinished = false;

/** Copy the AgentImage array into a local array, then start
the image loading over the network by trying to draw it into
the Graphics object argument.
@param  g An off-screen graphics context that we can draw into.
Used simply to get Java to load the image over the net.
@param  al  An applet that we can call back into to update the
status line with image loading progress reports.
@param  a An array of structures that contain image file URLs
when passed in, and which we fill with Image objects.
*/
public ImageLoader(AgentLauncher al,AgentImage a[],Graphics g){
   ai = a;
   agl = al;
   prefetchGC = g;
   for( int i = 0; i < ai.length; i++ )
      {
    // If the image already exists in this array, simply copy
    // it. The previous copy will be loaded.
     ai[i].image = null;
     for( int j = 0; j < i; j++ )
        {
        if( ai[i].FileName == ai[j].FileName )
           {
           ai[i].image = ai[j].image;
           break;
           }
        }
     if( ai[i].image != null )
        continue;

    // Now make sure the URL is valid.
     URL u;
     try {
      u = new URL( ai[i].FileName );
      // The URL is valid, get the image.
     agl.showStatus( "Getting hollow image "+u );
     ai[i].image = agl.getImage(u);
       boolean ret = g.drawImage(ai[i].image, 0, 0,al);
       }
     catch( MalformedURLException me ) {
         agl.bImageLoadingError = true;
         agl.sBadImage = new String( ai[i].FileName );
         break;
         }
```

```
    }
  }

/** Have all the bits for all the images in this array been
loaded over the network?
@return true if all the images have been loaded, false
otherwise.
*/
public boolean allLoaded() {
   for( int i = 0; i < ai.length; i++ )
     if( ai[i].loaded == false )
       return( false );
   return( true );
   }

/** Look through this loader's image array and if this image is
in there, then set its loaded flag to true.
@param  img The Image object that has been reported completely loaded.
@return true if the image was in this loaders array, false
otherwise.
*/
public boolean setImageLoaded( Image img ) {
   boolean bret = false;
   for( int i = 0; i < ai.length; i++ )
     if( img == ai[i].image )
       {
       System.out.println( "image "+ai[i].FileName+" loaded");
       agl.showStatus( ai[i].FileName+" loaded" );
       ai[i].loaded = true;
       bret = true;
       }
   return( bret );
   }
}


/** This class is really just a struct, used to hold a gif's
URL, an Image corresponding to all the bits in that file, and a
flag that tells us whether the image has been loaded over the
Net or not.
*/
class AgentImage extends Object {
/** The String URL of the GIF. */
public String FileName;
/** The hollow Image object that gets filled in by
Applet.getImage. */
```

```
public Image image;
/** flag that is true if the image has been loaded over the
net, false if it has not been loaded yet. */
public boolean loaded = false;

/** Set the String URL. The loaded flag and the Image object
will be set by the users of this class using that String URL.*/
public AgentImage( String file_n ) {
  FileName = file_n;
  }
}
```

The first thing to consider is when in the applet's execution trail do we want to load our images? Obviously, because image loading involves a lot of time-consuming network traffic, we only want to do it once per applet execution. There's only one method guaranteed to run only once, before the applet starts running—**Applet.init**. So that's where we invoke our **LoadAnimationImages** method.

The next thing to look at is the inheritance chain for **Applet**, shown in Chapter 5 as Figure 5.1. Back among its superclasses is **Component**. If we look at the declaration of **Component**, we see that it implements the **ImageObserver** interface shown in Table 6.3.

Like many interfaces, **ImageObserver** requires a single method—**imageUpdate**. In **Component**, **imageUpdate** simply repaints the **Component** whenever it gets called. We will override it and use it for a little different purpose.

Table 6.3 The ImageObserver Interface

Variable Type	Name	Description
int	ABORT	The image load aborted.
int	ALLBITS	All of the image has been loaded.
int	ERROR	There was an error loading the image.
int	FRAMEBITS	A complete frame in a multi-frame image has been loaded.
int	HEIGHT	The height of the image is available.
int	WIDTH	The width of the image is available.
int	PROPERTIES	The properties of the image are available.
int	SOMEBITS	Enough of the bits have arrived to draw a scaled image.

The next stop on our image loading journey is our own **ImageLoader** class. The purpose of **ImageLoader** is to consolidate the loading of an array of images into a single class. As such, we pass the constructor an AgentLauncher to use for updating the status line, an array of image file names, and a graphics context that it can draw those images into. The graphics context is an off-screen context, which we'll explain in a minute.

The **ImageLoader** constructor copies each image file name (provided by the AgentLauncher array instance variables **notstartedgifs**, **resultgifs** ...) into a local array and makes a URL out of it. If the URL is okay, it will call back to **Applet.getImage** to retrieve a hollow **Image** object. **getImage** does *not* load the image over the Net. The next call, **g.drawImage** is the key to this operation. **g** is our off-screen graphics context, and calling **drawImage** against **g** causes the browser to actually go and fetch the image over the Net *in a separate, asynchronous, image loading thread*. **drawImage** returns immediately, usually with a negative return value. We've told the graphics context to draw our image but it has essentially said, "Okay, I'll get around to it." We use an off-screen graphics context because we don't really want these images to appear on the screen—we just want to load them over the Net.

The last argument to **drawImage**, an **ImageObserver**, is the hook that allows us to know for certain when our images have actually been loaded. We've passed our AgentLauncher (which implements **ImageObserver** via its superclass **Component**) as this argument. What will happen now that we've called **drawImage**, and passed it an **ImageObserver**, is that the asynchronous thread that loads images will call **ImageObserver.imageUpdate** whenever there is some progress in loading the image.

So now we have a mechanism in place where the image is loading over the network, and the image loading thread is calling one of our methods at regular intervals to tell us how it's going. All we need to do now is force our main applet thread to block until the image loading thread has told us that all the images are loaded.

For this, we look to two places—our own **LoadAnimationImages** method and our implementation of the **ImageObserver.imageUpdate** method. In **LoadAnimationImages**, we create one of our **ImageLoader** objects for each animation (array of images). When the **ImageLoader** constructor returns, the asynchronous image loading thread has started loading the images for that animation over the Net. So by the time we reach the **while(notloaded)** loop in **LoadAnimationImages**, the asynchronous image loading thread is busy downloading bytes over the Net.

The **while** loop asks each **ImageLoader** if all of its images have been loaded yet. If all the images for all the **ImageLoaders** have been loaded, the loop terminates. If they haven't, we call **Object.wait**. What **wait** does is just that—wait. The thread in which **wait** was called blocks until it is notified by the aptly named method, **Object.notify**. So we reach the bottom of the **while** loop, and our main applet thread blocks in the call to **wait**.

Think about what is going on within the browser right now. The main applet thread is blocked, but the asynchronous image loading thread is still running. Not only is it running, but it is continually calling our **imageUpdate** method with progress reports on how the image loading is proceeding. The next step is to see what happens within **imageUpdate**.

The first argument to **imageUpdate** is the hollow **Image** object that the image-loading thread is trying to fill in. This argument tells us which image we're talking about. The second argument, **infoflags**, is the key. This argument tells us what state the loading of this image has reached. If we go back to the definition of the **ImageObserver** interface in Table 6.3, we see a number of integer constants defined that represent the various stages of image construction. There are only two states that interest us—**ERROR** and **ALLBITS**. If there is an image loading error (**infoflags==ERROR**), we abort the whole process by setting **bImageLoadingError**. This is a bit abrupt, but suffices for now. If the image has been completely loaded (**infoflags == ALLBITS**), we tell the **ImageLoaders** to mark this image as loaded. Then we close the circle by calling **Object.notify**.

Remember what's happening. The main applet thread is blocked in the call to **wait**, but the image-loading thread has invoked **imageUpdate**. When **imageUpdate** calls **notify**, the main applet thread wakes up and the call to **wait** returns. This is how **wait** and **notify** work; **wait** blocks and **notify** unblocks.

How does **imageUpdate**'s while loop terminate? The main applet thread is blocked in a call to **wait**. When the last bit of the last image has been loaded, the image-loading thread makes one last call to **imageUpdate** with **infoflags** set to **ALLBITS**. **imageUpdate** tells the **ImageLoaders** that this last image is done, which means that **ImageLoader.allLoaded** will now return true. Then **imageUpdate** unblocks the main applet thread by calling **notify**. Our call to **wait** returns; we run through all the **ImageLoaders** asking them if all their images have been loaded via **allLoaded**. They return true, and the loop exits. At this point all the bits for all the images are now in memory on the user's computer, and we can call **Component.drawImage** with complete confidence that the image will actually appear on the screen.

In any animation sequence you get two choices: Use predefined images, or draw the pictures yourself. In the AgentLauncher, we use a series of GIF files. The algorithm we'll use is to define an animation as a series of images, then roll through that array displaying each image in turn in order to give the illusion of movement.

Now the first question we have to confront with our animation is how "fine" we want our threading to be. Potentially, we could have many agents running, each getting an animation. Do we want each of those animations to be its own thread? We could do it that way but, on some systems, the overhead of even 15 or 20 additional threads could bring the system to a crawl. And the truth is, we can get the same effect by using a single new thread. In this case, the threaded object is a new subclass of **Panel—AnimationPanel**. Listing 6.8 shows the **AnimationPanel** class.

Listing 6.8 The AnimationPanel Class

```
/** A class for containing, laying out and animating a
collection of animations. Lays out animations out in a 10 by 10
grid, and animates by calling updateNextImage
against every animation in its collection.
*/
class AnimationPanel extends Panel implements Runnable {
/** The Vector of Animations */
   Vector a;

/** Constructor - Create a Vector for holding the animations,
and set us up as a grid layout 10 by 10.
*/
   public AnimationPanel() {
     a = new Vector(1);
     setLayout( new FlowLayout());
     }

/** Add an animation to this panel. Adds the animation
Component to this Container, re-lays out the Container and adds
the animation to our Vector of animations. Called only when a
new agent reports in. Agent state changes are handled by
replaceAnimation.
@return The number of animations in this Panel.
*/
   public int addAnimation( Animation an ) {
     add( an );
    layout();
     int ret = a.size();
```

```
    a.addElement( an );
    return( ret );
    }
```

```
/** Replace the animation at the specified index with the
supplied animation. Removes the animations Component from this
Container, removes the animation itself from our Vector of
animations, hides the Component, shows the new animation and
re-lays out this Container.
*/
  public void replaceAnimation( int index, Animation ani ) {
    System.out.println( "replacing animation at "+index );
    Component c = (Component)a.elementAt(index);
    c.hide();
    remove(c);
    add( ani, index );
    a.insertElementAt( ani, index );
    a.removeElementAt( index+1 );
    ani.show();
    layout();
    }
```

```
/** Our thread's run method sits in an infinite loop, sleeping
for 1/3 of a second, then running through all the animations in
our Vector of Animations setting them to the next image in the
sequence and telling them to repaint.
*/
  public void run() {
  Point pt = location();
  Dimension d = size();
    System.out.println( "size "+d.width+","+d.height);
  while (true) {
    for( int i = 0; i < a.size(); i++ )
      {
        Animation ani = (Animation)a.elementAt( i );
      ani.updateNextImage();
      }
    try {
    Thread.sleep(300);
      } catch (InterruptedException e) {
    break;
    }
    }
  }
}
```

As you can see, the whole thing is deceptively simple. The single instance variable—**a**—is a Vector of animations. In fact, **AnimationPanel** serves only two functions: to collect all the animations in one place and to "flip" each animation to the next **Image** at regular intervals.

We lay out the **Panel** in a **FlowLayout**, via **setLayout**. This ensures that our animations will retain their **preferredSize**, and that they'll line up in rows and columns as they get added to the **Panel**. When we want to add an animation to the **Panel,**, we call **addAnimation**, which adds the Animation to the **Panel** itself, re-lays out the **Panel** and adds the animation to our Vector of animations. This is only called when an agent first checks in from the field.

replaceAnimation is used whenever an agent changes state; for instance, when it reports results. This removes the **Component** from our **Container** and removes the animation from our Vector of animations.

Whenever an Agent checks in from the field, we call **addAnimation**, supplying the animation that fits the current state of the agent. Each state—NOTSTARTED, DISPATCHED, RUNNING, RESULTS, NORESULTS—has an animation associated with it. One of these animations will be the current one for each agent in the field.

The **Animation** class, shown in Listing 6.9, is itself a subclass of **Panel**.

Listing 6.9 The Animation Class

```
/** Class representing an animation. Each animation is a
series of frames of consistent and constant size that get
displayed for a fixed amount of time. There are two types of
animations: one-shot and looping. One-shot animations run
once, looping animations run continually until they are
stopped from outside.

@author John Rodley
@version 1.4 March 10 1996
*/

class Animation extends Panel {
/** Is this animation actually animating now? */
  public boolean bRunning;
/** The images comprising the stages of the animation. */
  public AgentImage images[];

/** An agentface to call back to process the mouse click. */
```

```
  AgentFace af;

/** If this animation runs only once, this gets set to true. If this
is a loop that restarts at the beginning, set this to false. */
  public boolean bOneShot;

/** This index indicates which frame of the animation will be displayed
next. */
  public int FrameNumber;
  int width;
  int height;

/** An Applet for us to call back to. */
  Applet a = null;

/** Has this frame already been displayed?  Set false in
nextImage, set true in paint. */
  boolean bDisplayed = false;

/** Constructor - store the applet to call back to
@param  al  An applet to call back to.
*/
  public Animation(Applet al) {
  System.out.println( "empty animation for copying" );
    a = al;
  }

/** Create an animation that is not animating right now. */
  public Animation(Applet al, AgentImage im[], AgentFace agf ){
    // Save the applet and AgentFace objects.
  a = al;
    af = agf;
  bRunning = true;
    FrameNumber = 0;
  images = im;
    width = images[0].image.getWidth(a);
    height = images[0].image.getHeight(a);
    resize( width, height );
  }

/** This method tells the LayoutManager the smallest size we
can be. In our case, it's the size of the image we're
displaying.
@return A Dimension - width and height.
*/
  public synchronized Dimension minimumSize() {
```

```
      return( new Dimension( width, height ));
      }

/** This method tells the LayoutManager the size we prefer
to be. In our case, it's the size of the image we're
displaying.
@return A Dimension - width and height.
*/
  public synchronized Dimension preferredSize() {
    return( new Dimension( width, height ));
    }

/** Paint a single frame of this animation within an existing Graphics
context. */
  public void paint(Graphics g) {
    try {
      if( FrameNumber >= images.length )
        FrameNumber = 0;

  if( images[FrameNumber].image == null )
    {
        System.out.println( "no image" );
      return;
    }
  g.drawImage( images[FrameNumber].image, 0, 0, a );
      }
    catch( ArrayIndexOutOfBoundsException e ) {
      System.out.println( "badindex "+FrameNumber);
      }
  bDisplayed = true;
  }

/** Go to the next image. Increments FrameNumber, rewinding
back to 0 if we've gone over the edge of the array.
*/
  public void nextImage() {
  if( !bDisplayed ) return;
  if( FrameNumber >= (images.length-1) )
    FrameNumber = 0;
  else
    FrameNumber++;
  bDisplayed = false;
    }

/** Go to the next image and display it.
*/
```

```
  public void updateNextImage() {
  nextImage();
    repaint();
  }

/** Called if the user clicks the mouse in this Panel.
@return false
*/
  public boolean mouseDown( Event e, int x, int y ) {
    af.clicked();
    return( false );
  }
}
```

As you can see, **Animation** does the dirty work of actually drawing the image onto the screen. All it's really designed to accomplish is to draw the proper **Image**, from an array of **Images**, into the graphics context whenever **paint** is called. The proper **Image** is indicated by the instance variable **FrameNumber**. In order to move along to the next **Image** in the sequence, our **AnimationPanel** calls **updateNextImage** at regular intervals. **updateNextImage** invokes **nextImage** to roll **FrameNumber** forward, then calls **Component.repaint**, which indirectly generates a call to **paint**.

preferredSize and **minimumSize** ensure that the **AnimationPanel**'s LayoutManager knows how much screen real estate to reserve for us.

paint actually draws the **Image** onto the screen. Because we use the **paint** method, rather than **update**, our **Component** is cleared before **paint** is invoked. The rest of the method is simple index checking and (possibly unnecessary) exception handling.

The last **Animation** method, **mouseDown**, is called whenever the mouse is clicked in our animation. **mouseDown** calls back to the **AgentFace** that owns it. Listing 6.10 shows the **AgentFace** class.

Listing 6.10   The AgentFace Class

```
/** A class that encapsulates the face that a dispatched agent
presents to the user. Contains a series of animations that
each represent a different possible state that the agent can be
in. At any time, only one of these animations will be running.
Clicking on the animation should take the user to the results
document for this agent. AgentFaces are uniquely identified by
the server name supplied to the constructor.
*/
```

```
class AgentFace extends Object {
  String StatusString = "";
  String serverName = "";
  Animation animation[];

  final int NOT_STARTED = 0;
  final int DISPATCHED = 1;
  final int RUNNING = 2;
  final int RETURNED_RESULTS = 3;
  final int RETURNED_NORESULTS = 4;
  AgentLauncher applet;
  String name;
  boolean bImageDisplay = true;
  public int index;
  public String url;

  int status = NOT_STARTED;

  public AgentFace( AgentLauncher ap, String ServerName, int index ) {
    name = new String( "AgentFace"+index );
  applet = ap;
    serverName = new String( ServerName );
    StatusString = new String( serverName+" Not started" );
    animation = new Animation[5];
  animation[NOT_STARTED] = new Animation( ap,
                                  ap.notStartedImages, this );
    animation[DISPATCHED] = new Animation( ap,
                                  ap.dispatchedImages, this );
  animation[RUNNING] = new Animation( ap,
                                  ap.runningImages, this );
  animation[RETURNED_RESULTS] = new Animation( ap,
                                  ap.resultImages, this);
  animation[RETURNED_NORESULTS] = new Animation( ap,
                                  ap.noResultImages, this );

    }

/** Called by the animation whenever the user clicks in the
animation. If the agent has finished work and has something to
report, this takes us over to that document, else it displays a
message box explaining what state the agent is in.
*/
  public boolean clicked() {
   String msg;
    MessageBox m;

    Frame f = ComponentUtil.getFrame(applet);
  switch( status ) {
    case NOT_STARTED:
```

```
          msg = new String( "Not started." );
            m = new MessageBox( f, msg );
          m.ShowAndLayout();
          break;
        case DISPATCHED:
            msg = new String( "Not running on server "+serverName+" yet." );
          m = new MessageBox( f, msg );
          m.ShowAndLayout();
          break;
      case RUNNING:
          msg = new String( "Server "+serverName+" not finished yet." );
          m = new MessageBox( f, msg );
            m.ShowAndLayout();
          break;
      case RETURNED_RESULTS:
          System.out.println( "Switching to URL "+url );
          AppletContext ac = applet.getAppletContext();
          ac.showDocument( url );
            break;
      case RETURNED_NORESULTS:
          msg = new String( "Agent on server "+serverName+
                                    " didn't find anything." );
          m = new MessageBox( f, msg );
            m.ShowAndLayout();
          break;
      }
   return( true );
      }


/** Changes the AgentFace's state to dispatched. */
  public void dispatched() {
   status = DISPATCHED;
     StatusString = new String( serverName+" Dispatched" );
   }
/** Changes the AgentFace's state to running. */
  public void running() {
   status = RUNNING;
   StatusString = new String( serverName+" Running" );
   }
/** Changes the AgentFace's state to returned with results. */
  public void returnedResults(String u) {
   url = new String(u);
     status = RETURNED_RESULTS;
   StatusString = new String(serverName+" Finished Results");
   }
/** Change the AgentFace's state to returned with no results.*/
  public void returnedNoResults() {
```

```
    status = RETURNED_NORESULTS;
      StatusString =
        new String( serverName+" Finished NO Results" );
  }


/** Return the animation that represents this agent's current
state.
@return An Animation.
*/
  public Animation getCurrentAnimation() {
    return( animation[status] );
  }
}
```

The point of **AgentFace** is to encapsulate the set of possible animations, and to keep track of which one is current for a particular agent. There is one **AgentFace** per agent, and each one is uniquely identified by the server name of the server the agent is running on. Listing 6.11 shows the **reportResult** method that changes the animation via the **AgentFace**'s status methods.

Listing 6.11 Changing the On-Screen Animation

```
/** A method called by the message processing code
(AgentDispatcher) to change an agent's state from running to
finished with or without results.
@param  url The URL of the results file. If null, there were
no results.
@param  server  The name of the server. We find the AgentFace
we need to change by searching on this name.
*/
  public void reportResult( String server, String url ) {
    for( int i = 0; i < ALVector.size(); i++ )
    {
    AgentFace af = (AgentFace)ALVector.elementAt(i);
      if( af.serverName.compareTo(server) == 0 )
        {
        if( url != null )
          af.returnedResults(url);
          else
            af.returnedNoResults();
        p.replaceAnimation( af.index, af.getCurrentAnimation());
        return;
        }
      }
    }
```

As it receives messages from an agent detailing the agent's progress, the AgentLauncher calls one of the status change methods in **AgentFace** (running, dispatched, returnedResults, or returnedNoResults), then it replaces the old animation with one that represents the new state. Listing 6.1 shows the AgentLauncher code (via AgentDispatcher) that calls **reportResult** upon receipt of a **ResultMessage**. This process completes the chain we've tried to build from the agent working out on a remote server, back to an animation running on-screen in front of the user who dispatched the agent. Messages come in over the socket, the AgentDispatcher calls into the AgentLauncher to change the **AgentFace**'s state, and the animation representing that agent changes.

Native Methods

The first thing I always look at when reviewing a new language like Java is how to get out of it. This is only natural, as most programmers are already productive in one language and most projects need some of the functionality of last year's language in the new product they're writing in next year's language. Windows GUI development languages, like Easel or Toolbook, usually provide the ability to make DLL calls, and Java provides an analogous escape hatch—native methods.

Native methods allow you to link dynamic libraries written in C, C++, or some other language via a method "wrapper." Basically, if your DLL call obeys certain rules about parameter passing, memory management, and such, you can write a method that simply calls out to that external DLL. Native methods are crucial for shrink-wrapped, standalone Java applications where your program is competing against code written to the native operating system API. Native methods, however, are not useful for the purposes of our application for two reasons. First and most important, by definition a native method is not portable and one of the base requirements for our application is that it run in any Java-capable browser. Second, and perhaps not so obvious, is the whole question of how you would get your native method onto a user's machine. The Java classloader is designed for moving java .class files, not Windows .DLL files. Thus, you could write the world's coolest native method, but any Java-capable browser trying to run your applet over the Net would throw an exception when it tried to (locally) load your native method.

Conclusion

Java makes threading simple and worthwhile. You can write Java applets the same way you used to write single-threaded applications in C or C++, but you'd be wasting much of the power of the language. The current generation of browsers are all multithreaded, and threading will only become more prevalent as a method of increasing the real and apparent efficiency of applications.

Chapter

7

Network
Communication

Network Communication

Network I/O is one of the keys to writing useful Java applets. Here we present a potpourri of applets that use Java's network I/O in interesting ways.

Every programming tool has a dirty little secret that makes using it less pleasant than the walk in the park promised by the marketing brochures. Basic has its spaghetti code and C has its wild pointers. Java is no different. The dirty little secret of Java applet writing is that browser security mechanisms make it nearly impossible to write a useful Java applet that doesn't connect back via sockets to a daemon on the server. Specifically, browsers can, and do, prevent applets from doing any file I/O. This means that any persistence that an applet requires has to be implemented in a server application (not an applet) to which the applet talks over the Net.

Java provides network communication through the package java.net. This package contains a number of useful classes. The basic ones that we're going to use and talk about are **URL**, **Socket**, **ServerSocket**, and **InetAddress**. The class hierarchy for the java.net package is shown in Figure 7.1.

Another package that is inextricably bound up with network I/O and I/O in general is the aptly named java.io package. As the various examples will show, whenever you do any kind of I/O, you will have to use one of the Stream classes provided in the java.io package. Figure 7.2 shows the java.io class hierarchy.

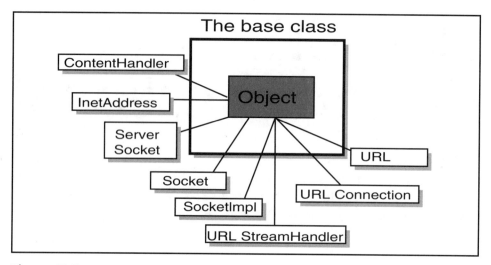

Figure 7.1

The **java.net** class hierarchy.

Using URLs

A URL, or *Uniform Resource Locator*, is basically just a network location. It tells you not only where something is, but *what* it is. For example, consider my home page URL:

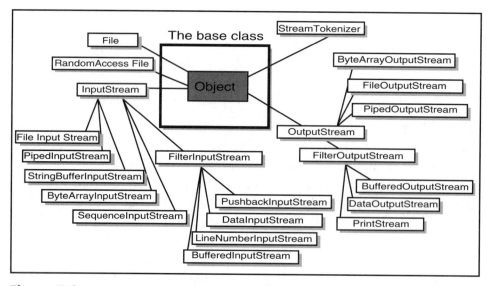

Figure 7.2

The **java.io** class hierarchy.

```
http://www.channel1.com/users/ajrodley/index.html
```

Briefly, the URL says that to use this "document," you connect to the http server on the machine named www.channel1.com, then tell it to send a stream of data made out of the file "/users/ajrodley/index.html."

Java's **URL** class takes this concept of an Internet location one step beyond. After all, a URL by itself can be easily represented by a **String**. A Java **URL** object, on the other hand, encompasses not just the address, but also the object at that address. Let's investigate URLs in more detail.

Word-Searching a URL

Many organizations are sitting on huge piles of information that they want to make available via the Web. After all, it's a perfect application of the technology, freeing information consumers from the time-consuming task of hauling themselves physically to the location (library, town hall ...) where the hard-copy information resides. For most companies in this situation, the easiest approach is to just dump the information out on the Web virtually unmodified from the hard-copy version. Although this is a valid approach, Java makes it easy to go one step beyond.

As a first step in adding value to a huge, raw document, you might want to add a word-search applet like the one shown in Listing 7.1, which scans a document for a particular word. Listing 7.2 shows the HTML code to load this applet.

Listing 7.1   Searching a Document for a Word

```
package chap7;

import java.awt.Graphics;
import java.awt.*;
import java.applet.Applet;
import java.net.*;
import java.lang.*;
import java.io.*;
import java.util.*;

/** A class to search for a word in a text document using only
URL.getContent to retrieve the document into a String.
@author John Rodley
@version 1.0 1/1/1996
```

```
*/
public class ch7_fig1 extends Applet {
String stringURL;
String desiredWord;
public final static String buttonLabel =
                     new String("Start Search");
TextField wordField;
Panel controlPanel;
Button searchButton;

/** Get the parameter "URL" from the applet tag, create a
panel with a text field for entering the word to search for,
and a button for starting the search.
*/
  public void init() {
    stringURL = new String( getParameter( "URL" ));
    if( stringURL == null ) {
      System.out.println( "URL parameter not set" );
      return;
      }
    controlPanel = new Panel();
    searchButton = new Button( buttonLabel );
    controlPanel.add( searchButton );
    wordField = new TextField( 25 );
    controlPanel.add( wordField);
    add( controlPanel );
  }


/** Do the search, using the URL provided in the URL parameter
and the search phrase set previously in the text field. Skip
the search if either of these variables is not set.
*/
void dosearch() {
  if( desiredWord == null ) {
    System.out.println( "find parameter not set" );
    return;
    }
  try {
    URL u = new URL(stringURL);
    try {
      Object o = u.getContent();
      if( o instanceof String ) {
        FindTheWord( desiredWord, (String)o );
        }
      }
```

```
      catch( IOException e ) {System.out.println( "ioex "+e);}
   }
   catch( MalformedURLException ue ) {System.out.println( "urlex "+ue);}
}



/** Search the supplied string for the specified sub-string.
Find by character position in the doc, as well as line
position. Report results to standard output.
@param  String  the phrase to search for
@param  String  a string that contains the ENTIRE document
*/
void FindTheWord( String find, String doc ) {
  int ret = doc.indexOf( find );
  if( ret != -1 ) {
    showStatus( "Found "+find+" at char offset "+ret );
    System.out.println( "found "+find+" at char offset "+ret );
    }

  // Split the doc into lines using a tokenizer with only \r
  // and \n as the delimiters.
  StringTokenizer lines = new StringTokenizer( doc, "\r\n" );
  int lineNo = 1;
  while( lines.hasMoreElements()) {
    String line = (String)lines.nextElement();
    // Create a second tokenizer, with space as the delimiter
    StringTokenizer words = new StringTokenizer( line );
    while( words.hasMoreElements()) {
      String word = (String)words.nextElement();
      if( word.toUpperCase().compareTo( find.toUpperCase())==0)
        {
        showStatus("found "+find+" on line "+lineNo );
        System.out.println( "found "+find+" on line "+ lineNo);
        }
      }
    lineNo++;
    }
  }


/** Handle the search button, starting a new search
if the start button is pushed.
*/
public boolean handleEvent(Event e) {
```

```
    if (e.id == Event.ACTION_EVENT) {
      if( e.target instanceof Button )
        {
        Button b = (Button )e.target;
        if( b.getLabel().compareTo( buttonLabel ) == 0 )
          {
          desiredWord = new String( wordField.getText());
          dosearch();
          }
        }
      }
    }
  return( false );
  }
}
```

Listing 7.2 The HTML Code That Loads the Word Finder Applet

```
<!DOCTYPE HTML PUBLIC "-//SQ//DTD HTML 2.0 HoTMetaL + extensions//EN">
<HTML><HEAD><TITLE>Chapter 7 - figure 1 - Finding a word in a
simple network text file.</TITLE>
</HEAD>
<BODY>
<applet code="chap7/ch7_fig1.class" width=600 height=600>
<param name=URL value="http://www.mymachine.com/temp/index.txt">
</applet>
</P>
</BODY></HTML>
```

The <applet> tag on the HTML page provides both the URL of a document to scan while a TextField gets the word to search for, and a Button starts the search.

One thing you need to note from Listing 7.2: The document we're scanning isn't an HTML document. We'll talk about that later.

Setting up the search requires getting the URL of the document we're scanning, and getting a word to scan for. In the **init** method, we get the URL via the **getParameter** method. We also set up a text field for entering the search word, and a button for starting the search. The text field and button arrangement requires us to implement a **handleEvent** method. As you can see, the event handler deals with a single event (among the many that can occur)—the user pressing the button labeled "Start Search."

Once we have a word to search for, and a string URL of a document to search, the next logical step is to retrieve the document. This is the purpose of the first part of the **dosearch** method, specifically the calls to the **URL** constructor and **URL.getContent**. The **URL** constructor actually connects to the document specified by our string URL. If the document doesn't exist, or we can't make a connection to it, the **URL** constructor throws a **MalformedURLException**, which we are required to catch. Having connected to the document, we then retrieve it via the call to **getContext**, where most of the functionality of this applet is actually embedded. When the file we're pointing at is simple text, what we get back from the call to **getContent** is a **String** that holds the entire text of that file.

Having read our whole file into a **String**, we simply pass that **String** into the method **FindTheWord** that searches for a word occurrence. Within **FindTheWord**, we use two different ways to find our word within the String. The first way is an exact match via **String.indexOf**:

```
int ret = doc.indexOf(find);
if( ret != -1 ) {
   showStatus( ... );
```

This approach searches the whole **String**, whitespace included, for the word, returning the character offset of the word within the string. Unfortunately, knowing the character offset of a word within a file is rarely useful.

What's usually called for in word searches is a line number within the document. Thus, within **FindTheWord**, we also implement a second, more useful search algorithm. This one uses **StringTokenizer** to turn the **String** representing our whole file into a Vector of lines. Then it turns each line into a Vector of words and compares each member of that Vector to the desired word.

The two search algorithms, **indexOf** and **compareTo,** will often find different things. **indexOf** will find the word within another word, while **compareTo** won't. **compareTo** combined with **toUpperCase** matches the words regardless of case.

The final thing to notice about our word-search applet is that we haven't talked at all about sockets, protocols, or daemons. All of the grunt work of connecting over the network and retrieving the file is handled entirely within **URL.getContent**.

Expanding the Search Beyond Simple Text

If you point the word search applet at a file with an .htm or .html extension, something very disturbing happens: **getContent** throws **ClassNotFound-**

Exception. This is because there is no content handler for content of type HTML. The steps **URL.getContent** goes through to deliver our **String** in Listing 7.1 are:

1. Make a connection over the Net via sockets.
2. Create a stream of characters flowing from the server to the applet.
3. Figure out that the stream is simple text and turn that stream of characters into a **String** object.

The problem with using this applet on HTML content is that Java figures out that the stream is HTML (not simple text), but it doesn't know how to create a sensible object from a stream of HTML text. This is unfortunate, but not insurmountable. Of the three steps, the first two are still available to us, regardless of the type of the URL's content. We just have to deal with the stream ourselves, rather than having **getContent** turn it into a **String**.

To do the same search and have it work whatever the content type, we have to modify the applet. Listing 7.3 shows those modifications.

Listing 7.3 Searching HTML Documents for a Word

```
package chap7;

import java.awt.Graphics;
import java.awt.*;
import java.applet.Applet;
import java.net.*;
import java.lang.*;
import java.io.*;
import java.util.*;

/** A class that searches the document specified in the URL
parameter for the word specified in the find parameter.
@author John Rodley
@version 1.0 1/1/1996
@see URL
@see InputStream
*/
public class ch7_fig3 extends Applet {
String stringURL;
String desiredWord;
public final static String buttonLabel =
                    new String("Start Search");
TextField wordField;
```

```
Panel controlPanel;
Button searchButton;

/** Get the parameter "URL" from the applet tag, create a
panel with a text field for entering the word to search for,
and a button for starting the search.
*/
  public void init() {
    stringURL = new String( getParameter( "URL" ));
    if( stringURL == null ) {
      System.out.println( "URL parameter not set" );
      return;
      }
    controlPanel = new Panel();
    searchButton = new Button( buttonLabel );
    controlPanel.add( searchButton );
    wordField = new TextField( 25 );
    controlPanel.add( wordField);
    add( controlPanel );
  }

/** Handle the search button, starting a new search
if the start button is pushed.
*/
public boolean handleEvent(Event e) {
  if (e.id == Event.ACTION_EVENT) {
    if( e.target instanceof Button )
      {
      Button b = (Button )e.target;
      if( b.getLabel().compareTo( buttonLabel ) == 0 )
        {
        desiredWord = new String( wordField.getText());
        dosearch();
        }
      }
    }
  return( false );
  }

/** Override of Applet.start. Gets the URL and search word
parameters, then opens a stream connection to the document at
that URL and passes the stream and the search word to the
FindWord method.
@see FindTheWord
@see URL
@see InputStream
```

```
*/
public void dosearch() {
  try {
    URL u = new URL(stringURL);
    System.out.println( "u="+u );
      try {
        InputStream is = u.openStream();
        FindTheWord( desiredWord, is );
      }
      catch( IOException e ) {System.out.println( "ioex "+e);}
    }
  catch( MalformedURLException e1 )
   {System.out.println( "mfuex "+e1);}
}

/** Find a word in an input stream, reporting the line number
to the standard output.
@arg  find  The word we're scanning the input stream for
@arg  is  An input stream
@see DataInputStream
@see StringTokenizer
@see String
*/
void FindTheWord( String find, InputStream is ) {
  int lineNo = 1;

  DataInputStream dis = new DataInputStream( is );
  while( true ) {
    try {
      String line = dis.readLine();
      if( line == null )
        break;
      StringTokenizer words = new StringTokenizer( line );
      while( words.hasMoreElements()) {
        String word = (String)words.nextElement();
        if( word.toUpperCase().compareTo( find.toUpperCase())
                            == 0)
          {
          showStatus("found "+find+" on line "+lineNo );
          System.out.println("found "+find+" on line "+lineNo);
          }
        }
      lineNo++;
      } catch( IOException e ) {break;}
    }
  }
}
```

We use the same basic structure as in Listing 7.1, getting the search word from a text field, and the URL from the **<applet>** tag. The real changes are to our content handling mechanisms—**dosearch** and **FindTheWord**. Within **dosearch**, we get rid of the call to **getContent** using the lower level call **URL.open Stream** instead.

```
URL u = new URL(stringURL);
    System.out.println( "u="+u );
      try {
        InputStream is = u.openStream();
```

This approach gets us the **InputStream** that **getContent** uses in Listing 7.1 to create an object appropriate to the URL's content. You can see now, how high-level the **URL.getContent** method really is. We could easily write our own version of it using the skeleton of **FindTheWord**, as shown in Listing 7.4.

Listing 7.4 Our Own Version of URL.getContent

```
String ourGetContent( InputStream is ) {
  String content = new String("");

  DataInputStream dis = new DataInputStream( is );
  while( true ) {
    try {
      String line = dis.readLine();
    if( line == null )
      break;
    content = new String(content+line);
} catch( IOException e ) {break;}
    }
return( content );
  }
```

The main difference between **URL.getContent** and our **FindTheWord** is that we embed a word search algorithm in **FindTheWord**. Within **FindTheWord** we turn the **InputStream** that **dosearch** got from our URL into a **DataInputStream**. This allows us to read the stream line by line rather than in byte or byte arrays, which are all the bare **InputStream** gives us. This technique is a common theme in Java I/O. The basic I/O object gives you an **Input/OutputStream** that you then turn into a more specialized stream, like **DataInputStream**, by passing the bare **Input/OutputStream** to the specialized stream constructor, as we do here in **FindTheWord**:

```
DataInputStream dis = new DataInputStream( is );
  while( true ) {
    try {
      String line = dis.readLine();
```

From this point, we use the same word search techniques as in Listing 7.1 to turn each line into a Vector of words and eventually compare the search word to each word in the document.

A Link-Checking Applet

Once you have access to the text of HTML documents on the Net, there are an endless number of interesting tasks you can take on. Because of the complex nature of my Web site, one of the most odious tasks I've had to deal with is checking all the links in my pages to make sure there aren't any dead ones. It's easy to get dead links in a page. A simple typo in the HREF tag will do it.

With a multi-level Web site containing many internal links, you really need an applet that will go through all the links—top-to-bottom—making sure the documents pointed to actually exist. We can develop an applet like this by combining the applets in Listing 7.1 and 7.3, as shown in Listing 7.5. Figure 7.3 shows the link-checking applet in action.

Listing 7.5   A Link-Checking Applet

```
package chap7;

import java.awt.Graphics;
import java.awt.*;
import java.applet.Applet;
import java.net.*;
import java.lang.*;
import java.io.*;
import java.util.*;


/** A class that prompts the user for a URL, then goes through
the, presumably HTML, content of that URL checking for links
to other WWW content and making sure that the documents those
links connect to actually exist and that all THEIR links are
valid.  This is recursive and potentially time-wasting.
@author John Rodley
@version 1.0 1/1/1996
@see TextField
```

```
@see Button
@see Panel
*/
public class ch7_fig5 extends Applet {

public static ch7_fig5 c7;

TextField urlEntryField;
Button checkButton;
Button skipButton;
public List lineList;
Panel topPanel;
public boolean bSkip = false;
String buttonLabel = new String( "Check URL" );
String skipLabel = new String( "Skip" );

/** Set up a text field for entering the URL to check, a button
to start the check, and a button to interrupt an undesired
check.
@see Panel
@see Button
@see TextField
*/
public void init() {
  c7 = this;

  setLayout( new BorderLayout());
  topPanel = new Panel();
  urlEntryField = new TextField( "http://", 60 );
  urlEntryField.setEditable( true );
  topPanel.add( urlEntryField );
  checkButton = new Button(buttonLabel);
  topPanel.add( checkButton );
  skipButton = new Button(skipLabel);
  topPanel.add( skipButton );
  lineList = new List(10, false);
  add( "North", topPanel );
  add( "Center", lineList );
  resize( 700, 400 );
  }

/** Handle the start and skip buttons, starting a new search
if the start button is pushed, and breaking out of a scan every
time the skip button is pressed.
*/
public boolean handleEvent(Event e) {
  if (e.id == Event.ACTION_EVENT) {
```

```
      if( e.target instanceof Button )
        {
        Button b = (Button )e.target;
        System.out.println( "button "+b );
        if( b.getLabel().compareTo( buttonLabel ) == 0 )
          clicked();
        if( b.getLabel().compareTo( skipLabel ) == 0 ) {
          System.out.println( "skip button clicked" );
          bSkip = true;
          }
        }
      }
  return( false );
  }


/** Actually start the search, getting the URL from the
text field, and setting off a recursive LinkFollower object.
@see LinkFollower
*/
public void clicked() {
  System.out.println( "Starting check run" );

  String stringURL = urlEntryField.getText();
  if( stringURL == null ) {
    showStatus( "URL ENTRY FIELD CANNOT BE EMPTY!!" );
    return;
    }
  if( stringURL.compareTo("" ) == 0 )
    {
    showStatus( "URL ENTRY FIELD CANNOT BE EMPTY!!" );
    return;
    }
  LinkFollower lf = new LinkFollower( this, stringURL );
  lf.start();
  }
}


/** A class that recursively follows all the links in an HTML
page to the very end.  This has circularity problems that are
not entirely solved, hence the skip button.  A HashTable
contains the list of all links that have been checked, and no
link should be checked twice.
@see HashTable
@author John Rodley
@version 1.0 1/10/1996
*/
class LinkFollower extends Thread {
```

```
String stringURL;
ch7_fig5 c;
static Hashtable hash;
String linkStrings[];

/** Constructor - creates the checked-link HashTable, and an
array of "keys" that we use to find links - HREF, IMG, and
applet.
@see HashTable
*/
public LinkFollower( ch7_fig5 ch, String url ) {
  hash = new Hashtable();
  linkStrings = new String[3];
  linkStrings[0] = new String("<A HREF=");
  linkStrings[1] = new String("<IMG SRC=");
  linkStrings[2] = new String("<applet code=");
  c = ch;
  stringURL = new String( url );
  }

/** The run loop for this LinkFollower thread.  This makes the
first call to the recursive method, FollowLinks.
@see FollowLinks
*/
public void run() {
  FollowLinks( stringURL );
  showOutput( "Check finished" );
  }

/** The recursive method that opens a stream from a URL, and
calls FindLinks with that stream as an arg.  FindLinks then
calls back to FollowLinks for each found link.  For each link,
add a line to the list box in the user interface describing
whether or not the link is valid.
@see URL
@see InputStream
*/
public void FollowLinks( String stringURL ) {
  String s;
  try {
    URL u = new URL(stringURL);
    Enumeration en = hash.elements();
    for( int i = 0; i < hash.size(); i++ ) {
              URL storedU = (URL)en.nextElement();
      if( u.sameFile(storedU) == true ) {
        s = new String( "already checked -> "+u );
        System.out.println( s );
```

```
            showOutput( s );
            return;
            }
        }
    hash.put( u.toString(), u );
    try {
        try {
            InputStream is = u.openStream();
            showOutput( "Link to URL OKAY -> "+u );
            FindLinks( u.toString(), is );
        }
        catch( FileNotFoundException e ) {
            showOutput( "Link to URL FILE NOT FOUND! -> "+u );
        }
    } catch( IOException e ) {
        showOutput( "Link to URL Error! -> "+u );
    }
    }
    catch( MalformedURLException e1 ) {
        showOutput( "Bad URL "+stringURL );
        }
    showOutput( "FollowLinks("+stringURL+") finished" );
}


/** Given an InputStream, grab each CRLF delimited line and
scan it for links to other URLs.  Calls FollowLinks for each
found URL.
@see InputStream
@see DataInputStream
@see FollowLinks
@see StringTokenizer
*/
void FindLinks( String url, InputStream is ) {
    int lineNo = 1;

    showOutput( "Checking file: "+url );

    // First get the base directory of this HTML doc
    int index = url.lastIndexOf( "/" );
    String baseDir = new String(url.substring( 0, index ));

    DataInputStream dis = new DataInputStream( is );
    while( true ) {
        try {
            if( c.bSkip == true ) {
                showOutput( "Interrupting "+url );
```

```
    c.bSkip = false;
    break;
    }
String line = dis.readLine();
if( line == null )
  break;
for( int i = 0; i < linkStrings.length; i++ ) {
  int startIndex = 0;
  while( true ) {
    int ret = line.indexOf(linkStrings[i],startIndex);
    if( ret == -1 )
      break;
    String subLine = new String( line.substring(ret));
    StringTokenizer st =
         new StringTokenizer(subLine,"<>");
    String element = (String)st.nextElement();
    st = new StringTokenizer( element, "=" );
    st.nextElement();
    st = new StringTokenizer( (String)st.nextElement());
    String ourLink =
         new String( (String )st.nextElement());
    int colon = ourLink.indexOf(":");
    int first = ourLink.indexOf("\"");
    int last = ourLink.lastIndexOf("\"");
    if( first != -1 && last != -1 && first != last ){
      ourLink =
           new String( ourLink.substring(first+1,last));
      }
    if( colon == -1 ) { // relative URL
      char ca[] = new char[1];
      ourLink.getChars( 0, 1, ca, 0);
      if( ca[0] == '#' ) {
        showOutput("skipping name relative link "+ourLink );
        startIndex = ret+1;
        continue;
        }
      else
        System.out.println("relative url baseDir = "+
                        baseDir+" ourLink = "+ourLink );
      ourLink = new String(baseDir+"/"+ourLink );
      }
    FollowLinks( ourLink );
    startIndex = ret+1;
    }
  }
lineNo++;
} catch( IOException e ) {break;}
```

```
    }
  showOutput( "Finished checking file: "+url );
  }

void showOutput( String s ) {
  c.lineList.addItem( s );
  System.out.println( s );
  }
 }
```

To make this applet check the links on a Web site, we enter the URL of a Web page in the text field, then press the start button to start it checking links. When the user presses the start button, the applet creates a **LinkFollower** object passing the **Applet** and **String** URL to the constructor. Once running (via **Thread.start**), the new **LinkFollower** object goes through the following steps:

1. Connect to the URL specified in the text field.

2. Download the document found there.

3. Scan the document **InputStream** for any of the strings that indicate a hyperlink.

4. If it finds one:

   Pull the target of the hyperlink from the text.

Figure 7.3
Link checker running against my home page.

Turn that hyperlink target into a URL.

Go back to step 2, using the new URL.

As you can see, this is clearly recursive. **FindLinks** calls **FollowLinks**, which calls back to **FindLinks**.

In parsing the HTML, we use the same basic technique we used in the word searches of Listing 7.1 and 7.3. Instead of the single search word, we look for any of three strings that indicate hyperlinks. These specific strings are defined in the **linkStrings** array, which we create in the **LinkFollower** constructor shown here:

```
linkStrings = new String[3];
  linkStrings[0] = new String("<A HREF=");
  linkStrings[1] = new String("<IMG SRC=");
  linkStrings[2] = new String("<applet code=");
```

This brute force parsing works surprisingly well, although it's a far cry from the kind of rigorous syntax checking a commercial product would need to do.

One of the biggest problems in writing an applet like this is a by-product of the structure of the Web itself—circular references. In the most basic case, if you have two pages that contain links to one another, an unsophisticated Web crawler will sit spinning in an endless loop.

Our checker takes a number of steps to try to prevent this. One is to store the URL of each site we visit, so that we never visit any page more than once. That's the purpose of the **HashTable** hash. In **FollowLinks**, we check each element of the **HashTable** against the URL we're about to check as follows:

```
URL u = new URL(stringURL);
    Enumeration en = hash.elements();
    for( int i = 0; i < hash.size(); i++ ) {
                URL storedU = (URL)en.nextElement();
      if( u.sameFile(storedU) == true ) {
        s = new String( "already checked -> "+u );
        System.out.println( s );
        showOutput( s );
        return;
        }
      }
    hash.put( u.toString(), u );
```

Now we could have just used **HashTable.contains** to see if this URL was already there. However, there are a number of different URLs that describe the same file. We try to cover this by calling **URL.sameFile**.

We also have to have a mechanism for breaking out of any unwanted branches in the Web site hyperlink structure. In my own Web site, I have links to both java.sun.com and microsoft.com. I certainly don't want to check the links to those Web sites along with my own. The simplest way to do that is to provide a skip button, which breaks you out of the lowest level of link-checking—the loop in **FindLinks** where lines are read and parsed.

The skip button is created in the **init** method, and as you would expect, clicking it causes an event that gets passed to **handleEvent**. When we detect a skip button press in **handleEvent**, we simply set the boolean, **bSkip**. The **LinkFollower** runs asynchronously in its own thread. When **bSkip** is set, the **LinkFollower** could be executing anywhere in the **run**, **FollowLinks**, or **FindLinks** methods, but more than likely it will be down in the **for** loop of **FindLinks**. Thus, we let **FindLinks** finish dealing with whatever line it's on, then check **bSkip** before starting the next line. If **bSkip** is set, we clear it and skip the rest of this document.

Using Sockets

Sockets are a form of interprocess communication that allows processes on different network hosts to communicate. They originated with Berkeley Unix and have spread to become the de facto standard for Internet communication. A form of sockets, Winsock, has also taken hold in the Windows world to the point that most Internet-capable Windows applications conform to some version of Winsock.

Sockets are actually an interface—a set of function calls that your application can call and be guaranteed a particular response. Each operating system that supports sockets implements them in its own way, but all present the same interface to applications that wish to use those sockets. Thus, socket libraries in both the System V and BSD versions of Unix provide a function called **gethostname**, though each implements it differently.

Socket libraries generally consist of about two dozen functions, but there are really only a few functions you need to understand to get going with sockets. Table 7.1 lists the key socket functions.

Table 7.1   Key Socket Functions

Function	Description
socket	Creates an endpoint, either client or server
connect	Connects this client to the server socket
bind	Binds the socket to a host name/port number
accept	Accepts connections on this server socket
listen	Listens for connections on this server socket
send	Sends some bytes
recv	Receives some bytes

Two connected sockets make a point-to-point communications channel. Each side of the conversation creates a socket (via **socket**). The server side **bind**s to a host name and port number, **listen**s for connections, and **accept**s them as they occur. The client side simply **connect**s to the host name and port number. When the **connect** returns, the two sides can then call **send** and **recv** to read and write the connection.

Sockets are at the heart of almost every instance of Internet communication. When, for instance, you point your Web browser at http://java.sun.com, the browser uses the socket interface to connect to a port on java.sun.com. Sockets are a simple, old, tried-and-true technology that make network programming fairly easy.

Socket Basics

There are two ends to each Java socket conversation: server and client. The server end is embodied in the **ServerSocket** class, while the client end is embodied in **Socket**. These two ends go through a specific set of steps to set up, conduct, and terminate a conversation, as shown here:

1. The server instantiates **ServerSocket** passing a local port number. This creates the socket and binds it to that local port number.

    ```
    ServerSocket ServerS = new ServerSocket( 1037 );
    ```

2. We accept connections to this server socket by calling **accept**.

    ```
    Socket AcceptedS = ServerS.accept();
    ```

3. The client instantiates **Socket**, passing a server name and port number. This creates a client end socket and connects it to the named port, on the named host. When this call returns, the two ends are connected.

    ```
    Socket ClientSocket = new Socket( "www.mymachine.com", 1037 );
    ```

4. **ServerSocket.accept** returns a **Socket**, which can now be used for I/O. Most applications will spawn a new thread to read and write this socket. The **ServerSocket** can continue to "accept" connections on the original socket.

```
byte b[] = new byte[100];
AcceptedS.getOutputStream().write( b );
```

From this point on, both server app and client applet can read and write the connected sockets. Of course, this is simplification of the steps C programs using the socket interface would go through. On the server side, Java's **ServerSocket** class compresses the socket creation, address binding, and listen calls into the constructor. On the client side, the **Socket** class compresses socket creation and connect into the constructor.

How does one side know when the conversation is over? Many protocols call for there to be a "goodbye," but depending on something like that won't get you very far. Lost connections are a fact of life. Fortunately, Java throws an **IOException** in almost any case where the network connection has been interrupted. You must catch and handle **IOException**s properly to write useable network communications code.

The Snitcher Applet

With those basic ideas well in hand, let's construct an application/applet combo that does some very simple socket communication. The purpose of this combination is to record the date, time, URL, and IP address of the user whenever someone accesses the HTML page in which this applet is embedded. This is one of the holy grails of Web publishers: to be able to know who is hitting their page and when. This applet, Snitcher, is unusual in that it has *no* user interface. The user never sees it.

The theory behind the system is simple enough. The server Java application (Snitch) is running all the time on the server accepting connections on port 1038. When a user loads the page with our applet in it, the applet starts up, gets the page URL, the host name, and IP address, and packages all that information in a message. Then it connects to the server socket and sends the message to the server, which stores it in a file from which it can be retrieved and analyzed. Listing 7.6 shows the Snitcher applet.

Listing 7.6   The Snitcher Applet

```java
package chap7;

import java.awt.Graphics;
import java.awt.*;
import java.applet.Applet;
import java.net.*;
import java.lang.*;
import java.io.*;
import java.util.*;

/** An applet that reports the host name and IP address of the
machine reading the HTML page back to the server from which
the HTML page was loaded.
@author John Rodley
@version 1.0 12/1/11996
*/
public class ch7_fig6 extends Applet {
boolean bAlreadyRan = false;
int port = 1038;

/** Resize the applet to almost nothing, and change the port
number that the applet will connect to, if the port parameter
is set in the applet tag.
*/
public void init() {
  String sPort = getParameter( "port" );
  if( sPort != null ) {
    Integer iPort = new Integer( sPort );
    port = iPort.intValue();
    }
  resize( 10, 10 );
  }

/** Check if the snitcher has already informed on this user and only
contact the server if we haven't run yet.  Tries to guarantee that
we only get one report for each time the page is loaded.
*/
public void start() {
  if( bAlreadyRan == false ) {
    snitch();
    bAlreadyRan = true;
    }
  }
```

```
/** Report the host name and IP address of this machine to the
server.
@see InetAddress
@see URL
@see PrintStream
@see Socket
@see Snitch
*/
void snitch() {
  // Get the local host name and IP address
  String sIpaddr = "Unknown ipaddr";
  try {
    InetAddress in = InetAddress.getLocalHost();
    sIpaddr = in.toString();
  } catch( UnknownHostException e )
    {System.out.println("exception "+e );}

  // Now get the URL of the HTML page we're running
  URL u = getDocumentBase();
  String sHost = new String( u.getHost());
  try {
    String snitchInfo = new String( u+" :::: "+sIpaddr);
    System.out.println( "reporting snitchinfo "+snitchInfo );
    Socket s = new Socket( sHost, port );
    PrintStream p = new PrintStream( s.getOutputStream());
    p.println( snitchInfo );
    s.close();
  } catch( IOException e )
    {System.out.println( "ioexception "+e ); }
  }
}
```

This applet is deceptively simple. Let's look at it in detail.

The applet needs to create a **Socket** that is connected to a **ServerSocket**. This means that we need to know the name of the server host and the port number it's accepting connections on. The port number is easy. We set that via a parameter in the **<applet>** HTML tag. The host name is a little trickier. As we've stated before (and will again), a security feature of some browsers requires that the server application run on the same host that the client applet is loaded from. This represents the "least-common-denominator" in network communication. Thus, we can get the name of the host simply by getting the URL of the HTML page, and then pulling the host name from that, as shown here:

```
// Now get the URL of the HTML page we're running
  URL u = getDocumentBase();
  String sHost = new String( u.getHost());
```

getDocumentBase, an **Applet** method, returns the URL of the HTML document, and **URL.getHost** gives the **String** version of the host to which the URL points.

Using InetAddress

Now that we're all set up to communicate with the server, we need to get the IP address and host name of the machine the browser (and the Snitcher applet) is running on so that we can create the message we'll actually send to the server. To do that, we need to use the **InetAddress** class. **InetAddress** is the interface between Java and the network name service. You can use it to turn a host name into an IP address or vice versa. The Snitcher applet uses the static method **InetAddress.getLocalHost** to get a complete description of the machine that the applet is running on. Notice that all we need to do to get the host name/IP address is call **InetAddress.toString**. This is a recurring theme in Java. It is also what happens if you append a non-**String** object to a **String** via the + operator as in:

```
InetAddress in = InetAddress.getLocalHost();
String s = "blah blah blah"+in;
```

Java calls **in.toString** in order to append it to the first string. Since we know where to connect, and what we want to say, the network communication boils down to four lines in the snitch method:

```
. Socket s = new Socket( sHost, port );
    PrintStream p = new PrintStream( s.getOutputStream());
    p.println( snitchInfo );
    s.close();
```

As in other I/O examples, we take a bare **OutputStream** returned by **Socket.getOutputStream**, turn it into a more capable Stream—in this case, a **PrintStream** just like **System.out**—and use that new Stream to write a **String** to the **Socket**.

The Snitch Application

That covers the client Snitcher applet, but we still need a server Snitch application for the Snitcher applet to talk to. Listing 7.7 shows the server Snitch application.

Listing 7.7 Standalone Server Snitch Application

```java
package chap7;

import java.awt.*;
import java.lang.*;
import java.util.*;
import java.net.*;
import java.io.*;


/** A standalone socket connection server that simply writes
everything it receives over the socket connection to a
day file. When the date changes, the server opens a new file.
The intent is that applets will connect, report the HTML
page's URL, date/time and the client's ip host name and IP
address allowing the Web page owner to know who hits his or her
page and when.

@version 1.0
@author John Rodley
@see ch7_fig4
*/

public class Snitch extends Thread {
public static ServerFrame f;
static public boolean bRun = true;
static Panel p;
MenuBar m;
SrvSocket s;
Acceptor acceptor;
public static Snitch currentSnitch;
String filename = "Report.web";
PrintStream ps;

/** The main function for this standalone application.
Corresponds directly to the main function in a C application.
@param  argv The arguments to this application.  Currently
takes none.
*/
public static void main(String argv[] ) {
  Snitch as = new Snitch();
  Properties p = System.getProperties();
```

```
  try {
  p.load(
   new FileInputStream("/users/default/.hotjava/properties"));
  } catch( IOException e ) {System.out.println("except "+e ); }
  System.out.println( "system properties "+p );

    String topDirectory = System.getProperty( "acl.read" );
    if( topDirectory == null ) {
      System.out.println( "can't read this machine" );
      }
    else
      System.out.println( "got "+topDirectory+" for acl.read");
  as.start();
  }

/** Constructor.  Creates a unique file via switchFiles for
logging, an acceptor thread for accepting connections on the
port, and a main window for user interaction.  Currently just
runs, and exits on command.
@see switchFiles
@see ServerFrame
@see Acceptor
@see awt.Frame
@see awt.MenuBar
@see awt.Panel
@see awt.Layout
@see awt.Menu
@see awt.MenuItem
*/
public Snitch() {
  switchFiles();
  currentSnitch = this;
  f = new ServerFrame();
  f.resize(300, 300);
  f.show();
  p = new Panel();
  p.reshape( 0, 0, 300, 300 );
  p.setLayout( new FlowLayout());
  f.add( p );
  m = new MenuBar();
  f.setMenuBar( m );
  Menu m1 = new Menu("File");
  m.add(m1);
  MenuItem m2 = new MenuItem( "Exit" );
  m1.add( m2 );
  acceptor = new Acceptor( this );
  acceptor.start();
```

```
  }

/** Reports a line of text received over the socket connection
to the unique log file created by switchFiles. Synchronized
so that entire entries are written as one lump.
@see Date
@see PrintStream
@see OutputStream
*/
public synchronized void Report( String msg ) {
  if( ps == null )
    return;
  Date d = new Date();
  ps.println( new String(d+" :::: "+msg) );
  }

/** Create a log file with a unique name formatted as:
  "M"  The letter M
  mm   One or two digit month 1-12
  "D"  The letter D
  dd   One or two digit day of month
  "Y"  The letter Y
  yy   One or two digit year offset from 1900
  ".w"  Dot and letter w
  hh   One or two digit hour
  mm   One or two digit minute
This gives us a file that's guaranteed to be unique both to
the day, and within the day so that the server can be stopped
and restarted within a day.
@see Date
@see File
@see FileOutputStream
@see PrintStream
*/
public void switchFiles() {
  Date d = new Date();

  filename = new String( "M"+(d.getMonth()+1)+"D"+d.getDate()+
      "Y"+d.getYear()+".w"+d.getHours()+""+d.getMinutes() );
  try {
    File fi = new File( filename );
    ps = new PrintStream( new FileOutputStream(fi) );
  } catch( IOException e )
    { System.out.println( "ioexception e "+e );}

  }
```

```
/** The run loop for the snitcher thread.  Wakes up once
per second and checks the date to see if we should switch log
files. This is far too often for the date checking, but
message processing is on hold while we sleep.  Thus, if we
change the sleep time to 1 minute, when the user closes
Snitch, it sits for a whole minute before closing the app --
unacceptable.
@see switchFiles
@see Date
@see Acceptor
*/
public void run() {
  boolean bLast = false;
  Date d = new Date();
  int lastday;
  int today;
  today = d.getDay();
  lastday = today;
  f.setTitle( "Snitch" );
  while( bRun == true ) {
    d = new Date();
    today = d.getDay();
    if( today != lastday )
      switchFiles();
    lastday = today;
    // Wake up once per minute and check the time
    try {Thread.sleep( 1000 );} catch( Exception e ) { }
    }
  acceptor.stop();
  System.out.println( "out of run loop" );
  f.dispose();
  System.exit(0);
  }
}

/** The frame window for this standalone application.  Exists
only to provide a way to kill the server.  Handles kill via
the system menu and the file menu.
@author John Rodley
@version 1.0
*/
class ServerFrame extends Frame {

/** Handle close from the system menu.
*/
```

```java
    public synchronized boolean handleEvent(Event evt) {
  if( evt.id == Event.MOUSE_UP ) {
    return( true );
    }
  else
    {
    if( evt.target instanceof Frame ) {
      if( evt.id == Event.WINDOW_DESTROY ) {
        Snitch.currentSnitch.bRun = false;
        System.out.println( "window destroy "+evt );
        return( true );
        }
      else
        return super.handleEvent(evt);
      }
    else
      return super.handleEvent(evt);
    }
  }

/** Handle exit from the file menu.
*/
public boolean action( Event evt, Object o ) {
  if( evt.target instanceof MenuItem )
    {
    if( evt.arg.toString().compareTo( "Exit" ) == 0 )
      {
      Snitch.currentSnitch.bRun = false;
      System.out.println( "action event "+evt );
      }
    else
      {
      }
    }
  return( true );
  }
}


/** Handle reading and closing a socket which has already been
accepted.
@see Report
@see Thread
@see AcceptedSocket
@author John Rodley
@version 1.0
*/
class SocketHandler extends Thread {
```

```
  public AcceptedSocket as;
  FileOutputStream outputFile;
  boolean bDispatcher = false;
  boolean bContinue = true;
/** Simply saves the Socket that's passed as an argument.
@arg  Socket  This socket is saved and used within the run method to
read from.
@see AcceptedSocket
@see Socket
*/
  public SocketHandler( Socket so ) {
   as = new AcceptedSocket( so );
  }


/** The run loop for this thread.  Does a single blocking read
from the Socket that was supplied to the constructor for a
maximum of 1024 bytes and then closes the socket and exits the
thread.  Passes whatever is read to Report for logging in the
day file.  The small, single read is done for security
purposes.  A malicious app could still flood the log, but it
would have to re-connect every time—an expensive and
dangerous proposition.
@see Report
*/
  public void run() {
    int ret;
    byte buffer[] = new byte[1024];

    if(( ret = as.readLine( buffer )) != 0 )
      {
      Snitch.currentSnitch.Report( new String(buffer,0,0,ret ));
      System.out.println( "read "+ new String(buffer,0,0,ret));
      }
    as.close();
    }

}


/** A thread that simply sits in a loop accepting connections
on the port and spawning other threads to read the accepted
socket.
@author John Rodley
@version 1.0
@see SrvSocket
@see SocketHandler
@see Snitch
*/
class Acceptor extends Thread {
```

```
   Snitch as;
   SrvSocket s;
/** Constructor - daemonize this thread and save the Snitch
for later use.
*/
   public Acceptor( Snitch a ) {
     setDaemon( true );
     as = a;
     }


/** The run loop for this thread.  Sits in a loop accepting
connections.  Whenever a client connects, we create a
SocketHandler thread using that accepted Socket and start the
thread up.  Runs until "stopped" from above.
@see Socket
@see SrvSocket
@see SocketHandler
*/
   public void run() {
     // set up the server socket
     s = new SrvSocket( 1038 );
     while( true ) {
       Socket newS = s.Accept();
       SocketHandler a = new SocketHandler( newS );
       a.start();
       }
     }
}



/** Class representing a server socket bound to a local port.
@see ServerSocket
@version 1.0 August 1, 1995
@author John Rodley
*/
class SrvSocket {
ServerSocket s;
Socket newS;

/** Constructor creates a ServerSocket bound to a local port.
@arg  port  The integer local port number that this socket will
be bound to.
@see ServerSocket
*/
public SrvSocket( int port ) {
  s = null;
  while( s == null ) {
    System.out.println( "Accepting on host port:"+port );
```

```
    try {
      s = new ServerSocket( port );
      } catch( IOException e )
        { System.out.println( "exception "+e ); }
    }
  }

/** Accept a connection on this port and return the new
socket.  Swallow any exceptions.
@see Socket
@see Socket.accept
*/
public Socket Accept() {
  try {
    newS = s.accept();
    System.out.println( "Accepted on host port" );
    } catch( IOException e )
      { System.out.println( "exception "+e ); }
  return( newS );
  }
}

/** A socket that has been accepted, meaning that there is a
client now attached to it.
@see InputStream
@see OutputStream
@author John Rodley
@version 1.0
*/
class AcceptedSocket {
public InputStream inputStream;
public OutputStream outputStream;
public DataInputStream dis;
Socket s;

/** Constructor - creates input and output streams that read
and write can use.
@arg  so  The accepted Socket, saved for further use.
@see InputStream
@see OutputStream
*/
public AcceptedSocket( Socket so ) {
  s = so;
  try {
    inputStream = s.getInputStream();
    outputStream = s.getOutputStream();
    } catch( IOException e )
      { System.out.println( "exception "+e); }
```

```
    }

/** Read a line terminated by one of the usual suspects - \r
and/or \n.  Accomplish this by making a DataInputStream from
our base InputStream.
@see DataInputStream
*/
public int readLine( byte buffer[] ) {
  int ret = -1;
  String s = new String("");

  try {
    dis = new DataInputStream(inputStream);
    s = dis.readLine();
    s.getBytes( 0, s.length(), buffer, 0 );
    } catch( IOException e )
     { System.out.println("exception "+e); return( -1 );}
  return( s.length());
  }

/** Read an array of bytes from the socket.
@return The number of bytes read.
*/
public int read(byte buffer[], int length) {
  try {
    return( inputStream.read(buffer));
    } catch( IOException e )
     { System.out.println("exception "+e); return( -1 ); }
  }

/** Write an array of bytes to the socket. */
public void write(byte buffer[], int length) {
  try {
    outputStream.write(buffer, 0, length);
    } catch( IOException e )
     { System.out.println( "exception "+e); }
  }

/** Close the socket. */
public void close() {
  try {
    s.close();
    } catch( IOException e )
     { System.out.println( "exception "+e); }
  }
}
```

The starting point for any standalone application is the **main** method. Snitch's **main** method accomplishes the following tasks:

- Loads a set of "properties" into the **System**'s properties list
- Gets the path of the directory in which the day file will be created by query ing the property "*acl.read*"
- Instantiates the **Snitch** class
- Starts the new **Snitch** instance by calling **Thread.start**

A close look at **Snitch.java** reveals a basic skeleton that all server applications follow. The top level thread does almost nothing except create a **Frame** object (window) for accepting user input, and create another thread to accept connections to a **ServerSocket**. This is what happens in the Snitch constructor. We create our frame window and populate it with child windows, in this case a menu and some menu items. We also create an acceptor thread, and set it running.

The **Acceptor** class merely creates a **ServerSocket** on the local host bound to port number 1038. Each time a client applet connects to this server socket, the acceptor thread creates a new thread to read the port and deal with whatever the client sends us, in this case, writing a line of text to the day file.

Like the **File** class, the **Socket** class provides two methods, **getInputStream** and **getOutputStream**, that provide a base object through which we can do whatever style of I/O we wish. The AgentServer, for the most part, does non-delimited, byte-level I/O using the bare **InputStream**. Snitch, on the other hand, receives CRLF-delimited lines of text from its client applets. Thus, it needs to create a **DataInputStream** from the **Socket**'s bare **InputStream**, and use **DataInputStream.readLine** rather than **InputStream.read**. You will find that almost all I/O operates this way. You take a bare **InputStream** or **OutputStream**, then create a more sophisticated, higher-level stream, like **DataInputStream**, using that bare stream.

The other big difference between Snitch and more complicated server applications like AgentServer is that we do only a single **readLine** before closing the socket; most servers keep reading the socket until the client applet disconnects.

File I/O

Something in the server Snitch application that we haven't seen before is file I/O via the **File** class. File I/O is not useful to applets because the browser **SecurityManagers** generally do not allow applets to use it. Period. When you're writing a Java standalone application like Snitch, on the other hand, you're free to do whatever I/O you might want. Snitch's use of file I/O is limited to:

- Creating a new day file
- Writing whatever lines come over the **Socket** into that day file

Creating the new day file is embodied in the **switchFiles** method.

```
public void switchFiles() {
  Date d = new Date();

  filename = new String( "M"+(d.getMonth()+1)+"D"+d.getDate()+
      "Y"+d.getYear()+".w"+d.getHours()+""+d.getMinutes() );
  try {
    File fi = new File( filename );
    ps = new PrintStream( new FileOutputStream(fi) );
  } catch( IOException e )
    { System.out.println( "ioexception e "+e );}


}
```

The point of **switchFiles** is to create a file that will be unique and have a name that will indicate what date it is associated with. In normal operation, the system would create one day file for each day. Since the day file name also contains an hour/minute indicator, you can stop and restart the server within a day and end up with two day files for one day. As with all I/O, we create the basic I/O object, get a base Stream object (in this case, a **FileOutputStream**) and create a higher-level Stream (in this case, a **PrintStream**) against which to do our actual I/O.

When does **switchFiles** get called? Well, it gets called once at startup. What happens in normal running then is that the main loop of Snitch simply sleeps for a second, then wakes up and checks the time. If we've rolled past midnight, the main loop calls **switchFiles** to create a new day file.

To Block or Not to Block

One of the key characteristics of any I/O operation is whether or not it blocks. If you call **InputStream.readLine**, no matter how many bytes it does read, it will not return until it reads a line terminator. It "blocks" until the line terminator is read. If **readLine** were non-blocking, it would return immediately whether or not it had read a line terminator.

Many coders, especially those who grew up in the bad old days of single threading, prefer to write their communication code as non-blocking. In single-threaded systems, there are very good reasons for this, one being that code that blocks often fails to unblock.

That reasoning doesn't hold up in Java. Any thread that has blocked should be able to be unblocked by calling **Thread.stop** (throwing a **ThreadDeath** at it). Java also doesn't support many of the system calls (**select** and **available**, to name two) that Unix coders used to rely on to write non-blocking I/O.

Almost all Java I/O calls block, including socket connect, stream read, and stream write. Some allow the operation to time out, but for the most part, you are literally required to thread and block.

Writing AgentServer

We now have everything we need to write the agent server—a standalone application for loading and running agents that are sent to it over the Net. Listing 7.8 shows the final AgentServer code. This is a long listing, but for the most part it's a combination of things we've already seen.

Listing 7.8   The AgentServer Application

```
package agent.Server;

import java.awt.*;
import java.lang.*;
import agent.util.*;
import agent.Agent.*;
import agent.Server.*;
import java.util.*;
import java.net.*;
import java.io.*;

/** A standalone application for loading and running Agents
that are sent to it over the Net.
@author John Rodley
@version 1.0 12/1/1995
*/
public class AgentServer extends Thread {
```

```
public static ServerFrame f;
static public boolean bRun = true;
public static AgentServer currentAgentServer;
static Panel p;
MenuBar m;
SrvSocket s;
Acceptor acceptor;

Vector runningAgents;
Vector dispatchedAgents;

public static Vector serverList = new Vector( 1 );

/** The main loop for this standalone application.  Creates one
AgentServer, then sets it running via Thread.start.
@see Thread
*/
public static void main(String argv[] ) {
  AgentServer as = new AgentServer();
  as.start();
  }

/** Constructor, builds the list of AgentServers, builds all
the screen elements, including menu and menu items. For now,
this app only handles exit from the menu.  Instantiates an
acceptor thread that listens to the AgentServer port where
agents to be loaded will come in.
@see Frame
@see Panel
@see MenuBar
@see MenuItem
@see Acceptor
*/
public AgentServer() {
  LoadServerList();
  runningAgents = new Vector(1);
  dispatchedAgents = new Vector(1);
  System.out.println( "AgentServer constructor" );
  currentAgentServer = this;
  f = new ServerFrame();
  f.resize(300, 300);
  f.show();
  p = new Panel();
  p.reshape( 0, 0, 300, 300 );
  p.setLayout( new FlowLayout());
  f.add( p );
  m = new MenuBar();
```

```
   f.setMenuBar( m );
   Menu m1 = new Menu("File");
   m.add(m1);
   MenuItem m2 = new MenuItem( "Load test" );
   m1.add( m2 );
   m2 = new MenuItem( "Exit" );
   m1.add( m2 );
   acceptor = new Acceptor( this );
   acceptor.start();
   }


/** Load the list of agent servers we know about from the file
servers.lst in the directory specified by acl.read in the
properties file.
*/
void LoadServerList() {
  Properties p = System.getProperties();

  try {
  p.load(
   new FileInputStream("/users/default/.hotjava/properties"));
  } catch( IOException e ) {System.out.println("except "+e ); }
  System.out.println( "system properties "+p );

    String topDirectory = System.getProperty( "acl.read" );
    if( topDirectory == null ) {
      System.out.println( "can't read this machine" );
      }
    else
      System.out.println( "got "+topDirectory+" for acl.read");

  try {
    File f = new File( topDirectory+"/servers.lst" );
    FileInputStream fis = new FileInputStream( f );
    DataInputStream dis = new DataInputStream( fis );
    while( true ) {
      try {
        String s = dis.readLine();
        StringTokenizer st;
        // All lines or of the form "<servername>:<port>"
        st = new StringTokenizer( s, ":" );
  try {
          String server = (String)st.nextElement();
          Integer IPort=new Integer((String)st.nextElement());
          System.out.println( "adding "+server+":"+IPort );
          serverList.addElement(
```

```
                  new ServerEntry( server, IPort.intValue()));
            } catch( NoSuchElementException e ) { break; }
         } catch( IOException e ) { break; }
      }
   } catch( IOException e )
      { System.out.println( "Bad serverlist file" );
         return; }
}


/** Test the loading of classes at this site by allowing the
user to choose a class file to load, then creating/parsing a
LoadMessage from that class file. DEBUGGING method.
@see LoadMessage
@see FileDialog
*/
public void LoadTest() {
   System.out.println( "Load test" );

// The FileDialog doesn't work in W95 or NT
   FileDialog fd = new FileDialog(f, "LoadTest");
   fd.setDirectory( "/agent/classes/beta/agent" );
   fd.show();
   if( fd.getFile() != null ) {
      System.out.println( "Load test - "+fd.getFile() );
      try {
         System.out.println( "button ok hit" );
         LoadMessage lm = new LoadMessage();
         lm.LoadClassFromFile( fd.getFile() );
         byte[] b = lm.getMessageBytes();
//       SocketHandler.ClientProcess( b, b.length );
      } catch( Exception e )
         { System.out.println( "exception "+e ); }
   }
   else
      System.out.println( "getFile == null" );
   }


/** Notify the AgentLauncher, via the dispatching agent server
that the agent has finished running and has the specified
results to report.
@param rm A results message containing the results page URL
@see ResultsMessage
*/
public void notifyResults( ResultMessage rm ) {
   for( int i = 0; i < dispatchedAgents.size(); i++ ) {
      DispatchedAgent da =
         (DispatchedAgent)dispatchedAgents.elementAt(i);
```

```java
    if( da.id.compareTo(rm.sid) == 0 ) {
      try {
        da.sh.as.outputStream.write(rm.getMessageBytes());
        return;
      } catch( IOException e )
        {System.out.println("exception "+e ); }
      break;
      }
    }
  System.out.println( "No launcher to notify "+rm.sid );
  }

/** Notify the AgentLauncher, via the dispatching agent server
that the agent has started running.
@param sm A StartMessage
@see StartMessage
*/
public void notifyStart( StartMessage sm ) {
  for( int i = 0; i < dispatchedAgents.size(); i++ ) {
    DispatchedAgent da =
      (DispatchedAgent)dispatchedAgents.elementAt(i);
    if( da.id.compareTo(sm.sid) == 0 ) {
      try {
        da.sh.as.outputStream.write(sm.getMessageBytes());
        return;
      } catch( IOException e )
        {System.out.println("exception "+e ); }
      break;
      }
    }
  System.out.println( "No launcher to notify "+sm.sid );
  }

/** Add an Agent to the list, using the specified ID and
SocketHandler.
@see SocketHandler
*/
public void addDispatchedAgent( String id, SocketHandler sh ) {
  dispatchedAgents.addElement( new DispatchedAgent( id, sh ));
  }

/** Delete an agent from the list of dispatched agents
because it's ended.
@param id The String id of the terminating Agent.
*/
public void deleteDispatchedAgent( String id ) {
  for( int i = 0; i < dispatchedAgents.size(); i++ ) {
```

```
      DispatchedAgent da =
        (DispatchedAgent)dispatchedAgents.elementAt(i);
    if( da.id.compareTo(id) == 0 ) {
      da.sh.stop();
      dispatchedAgents.removeElementAt(i);
      break;
      }
    }
  }

/** Delete an agent from the list of dispatched agents
because of a socket exception.
@param sh The SocketHandler that generated the exception.
*/
public void deleteDispatchedAgent( SocketHandler sh ) {
  for( int i = 0; i < dispatchedAgents.size(); i++ ) {
    DispatchedAgent da =
      (DispatchedAgent)dispatchedAgents.elementAt(i);
    if( da.sh == sh ) {
      da.sh.stop();
      dispatchedAgents.removeElementAt(i);
      break;
      }
    }
  }

/** Add an agent to the list of agents running on this machine.
@param id The String ID of this running agent.
*/
public void addRunningAgent( String id ) {
  System.out.println( "addAgent ("+runningAgents.size()+")");
  runningAgents.addElement(new RunningAgent( id ));
  p.layout();
  f.layout();
  f.show();
  }

/** Delete an agent from the list of running agents.  The
Agent thread MUST BE STOPPED already when you get here.
@param id The String id of the running agent.
*/
public void deleteRunningAgent( String id ) {
  System.out.println("deleteAgent ("+runningAgents.size()+")");
  for( int i = 0; i < runningAgents.size(); i++ )
    {
    RunningAgent ra =
      (RunningAgent )runningAgents.elementAt(i);
```

```
        if( ra.id.compareTo(id) == 0 )
          {
          runningAgents.removeElementAt(i);
          p.show();
          p.layout();
          System.out.println( "deleting runningAgent at "+i );
          break;
          }
        }
      System.out.println( "end deleteAgent ("+
          runningAgents.size()+")");
      }


/** The main loop for the AgentServer. Sits in a loop,
sleeping for 1 second, then waking up to check whether the user
interface has been terminated.
*/
public void run() {
  while( bRun == true ) {
    try {
    f.setTitle( "AgentServer: "+
      runningAgents.size()+" agents running" );
    Thread.sleep( 1000 );
      } catch( Exception e ) { }
    }
  System.out.println( "out of run loop" );
  f.dispose();
  System.exit(0);
  }
}



/** The main window functionality - window creation/refresh
handling, application exit handling ...
@see Frame
*/
class ServerFrame extends Frame {

/** Handle any events that might come up. Right now, only
deals with WINDOW_DESTROY, which is what happens when the user
tries to close the application via the system menu.
*/
 public synchronized boolean handleEvent(Event evt) {
  if( evt.id == Event.MOUSE_UP ) {
    return( true );
    }
  else
```

```
    {
    if( evt.target instanceof Frame ) {
      if( evt.id == Event.WINDOW_DESTROY ) {
        AgentServer.currentAgentServer.bRun = false;
        System.out.println( "window destroy "+evt );
        return( true );
        }
      else
        return super.handleEvent(evt);
      }
    else
      return super.handleEvent(evt);
    }
  }


/** Handle any menu item picks. Right now, only has two, Exit
and Load Test.  Exit sets the agentServers bRun flag to false,
causing the AgentServer.run to fall out of the endless while
loop.
@see AgentServer
*/
public boolean action( Event evt, Object o ) {
  if( evt.target instanceof MenuItem )
    {
    if( evt.arg.toString().compareTo( "Exit" ) == 0 )
      {
      AgentServer.currentAgentServer.bRun = false;
      System.out.println( "action event "+evt );
      }
    else
      {
      if(evt.arg.toString().compareTo( "Load test" ) == 0 )
        {
        AgentServer.currentAgentServer.LoadTest();
        System.out.println( "action event "+evt );
        }
      }
    }
  return( true );
  }


  }


/** A class that encapsulates the AgentContext interface
routines that the AgentServer needs to implement.
@see AgentContext
*/
```

```
class SepContext implements AgentContext {
  FileOutputStream outputFile;
  PrintStream printStream;
  DataOutputStream outputData;
  String dispatchingHost;
  int port;
  String AgentID;
  boolean bDispatched = false;
  boolean bReportedResults = false;

/** Creates an interface to the AgentServer that knows the
Agent's ID and dispatching host.
*/
  public SepContext( String id, String dHost, int dport ) {
    AgentID = new String( id );
    dispatchingHost = new String( dHost );
    port = dport;
    }

/** Send a lump of bytes to the dispatching host for this
Agent.
@param msg A byte array, usually obtained via
Message.getBytes().
@see Message
@see Socket
*/
public void sendMessage( byte msg[] ) {
  try {
  Socket s = new Socket( dispatchingHost, port );
  s.getOutputStream().write( msg );
  } catch( IOException e ) {System.out.println("except "+e ); }
  }

/*** The AgentContext Interface Implementation ***********/

/** Report this agent starting work on this AgentServer.
Implementation of AgentContext interface method.
*/
public void reportStart( String dummy ) {
  String fname =
    new String( System.getProperty("acl.write")+"test.html" );
  try {
    outputFile = new FileOutputStream( fname );
    printStream = new PrintStream(outputFile);
    outputData = new DataOutputStream( outputFile );
    try {
      InetAddress in = InetAddress.getLocalHost();
```

```
      String server = new String(in.getHost name());
      StartMessage sm = new StartMessage(AgentID, server);
      sm.createMessage();
      sendMessage( sm.getMessageBytes() );
   } catch( UnknownHostException e )
     {System.out.println("UNK ex"+e);}
 } catch( IOException e )
   {System.out.println("exception "+e);return;}

 return;
 }


/** Report this Agent finishing work on this AgentServer.
Implementation of AgentContext method.
@param url The string url of the results file.  If null, then
there were no results generated.
@param price The price that will be charged to view the results
file.
@param comment Whatever comment the Agent wants to make about
this particular run.
*/
public void reportFinish( String dummy, String url, int price,
          String comment ){
  try {
    outputFile.close();
  } catch( IOException e ) {System.out.println("Except "+e ); }
  outputFile = null;
  outputData = null;
  try {
    InetAddress in = InetAddress.getLocalHost();
    String server = new String(in.getHost name());
    ResultMessage rm = new ResultMessage(AgentID, url, price,
        comment, server);
    rm.createMessage();
    sendMessage( rm.getMessageBytes() );
  } catch( UnknownHostException e )
    {System.out.println("UNK ex"+e);}
  bReportedResults = true;
  if( bDispatched == true )
    AgentServer.currentAgentServer.deleteRunningAgent(AgentID);
  return;
  }


/** Return the string URL of the results file that this Agent
has been using. This URL will eventually be passed to
reportFinish.
@param AgentID The string id of this agent.
```

```
*/
public String getResultsURL( String AgentID ) {
  try {
    InetAddress in = InetAddress.getLocalHost();
    StringTokenizer st = new StringTokenizer(
                                    in.toString(), "/");
    st.nextElement();
    String sipaddr = (String)st.nextElement();
    String furl = new String( "http://"+sipaddr+
       System.getProperty("acl.write")+"test.html" );
    return( furl );
    } catch( UnknownHostException e ) { return( null ); }
  }

/** Write a string to the results file.
@param resultString The string to write to the output file.
Should be valid HTML.
@return True if success, false otherwise.
*/
public boolean writeOutput( String resultString ) {
  if( outputFile == null || outputData == null )
    return( false );
  printStream.println( resultString );
  return( true );
  }

/** Write a byte array to the results file.
@param resultBytes The bytes to write, should be valid HTML.
@return true if success, false otherwise.
*/
public boolean writeOutput( byte resultBytes[] ) {
  if( outputFile == null || outputData == null )
    return( false );
  try {
    outputData.write( resultBytes, 0, resultBytes.length);
    return( true );
  } catch( IOException e ) {return( false ); }
  }

/** Dispatch this agent to all the servers on this AgentServer's
list. If this Agent has already reported results, we terminate
it and forget about it.
@return false
*/
public boolean dispatch() {
  bDispatched = true;
  if( bReportedResults == true )
```

```
      AgentServer.currentAgentServer.deleteRunningAgent( AgentID );
    return( false );
    }
    }


/** A thread that handles the connection to a client's socket.
This is the thread that actually reads the socket and processes
incoming messages.
*/
class SocketHandler extends Thread {
  public Label label;
  public AcceptedSocket as;
  FileOutputStream outputFile;
  boolean bDispatcher = false;

/** Constructor takes a socket to which a client has already
connected.
@param so A socket that is already connected and ready for
read/write.
*/
  public SocketHandler( Socket so ) {
    as = new AcceptedSocket( so );
    label = new Label( "This is the label" );
    }

/** The main run loop for the socket handler, reads the socket
until the client disconnects.
*/
  public void run() {
    byte buffer[] = new byte[8192];
    boolean bContinue = true;
    while( bContinue == true ) {
      int ret;
      if(( ret = as.read( buffer, buffer.length )) != 0 )
        {
        if( ret < 0 )
          {
          if( bDispatcher )
            AgentServer.currentAgentServer.deleteDispatchedAgent(this);
          System.out.println( "connection lost");
          break;
          }
        bContinue = ClientProcess( buffer, ret );
        }
      }
    as.close();
    }
```

```
/** Send a message to all the agent servers on the list. Used
by dispatch, which creates a LoadMessage, then passes that
message's byte array here.
@param msg The lump of bytes to send to everyone.
*/
public static void SendToAll( byte msg[] ) {
  Vector v = AgentServer.currentAgentServer.serverList;
  for( int i = 0; i < v.size(); i++ ) {
    ServerEntry s = (ServerEntry )v.elementAt( i );
    s.send( msg );
    }

  System.out.println( "sending message to all" );
  }


/** Parse and process a message from the client. Follows the
basic system of: read 4 bytes and figure out the message type,
instantiate a message class appropriate to the type, then tell
that new instance to parse the lump. Deal with the parsed
message by looking at public members of the new class and
acting appropriately.
@param b An array of bytes read over the socket.
@param numbytes The number of read-bytes in b.

*/
public boolean ClientProcess( byte b[], int numbytes ) {

String command;
int currentOffset = 0;
String s;
int messageStart;
boolean bret = false;

while( currentOffset != numbytes ) {
  messageStart = currentOffset;
  System.out.println( "currentOffset "+currentOffset+
      " numbytes "+numbytes );
  // Every message starts with 4 bytes of command
  command = new String( b, 0, currentOffset, 4 );
  currentOffset += LoadMessage.PREFIX_SIZE;

  // Followed by 10 bytes ASCII length—length of the whole message
  // including command
  String sLength = new String( b, 0, currentOffset, 10 );
  currentOffset += LoadMessage.LOADLEN_SIZE;
  System.out.println( "got "+command+" of length "+sLength );
```

```
if( command.compareTo( LoadMessage.LOAD_PREFIX ) == 0 ) {
  LoadMessage lm = new LoadMessage();
  Object o = lm.parse( b, currentOffset );
  if( o instanceof Agent ) {
    Agent a = (Agent)o;
    AgentServer.currentAgentServer.addRunningAgent(lm.sid);
    a.setAgentContext( new SepContext( lm.sid,
      lm.dispatching_server_name,
        lm.dispatching_server_port ));
    a.setArguments( lm.vargs );
    a.start();
    }
  }
else
  {
  if( command.compareTo( KillMessage.KILL_PREFIX ) == 0 ) {
    KillMessage km = new KillMessage( "" );
    String id = km.parse( b, currentOffset );
    System.out.println( "got kill message for agent "+id );
    AgentServer.currentAgentServer.deleteRunningAgent( id );
    AgentServer.currentAgentServer.deleteDispatchedAgent(id);
    }
  else {
    if(command.compareTo(DispatchMessage.DISPATCH_PREFIX)==0)
      {
      bDispatcher = true;
      DispatchMessage dm = new DispatchMessage("","", null);
      if( dm.parse( b, currentOffset ) == true ){
        System.out.println("got good dispatch message");
        AgentServer.currentAgentServer.addDispatchedAgent(
                dm.id, this);
        try {
          InetAddress in = InetAddress.getLocalHost();
          StringTokenizer st = new StringTokenizer(
                                    in.toString(), "/");
          st.nextElement();
          String sipaddr = (String)st.nextElement();
          LoadMessage lm = new LoadMessage( dm.name,
            dm.id,dm.sig,dm.args,sipaddr,1037 );
          byte msg[] = lm.getMessageBytes();
          SendToAll( msg );
          bret = true;
          } catch( UnknownHostException e ) {
            System.out.println( "inet problem" ); }
        }
      else {
        System.out.println( "got bad dispatch message" );
```

```
                }
              }
          else
            {
            if(command.compareTo(ResultMessage.RESULT_PREFIX)==0)
              {
              ResultMessage rm = new ResultMessage();
              rm.parse( b, currentOffset );
              AgentServer.currentAgentServer.notifyResults( rm );
              }
            else
              {
              if(command.compareTo(StartMessage.START_PREFIX )==0)
                {
                System.out.println("starting");
                StartMessage sm = new StartMessage();
                sm.parse( b, currentOffset );
                AgentServer.currentAgentServer.notifyStart( sm );
                }
              else
                System.out.println( "Message is BOGUS");
              }
            }
        }
      }
  Integer il = new Integer( sLength );
  currentOffset = messageStart + il.intValue();
  } // while bytesused
  return( bret );
}
}


/** A class that sits accepting connections on a port, spawning
a SocketHandler for each client connection that comes in. Each
AgentServer should only create one of these.
*/
class Acceptor extends Thread {
  AgentServer as;
  SrvSocket s;

/** Constructor -
@param a An agent server for us to call back to.
*/
  public Acceptor( AgentServer a ) {
    setDaemon( true );
    as = a;
    }
```

```
/** Main run loop for acceptor. Creates the server socket,
then sits in a SrvSocket.Accept loop forever.
@see SrvSocket
*/
  public void run() {
    // set up the server socket
    s = new SrvSocket( 1037 );
    while( true ) {
      Socket newS = s.Accept();
      SocketHandler a = new SocketHandler( newS );
      a.start();
      }
    }
}


/** A class representing an AgentServer server socket. All
this really does for now is eat exceptions.
*/
class SrvSocket {
ServerSocket s;
Socket newS;

/** Class representing a socket. This can be either a network
socket, or a local pipe. If the network socket can't be
connected to, a local pipe is created along with a robot.
@version 1.0 August 1, 1995
@author John Rodley
*/
public SrvSocket( int port ) {
  int i = 0;

  s = null;
  while( s == null ) {
    System.out.println( "Accepting on host port:"+port );
    try {
      s = new ServerSocket( port );
      } catch( IOException e )
        { System.out.println( "exception "+e ); }
    }
  }

public Socket Accept() {
  try {
    newS = s.accept();
    System.out.println( "Accepted on host port" );
    } catch( IOException e )
      { System.out.println( "exception "+e ); }
```

```
    return( newS );
  }
}


/** A socket that has been accepted, and is thus connected. We
create one of these from the return from SrvSocket.Accept.
*/
class AcceptedSocket {
public InputStream inputStream;
public OutputStream outputStream;
Socket s;

/** Constructor, save the Socket, and gets input and output
streams from it for future use.
@param so This is usually the return from SrvSocket.Accept, a
connected Socket.
@see Socket
@see SrvSocket
@see ServerSocket
*/
public AcceptedSocket( Socket so ) {
  s = so;
  try {
    inputStream = s.getInputStream();
    outputStream = s.getOutputStream();
    } catch( IOException e )
      { System.out.println( "exception "+e); }
  }

/** Read an array of bytes from the socket/pipe. */
public int read(byte buffer[], int length) {
  try {
    return( inputStream.read(buffer));
    } catch( IOException e )
      { System.out.println("exception "+e); return( -1 ); }
  }

/** Write an array of bytes to the socket/pipe. */
public void write(byte buffer[], int length) {
  try {
    outputStream.write(buffer, 0, length);
    } catch( IOException e )
      { System.out.println( "exception "+e); }
  }

/** Close the socket/pipe. */
```

```
public void close() {
  try {
    s.close();
    } catch( IOException e )
      { System.out.println( "exception "+e); }
  }
}


/** An entry in the list of AgentServers.  A list of these is
used to dispatch Agents.
@author John Rodley
@version 1.0 11/1/1995
*/
class ServerEntry {
  String host name;
  int port;

/** Save the host name and port of the AgentServer. */
  public ServerEntry( String host, int pt ) {
    host name = new String( host );
    port = pt;
    }

/** Send a lump of bytes to this AgentServer */
  public void send( byte msg[] ) {
    System.out.println( "sending to "+host name+":"+port );
    try {
      Socket so = new Socket( host name, port );
      so.getOutputStream().write( msg );
    } catch( IOException e)
      { System.out.println( "io exception"+e ); }
    }
  }


/** An Agent running on this machine.
@version 1.0 11/1/1995
@author John Rodley
*/
class RunningAgent {
  public String id;
  public RunningAgent( String AgentID ) {
    id = new String( AgentID );
    }
  }


/** An Agent dispatched from this machine. */
class DispatchedAgent {
```

```
public String id;
public SocketHandler sh;
public DispatchedAgent(String AgentID, SocketHandler s ) {
  id = new String( AgentID );
  sh = s;
  }
}
```

The AgentServer follows the same skeletal form as the example in Listing 7.7. The top-level thread creates a frame window for accepting user input in the **AgentServer** constructor. This frame window deals with only two events in its **handleEvent** method—the Exit menu item choice and the Load Test menu item choice, which allows you to manually load a local class file via the **ClassLoader** mechanism (discussed in Chapter 9).

The **AgentServer** constructor also creates a single instance of our own **Acceptor** class, which accepts connections to a **ServerSocket**, via **SrvSocket**. Each time a client connects to the server socket, the acceptor thread creates a new thread, an instance of its own **SocketHandler** class, to read the port and deal with whatever the client sends us. The **SocketHandler** passes each received message through **ClientProcess** where it gets parsed and acted upon. The main difference between the AgentServer and the skeletal Snitch application in Listing 7.7 is that the AgentServer has a pile of housekeeping code for dealing with the sets of running and dispatched agents, and another huge set of message handling code (described shortly) that the Snitch doesn't need.

Client-Side Network I/O in the AgentLauncher

The AgentLauncher's network I/O is embodied in a single private class, **AgentDispatcher**, shown in Listing 7.9.

Listing 7.9 The AgentDispatcher Class

```
/** There is one AgentDispatcher active at any one time. It
maintains a CONSTANT connection from the AgentLauncher to the
Dispatching AgentServer.
@version 1.0
@author John Rodley 12/1/1995
*/
class AgentDispatcher extends Thread {
  Socket s;
  public AgentDispatcher( String ServerName, int port ) {
    try {
```

```
          s = new Socket( InetAddress.getByName(ServerName ),port );
        } catch( IOException e )
          {System.out.println("exception "+e ); }
      }


/** Dispatch a kill message to all servers telling them to
terminate the named Agent with prejudice.
*/
   public void StopAgent(String id) {
     KillMessage km = new KillMessage(id);
     try { s.getOutputStream().write( km.getMessageBytes()); }
     catch( IOException e )
         { System.out.println( "stop output exception "+e); }
     try { s.close(); }
     catch( IOException e1 )
         { System.out.println( "stop close exception "+e1); }
     }


/** Tell the dispatching agent server to dispatch this agent.
*/
   public void Dispatch( String Name, String ID, Vector Args ) {
     DispatchMessage dm = new DispatchMessage(Name,ID,Args);
     try { s.getOutputStream().write( dm.getMessageBytes()); }
     catch( IOException e )
         { System.out.println( "stop output exception "+e); }
     }


/** The main run loop for this thread. Sits in a loop reading
the socket and processing messages. The only messages that
should come in over this socket are StartMessage and
ResultsMessage.
*/
   public void run() {
     System.out.println("agentdispatcher running");
     byte buffer[] = new byte[8192];
     while( true ) {
       try {
       int ret;
       if(( ret = s.getInputStream().read( buffer )) != 0 )
         {
         if( ret < 0 )
           {
           System.out.println( "connection lost");
           break;
           }
         ClientProcess( buffer, ret );
         }
```

```
      } catch( IOException e ) {
        System.out.println( "IOexception "+e );
        break;
        }
      }
    try{s.close();}
    catch(Exception e)
        { System.out.println("close exception "+e);}
    }

/** Parse a message from the dispatching agent server. Only
valid message types are Start and Results. Take appropriate
action for each message type, updating the AgentLauncher
display.
*/
public void ClientProcess( byte b[], int numbytes ) {

String command;
int currentOffset = 0;
String s;
int messageStart;
boolean bret = false;

System.out.println( "ClientProcess" );
while( currentOffset != numbytes ) {
  messageStart = currentOffset;
  // Every message starts with 4 bytes of command
  command = new String( b, 0, currentOffset, 4 );
  currentOffset += LoadMessage.PREFIX_SIZE;

  // Followed by 10 bytes ASCII length of the whole message
  // including command
  String sLength = new String( b, 0, currentOffset, 10 );
  currentOffset += LoadMessage.LOADLEN_SIZE;
  System.out.println( "got "+command+" of length "+sLength );

  if( command.compareTo(ResultMessage.RESULT_PREFIX ) == 0 )
    {
    ResultMessage rm = new ResultMessage();
    rm.parse( b, currentOffset );
    AgentLauncher.currentAgentLauncher.reportResult(
            rm.server, rm.theURL);
    }
  else
    {
    if( command.compareTo(StartMessage.START_PREFIX ) == 0 )
      {
```

```
        StartMessage sm = new StartMessage();
        sm.parse( b, currentOffset );
      AgentLauncher.currentAgentLauncher.addAgentFace(sm.server);
        }
    else
      System.out.println( "Message is BOGUS");
    }
  Integer il = new Integer( sLength );
  currentOffset = messageStart + il.intValue();
  } // while bytesused
  }
}
```

The **AgentDispatcher** constructor creates a client socket and connects it to the specified port on the specified host. All the remaining code in the **AgentDispatcher** is concerned with creating and sending, or receiving and processing messages.

AgentLaunchers can send only two message types, dispatch and kill. The dispatch message tells the dispatching agent server to dispatch the agent named in the message, with the ID supplied in the message. The kill message tells the dispatching agent server to kill the agent with the ID supplied in the message. Both of these messages are re-transmitted to all the other agent servers. The AgentLauncher's **AgentDispatcher** has one method to send each of these messages.

As in the AgentServer, the socket reading thread sits in a loop reading the socket and passing messages into the **ClientProcess** method. AgentLaunchers can also receive only two message types, start and result. Each of these causes a call back into the AgentLauncher once the message has been parsed. Within **ClientProcess**, the message gets parsed just enough to determine what type it is, then it gets passed to the constructor for the particular message type. The message creation and parsing in the message classes is some of the longest and most tedious code in the whole agent system.

The Message Classes

With the socket handling structure we've already outlined, we now have the parts of the agent network connected. What we need to do now is to define a protocol and a set of messages that will get all these connected computers working together.

Any messaging system can be split into two pieces: the protocol and the actual message structure. Table 7.3 shows the messages supported by the Agent system.

Table 7.3 Messages Supported by the Agent System

Message	Direction	Meaning
QueryAgentList	AgentLauncher -> dispatching AgentServer	Send me the list of agents that this AgentServer can dispatch.
AgentList	dispatching AgentServer -> AgentLauncher	Here is the list of agents that this AgentServer can dispatch.
Dispatch	AgentLauncher-> dispatching AgentServer	Dispatch the named class to all your servers.
Load	AgentServer-> AgentServer	Load and run the supplied class.
Kill	AgentLauncher-> AgentServer	Kill the named agent.
Start	AgentServer-> dispatching AgentServer -> AgentLauncher	The named agent has started work.
Result	AgentServer-> dispatching AgentServer -> AgentLauncher	The named agent is reporting results in the named URL.

Table 7.3 also gives a rough idea of the protocol the system uses. The **QueryAgentList** and **AgentList** messages are the only query-response pairs in the system. All the other messages can arrive in any order. In the normal course of events, the AgentLauncher and its dispatching AgentServer exchange a **QueryAgentList/AgentList** message pair. Then, the AgentLauncher sends its AgentServer a **Dispatch** message. At that point, the dispatching AgentServer sends out a number of **Load** messages. As servers process the **Load** messages and start running the Agents, they begin sending **Start** messages back to the AgentLauncher. As each agent finishes, it sends back a result message.

The other half of any messaging system is the actual message structure, shown in Table 7.4. Each message has a header that tells what type of message it is, and how long it is. The header is followed by a series of fields. Each field has a header that tells what it is, and how long the data portion of the field is. The order of the fields *is* significant.

It only makes sense for the AgentServer and AgentLauncher to share the message classes, so we split them into their own package, agent.util. Listing 7.10 shows the base message class.

Table 7.4 The Message Structure

Fields	Size	Description
Message type	4 bytes	ASCII message type description; for example, "Disp."
Size of length	4 bytes	ASCII integer describing the length of the length field.
length	Size of length bytes	ASCII integer describing the size of the entire message.
Field type	4 bytes	ASCII field type description, for example. "Clas."
Size of length	4 bytes	ASCII integer describing the length of the length field.
length	Size of length bytes	ASCII integer describing the length of the data portion of the field.
Data	length bytes	The actual data of the message; that is, the bytecodes transmitted when sending a load message, or the string URL when reporting results.

Listing 7.10 The Base Message Classes

```
package agent.util;

import java.awt.*;
import java.lang.*;
import agent.util.*;
import java.util.*;
import java.net.*;
import java.io.*;

/** An abstract class for the messages that AgentServers
exchange with each other and with AgentLaunchers. Provides a
couple of utility functions to aid in message construction.
@version 1.0 12/1/1995
@author John Rodley
*/
public abstract class Message {
  protected byte command[];
  byte sig[];
  int i, j;
  protected byte msg[];
  public static final int PREFIX_SIZE=4;

/** Message senders call this function to force the
construction of an actual message within the msg instance
variable.  Implementors MAY put message creation into the
constructor if they wish, and leave createMessage as an empty
method.  Current implementations put all message creation code
here.
```

```
*/
public abstract void createMessage();

/** Make a string that is a valid field prefix in the format:
  FieldName
  Length of length
@return String  String representation of the field prefix.  Use
String.getBytes on this String and resulting bytes go straight
into the message right before the field data.
*/
public String makePrefix( String prefix,
        int fieldlen, int lensize ) {
  String s =
    new String(prefix+ZeroPadToLength(fieldlen,lensize));
  return( s );
  }


/** All field and message length indicators are sent as
zero-padded ascii integers. This turns the supplied number
into a string and zero pads it to the specified length.
@param  int the number that needs to be converted to a string
@param  int
@return String
*/
public String ZeroPadToLength( int num, int length ) {
  char c[] = new char[length+1];
  for( int i = 0; i < c.length; i++ )
   c[i] = '0';
  String s = new String( c );

  byte b[] = new byte[length];
  Integer I = new Integer( num );
  String s1 = new String( I.toString());
  if( s1.length() >= length )
    return( s1 );
  int pad = length - s1.length();
  s.getBytes( 0, pad, b, 0 );
  s1.getBytes( 0, s1.length(), b, pad );
  String s3 = new String( b, 0 );
  return( s3 );
  }

/** Return a lump of bytes that is a valid message of this
type. Depends on createMessage to fill in the instance
variable msg.
@return A lump of message bytes, suitable for transmission.
*/
```

```
public byte[] getMessageBytes() {
  createMessage();
  return( msg );
  }
}
```

We create one public class for each message. This class contains methods for
both the message construction and parsing. To create a message from scratch, we
use the constructor that takes the constituent fields as arguments, then call
getMessageBytes to get a lump of bytes suitable for network transmission. To
parse a message, we call the do-nothing constructor, then call parse to break the
message into constituent fields.

The message classes all subclass the base abstract class **Message**. **Message**, for the
most part, merely enforces an interface—in this case, the **getMessageBytes**
method for getting a lump of bytes to transmit over the network. If not for the
utility methods, **makePrefix** and **zeroPadToLength**, **Message** could have been
written as an interface rather than as a class. Listing 7.11 shows the actual implementation of the derived message classes.

Listing 7.11   The Derived Message Classes

```
package agent.util;

import java.awt.*;
import java.lang.*;
import agent.util.*;
import java.util.*;
import java.net.*;
import java.io.*;

/** A message that supplies the receiver with a list of
dispatchable agents available on this server.  It is sent to
provoke a responding AgentListMessage. Message format:

  Description  Data       Length
  The command  Load       4 bytes
  The length   10 bytes   ascii int

Class contains both message construction and message parsing
methods.

@version 1.0 1/1/1996
@author John Rodley
```

```
@see QueryAgentListMessage
@see Message
*/
public class QueryAgentListMessage extends Message{
  public static final int PREFIX_SIZE=4;
  public static final String QALS_PREFIX = new String("QALs");

  public static final int QALSLEN_SIZE=10;

/** There is nothing to parse in a QueryAgentList message.
The message prefix, QALs is the message.
*/
public void parse(byte b[], int currentOffset) { return; }

/** Actually fill the byte array "msg" with ALL the bytes that
make up this load message.  Expects NO instance variables to
already be filled with valid data.
*/
public void createMessage() {
  String s;
  int totallength = 0;

  totallength = PREFIX_SIZE+QALSLEN_SIZE;
  s = makePrefix( QALS_PREFIX, totallength, 10 );
  command = new byte[s.length()];
  s.getBytes( 0, s.length(), command, 0 );

  msg = new byte[totallength];
  int currentOffset = 0;
  for( i = 0; i < command.length; i++ )
    msg[currentOffset++] = command[i];
  }
}
package agent.util;

import java.awt.*;
import java.lang.*;
import agent.util.*;
import java.util.*;
import java.net.*;
import java.io.*;

/** A message that supplies the receiver with a list of
dispatchable agents available on this server. It is sent in
response to a QueryAgentListMessage. Message format:

Description  Data  Length
```

```
The command   Load  4 bytes
The length    10 bytes ascii int

filename FNam  4 bytes
length        4 bytes ascii int
filename      length bytes
description  Desc  4 bytes
length        4 bytes ascii int
description      length bytes
```

Class contains both message construction and message parsing
methods.

```
@version 1.0 1/1/1996
@author John Rodley
@see QueryAgentListMessage
@see Message
*/
public class AgentListMessage extends Message{
  public static final int PREFIX_SIZE=4;
  public static final String ALST_PREFIX = new String("ALst");
  public static final String FNAM_PREFIX = new String("FNam");
  public static final String DESC_PREFIX = new String("Desc");

  public static final int ALSTLEN_SIZE=10;
  public static final int FNAMLEN_SIZE=4;
  public static final int DESCLEN_SIZE=4;
  public Vector filenames;
  public Vector descriptions;
  byte bfnam[];
  byte bdesc[];

  public AgentListMessage() { };

/** This is the constructor used by an AgentServer that wishes
to SEND a AgentList message. Supply the name of the lead
class, the id, the signature, arguments, dispatching server,
and port.
*/
  public AgentListMessage( Vector fnames, Vector descs ) {
    filenames = fnames;
    descriptions = descs;
    }

/** Parse the supplied byte array as if it were an AgentList
message. Start parsing at the supplied currentOffset.
```

```
currentOffset should point to the FIRST byte of the SECOND
field in a message, i.e. to the first character in the word
"FNam".  Fills the instance variables:
  filenames
  descriptions
with data from the message.
*/
public void parse(byte b[], int currentOffset) {
String command;
String s;

filenames = new Vector(1);
descriptions = new Vector(1);

while( currentOffset < b.length ) {
  s = new String( b, 0, currentOffset, PREFIX_SIZE );
  System.out.println( "next field "+s);
  currentOffset += PREFIX_SIZE;

  if( s.compareTo( FNAM_PREFIX ) == 0 )
    {
    String sl = new String( b, 0, currentOffset, FNAMLEN_SIZE);
    System.out.println("currOff "+currentOffset+" sl = "+sl);
    currentOffset+=FNAMLEN_SIZE;
    Integer length = new Integer( sl );
    bfnam = new byte[length.intValue()];
    for( int i = 0; i < length.intValue(); i++ )
      bfnam[i] = b[currentOffset++];
    filenames.addElement( new String( bfnam, 0 ));
    s = new String( b, 0, currentOffset, PREFIX_SIZE );
    System.out.println( "next field "+s);
    currentOffset += PREFIX_SIZE;
    }
  else {
    System.out.println( "out of sync at FNAM" );
    break;
    }

  if( s.compareTo( DESC_PREFIX ) == 0 )
    {
    String sl = new String( b, 0, currentOffset, FNAMLEN_SIZE);
    System.out.println("currOff "+currentOffset+" sl = "+sl);
    currentOffset+=DESCLEN_SIZE;
    Integer length = new Integer( sl );
    bdesc = new byte[length.intValue()];
    for( int i = 0; i < length.intValue(); i++ )
```

```
      bdesc[i] = b[currentOffset++];
    descriptions.addElement( new String( bdesc, 0 ));
    s = new String( b, 0, currentOffset, PREFIX_SIZE );
    System.out.println( "next field "+s);
    currentOffset += PREFIX_SIZE;
    }
  else {
    System.out.println( "out of sync at DESC" );
    break;
    }
  }
}

/** Actually fill the byte array "msg" with ALL the bytes that
make up this load message. Expects the instance variables:
  filenames
  descriptions
to already be filled with valid data.
*/
public void createMessage() {
  String s;
  int totallength = 0;

  if(filenames == null || descriptions == null) {
    System.out.println( "No msg data loaded" );
    return;
    }

  totallength = PREFIX_SIZE+ALSTLEN_SIZE;
  byte bbfnam[][] = new byte[filenames.size()][];
  byte bbdesc[][] = new byte[filenames.size()][];
  for( int i = 0; i < filenames.size(); i++ ) {
    String sf = (String)filenames.elementAt(i);
    s = makePrefix( FNAM_PREFIX, sf.length(), FNAMLEN_SIZE );
    bbfnam[i] = new byte[s.length()+sf.length()];
    s.getBytes(0,s.length(),bbfnam[i], 0 );
    sf.getBytes(0,sf.length(), bbfnam[i], s.length());
    totallength += bbfnam[i].length;

    sf = (String)descriptions.elementAt(i);
    s = makePrefix( DESC_PREFIX, sf.length(), DESCLEN_SIZE );
    bbdesc[i] = new byte[s.length()+sf.length()];
    s.getBytes(0,s.length(),bbdesc[i], 0 );
    sf.getBytes(0,sf.length(), bbdesc[i], s.length());
    totallength += bbdesc[i].length;
    }
```

```
      s = makePrefix( ALST_PREFIX, totallength, 10 );
  command = new byte[s.length()];
  s.getBytes( 0, s.length(), command, 0 );

  msg = new byte[totallength];
  int currentOffset = 0;
  for( i = 0; i < command.length; i++ )
    msg[currentOffset++] = command[i];

  for( j = 0; j < bbfnam.length; j++ ) {
    for( i = 0; i < bbfnam[j].length; i++ )
      msg[currentOffset++] = bbfnam[j][i];
    for( i = 0; i < bbdesc[j].length; i++ )
      msg[currentOffset++] = bbdesc[j][i];
    }
  }
}
package agent.util;

import java.awt.*;
import java.lang.*;
import agent.util.*;
import java.util.*;
import java.net.*;
import java.io.*;

/** A results message, sent from running Agent back to
AgentLauncher and containing a URL that holds the results of
the Agent's work.
// Format of the results command:
// The command  Resu  4 bytes
// The length   10 bytes ascii int
// The arguments
           ID
// Field hdr  ID__  4 bytes
// length   4 bytes ascii int
// ID data  length bytes

           URL
// Field hdr  URL_  4 bytes
// The length   4 bytes
// The URL data    length bytes

           Price
// Field hdr  Pric_ 4 bytes
// length   4 bytes ascii int
```

```
// Price data   length bytes


              Comment
// Field hdr  Comm_  4 bytes
// length    4 bytes ascii int
// Comment data   length bytes


              Server name
// Field hdr  Srv_  4 bytes
// The length    4 bytes
// The Server data      length bytes
@see Message
*/
public class ResultMessage extends Message{
  public static final int PREFIX_SIZE=4;
  public static final int LOADLEN_SIZE=10;
  public static final int IDLEN_SIZE = 4;
  public static final int PRICELEN_SIZE = 4;
  public static final int URLLEN_SIZE = 4;
  public static final int COMMENTLEN_SIZE = 4;
  public static final int SERVERLEN_SIZE = 4;
  public static final String ClassPath =
      new String( "/agent/classes/rel/" );

  public static final String ID_PREFIX=new String( "ID__" );
  public static final String PRICE_PREFIX=new String("Pric");
  public static final String COMMENT_PREFIX=new String("Comm");
  public static final String URL_PREFIX=new String("URL_");
  public static final String RESULT_PREFIX=new String("Resu");
  public static final String SERVER_PREFIX=new String("Serv");

  public String sid;
  public String comment;
  public int price;
  public String theURL = null;
  public String server;

  byte burl[];
  byte bcomment[];
  byte bprice[];
  byte bsid[];
  byte bserver[];

  public ResultMessage() { };
  public ResultMessage(String AgentID, String u, int p,
        String c,String srv)
```

```
    {
    System.out.println( "resultmsg "+AgentID+" u "+u );
    sid = new String( AgentID );
    if( u != null )
      theURL = new String( u );
    price = p;
    comment = new String( c );
    server = new String( srv );
    }

/** Parse the ResultsMessage passed in as a byte array. Simply
fills in the public instance variables:
  sid
  comment
  price
  theURL
  server
which the caller can then use as needed.
@param b The array of bytes containing ResultsMessage data.
@param currentOffset The offset of the SECOND field in the
message, i.e. the first Results-specific field.  We've already
parsed the message type field; that's how we got here.
*/
public void parse(byte b[], int currentOffset) {
String command;
byte sig[];
byte clas[];
String s;


  // Followed by some number of byte array arguments
  s = new String( b, 0, currentOffset, PREFIX_SIZE );
  System.out.println( "next field "+s);
  currentOffset += PREFIX_SIZE;

  if( s.compareTo( ID_PREFIX ) == 0 )
    {
    String sl = new String( b, 0, currentOffset,IDLEN_SIZE );
    currentOffset += IDLEN_SIZE;
    Integer length = new Integer( sl );
    System.out.println( "got id of length "+length );
    bsid = new byte[length.intValue()];
    for( int i = 0; i < length.intValue(); i++ ) {
      bsid[i] = b[currentOffset++];
      }
    sid = new String( bsid, 0 );
```

```
      }
    else
      System.out.println( "out of sync at ID" );


    s = new String( b, 0, currentOffset, PREFIX_SIZE );
    currentOffset += PREFIX_SIZE;
    System.out.println( "next field "+s);

    if( s.compareTo( URL_PREFIX ) == 0 )
      {
      String s1 = new String( b, 0, currentOffset,URLLEN_SIZE);
      currentOffset += URLLEN_SIZE;
      Integer length = new Integer( s1 );
      System.out.println( "got url of length "+length );
      burl = new byte[length.intValue()];
      for( int i = 0; i < length.intValue(); i++ ) {
        burl[i] = b[currentOffset++];
        }
      theURL = new String( burl, 0 );

      s = new String( b, 0, currentOffset, PREFIX_SIZE );
      currentOffset += PREFIX_SIZE;
      System.out.println( "next field "+s);
      }
    else
      System.out.println( "No results here!" );



    if( s.compareTo( PRICE_PREFIX ) == 0 )
      {
      String s1 = new String( b, 0, currentOffset,PRICELEN_SIZE);
      currentOffset += PRICELEN_SIZE;
      Integer length = new Integer( s1 );
      System.out.println( "got price of length "+length );
      bprice = new byte[length.intValue()];
      for( int i = 0; i < length.intValue(); i++ ) {
        bprice[i] = b[currentOffset++];
        }
      String sprice = new String( bprice, 0 );
      Integer J = new Integer( sprice );
      price = J.intValue();
      }
    else
      System.out.println( "out of sync at price" );
```

```
s = new String( b, 0, currentOffset, PREFIX_SIZE );
currentOffset += PREFIX_SIZE;
System.out.println( "next field "+s);

if( s.compareTo( COMMENT_PREFIX ) == 0 )
  {
  String sl = new String(b,0,currentOffset,COMMENTLEN_SIZE);
  currentOffset += COMMENTLEN_SIZE;
  Integer length = new Integer( sl );
  System.out.println( "got comment of length "+length );
  bcomment = new byte[length.intValue()];
  for( int i = 0; i < length.intValue(); i++ ) {
    bcomment[i] = b[currentOffset++];
    }
  comment = new String( bcomment, 0 );
  }
else
  System.out.println( "out of sync at comment" );

s = new String( b, 0, currentOffset, PREFIX_SIZE );
currentOffset += PREFIX_SIZE;
System.out.println( "next field "+s);

if( s.compareTo( SERVER_PREFIX ) == 0 )
  {
  String sl = new String(b,0,currentOffset,SERVERLEN_SIZE);
  currentOffset += SERVERLEN_SIZE;
  Integer length = new Integer( sl );
  System.out.println( "got server of length "+length );
  bserver = new byte[length.intValue()];
  for( int i = 0; i < length.intValue(); i++ ) {
    bserver[i] = b[currentOffset++];
    }
  server = new String( bserver, 0 );
  }
else
  System.out.println( "out of sync at server" );
}

/** Create the message byte array using the public instance
variables:
  sid
  comment
  price
  theURL
  server
```

```
that must already have been filled in. When this method is
through, the byte array msg is ready to be sent over the Net.
*/
public void createMessage() {
  String s;
  int totallength = 0;

// the load command
  totallength = PREFIX_SIZE+LOADLEN_SIZE;

// the AgentID
  s = makePrefix( ID_PREFIX, sid.length(), IDLEN_SIZE );
  bsid = new byte[s.length()+sid.length()];
  s.getBytes(0,s.length(),bsid, 0 );
  sid.getBytes(0,sid.length(), bsid, s.length());
  totallength += bsid.length;

// the URL
  if( theURL != null ) {
    s = makePrefix( URL_PREFIX, theURL.length(), URLLEN_SIZE );
    burl = new byte[s.length()+theURL.length()];
    s.getBytes(0,s.length(),burl, 0 );
    theURL.getBytes(0,theURL.length(), burl, s.length());
    totallength += burl.length;
    }

// the price
  String sprice = new String( new Integer(price).toString());
  s = makePrefix( PRICE_PREFIX, sprice.length(),PRICELEN_SIZE);
  bprice = new byte[s.length()+sprice.length()];
  s.getBytes(0,s.length(),bprice, 0 );
  sprice.getBytes(0,sprice.length(), bprice, s.length());
  totallength += bprice.length;

// the comment
  s = makePrefix(COMMENT_PREFIX,comment.length(),
            COMMENTLEN_SIZE);
  bcomment = new byte[s.length()+comment.length()];
  s.getBytes(0,s.length(),bcomment, 0 );
  comment.getBytes(0,comment.length(), bcomment, s.length());
  totallength += bcomment.length;

// the server
  s = makePrefix( SERVER_PREFIX, server.length(),
      SERVERLEN_SIZE );
  bserver = new byte[s.length()+server.length()];
```

```
    s.getBytes(0,s.length(),bserver, 0 );
    server.getBytes(0,server.length(), bserver, s.length());
    totallength += bserver.length;

// the raw class data is already set via LoadClassFromFile

    s = makePrefix( RESULT_PREFIX, totallength, 10 );
    command = new byte[s.length()];
    s.getBytes( 0, s.length(), command, 0 );

    msg = new byte[totallength];
    int currentOffset = 0;
    for( i = 0; i < command.length; i++ )
      msg[currentOffset++] = command[i];
    for( i = 0; i < bsid.length; i++ )
      msg[currentOffset++] = bsid[i];
    if( theURL != null ) {
      for( i = 0; i < burl.length; i++ )
        msg[currentOffset++] = burl[i];
      }
    for( i = 0; i < bprice.length; i++ )
      msg[currentOffset++] = bprice[i];
    for( i = 0; i < bcomment.length; i++ )
      msg[currentOffset++] = bcomment[i];
    for( i = 0; i < bserver.length; i++ )
      msg[currentOffset++] = bserver[i];
    }
}


package agent.util;

import java.util.*;
import java.io.*;
import java.net.*;
import java.applet.*;
import java.awt.*;
import agent.util.*;
import agent.Launcher.*;
import agent.Agent.*;

/** A message from an AgentLauncher telling the AgentServer
recipient to dispatch the agent named in the message to all
the AgentServers in it's list. Format:

Message hdr Disp 4 bytes
```

```
length of length  4 bytes ASCII integer
length   length bytes ASCII integer


          Class File Name
Field hdr Name 4 bytes
length  4 bytes ASCII Integer
Name data  length bytes


          Agent ID
Field hdr ID__ 4 bytes
length 4 bytes ASCII integer
ID data  length bytes


          Argument
Field hdr Arg_ 4 bytes
length 4 bytes ASCII integer
Argument data  length bytes

@version 1.0
@author John Rodley 12/1/1995
*/
public class DispatchMessage extends Message  {
 public static final String DISPATCH_PREFIX=new String("Disp");
 public static final String ID_PREFIX = new String( "ID__" );
 public static final String NAME_PREFIX = new String( "Name" );
 public static final int IDLEN_SIZE = 4;
 public static final int NAMELEN_SIZE = 4;
 public static final int ARGLEN_SIZE = 4;
 public static final String ARG_PREFIX = new String( "Arg_" );
 String s;
 public String name;
 public String id;
 public String sig = new String("XXX");
 byte bname[];
 byte bid[];
 public Vector args;

/** Save the name, id, and arguments for future use in
createMessage.
@param Name The String filename of the lead .class file.
@param ID The id of this Agent, set by AgentLauncher
@param Args A vector of argument data, significant ONLY to the
Agent itself.
*/
  public DispatchMessage( String Name, String ID, Vector Args )
    {
```

```
      name = new String( Name );
      id = new String( ID );
      args = Args;
      }

/** Create a useable message from the instance variables:
 id
 args
 name
When this method is done, the msg byte array contains a message
that can be sent over the wire.
*/
  public void createMessage() {
    int totallength = 0;
    s = makePrefix( DISPATCH_PREFIX, totallength, 10 );
    totallength = s.length();
    s = makePrefix( ID_PREFIX, id.length(), IDLEN_SIZE );
    bid = new byte[s.length()+id.length()];
    s.getBytes( 0, s.length(), bid, 0 );
    id.getBytes( 0, id.length(), bid, s.length());
    totallength += s.length();
    totallength += id.length();

    s = makePrefix( NAME_PREFIX, name.length(), NAMELEN_SIZE );
    bname = new byte[s.length()+name.length()];
    s.getBytes( 0, s.length(), bname, 0 );
    name.getBytes( 0, name.length(), bname, s.length());
    totallength += s.length();
    totallength += name.length();

// the arguments
    byte bargs[][] = new byte[args.size()][];
    for( i = 0; i < args.size(); i++ ) {
      byte arg[] = (byte[])args.elementAt(i);
      s = makePrefix( ARG_PREFIX, arg.length, ARGLEN_SIZE );
      bargs[i] = new byte[arg.length+s.length()];
      s.getBytes( 0, s.length(), bargs[i], 0 );
      for( int k = 0; k < arg.length; k++ )
        bargs[i][k+s.length()] = arg[k];
      totallength += s.length();
      totallength += arg.length;
      }

// redo the message header with proper totallength
    s = makePrefix( DISPATCH_PREFIX, totallength, 10 );
    command = new byte[s.length()];
```

```
      s.getBytes( 0, s.length(), command, 0 );
      msg = new byte[totallength];

      int currentOffset = 0;
      for( i = 0; i < command.length; i++ )
        msg[currentOffset++] = command[i];
      for( i = 0; i < bid.length; i++ )
        msg[currentOffset++] = bid[i];
      for( i = 0; i < bname.length; i++ )
        msg[currentOffset++] = bname[i];
      for( i = 0; i < args.size(); i++ )
        for( j = 0; j < bargs[i].length; j++ )
          msg[currentOffset++] = bargs[i][j];
    }

/** Parse the supplied byte array as if it were a dispatch
message.
@param b An array of bytes containing message data.
@param co The offset of the SECOND field in the message.
@return true if successful, false otherwise
*/
  public boolean parse(byte b[], int co) {
    int currentOffset = co;

    args = new Vector(1);
    name = null;
    // We enter here with byte[currentOffset] at the byte
    // right after the length.
    byte prefix[] = new byte[4];
    for( int i = 0; i < 4; i++ )
      prefix[i] = b[currentOffset++];
    String sprefix = new String( prefix, 0 );
    if( sprefix.compareTo( ID_PREFIX ) == 0 ) {
      byte bsize[] = new byte[IDLEN_SIZE];
      for( i = 0; i < IDLEN_SIZE; i++ ) {
        bsize[i] = b[currentOffset++];
        }
      String ssize = new String( bsize, 0 );
      Integer isize = new Integer( ssize );
      byte bid[] = new byte[isize.intValue()];
      for( i = 0; i < isize.intValue(); i++ ) {
        bid[i] = b[currentOffset++];
        }
      id = new String( bid, 0 );
      }
    else {
```

```
     System.out.println( "out of sync at prefix " );
     return (false);
     }

// Followed by some number of byte array arguments
sprefix = new String( b, 0, currentOffset, PREFIX_SIZE );
currentOffset += PREFIX_SIZE;

if( sprefix.compareTo( NAME_PREFIX ) == 0 ) {
  byte bsize[] = new byte[NAMELEN_SIZE];
  for( i = 0; i < NAMELEN_SIZE; i++ ) {
    bsize[i] = b[currentOffset++];
    }
  String ssize = new String( bsize, 0 );
  Integer isize = new Integer( ssize );
  byte bname[] = new byte[isize.intValue()];
  for( i = 0; i < isize.intValue(); i++ ) {
    bname[i] = b[currentOffset++];
    }
  name = new String( bname, 0 );
  }
else {
  System.out.println( "out of sync at name " );
  return(false);
    }

// Followed by some number of byte array arguments
s = new String( b, 0, currentOffset, PREFIX_SIZE );
currentOffset += PREFIX_SIZE;

while( s.compareTo( ARG_PREFIX ) == 0 )
  {
  // the next thing is ASCII 4 bytes of length
  String sl = new String( b, 0, currentOffset,ARGLEN_SIZE);
  currentOffset+=ARGLEN_SIZE;
  Integer length = new Integer( sl );
  byte arg[] = new byte[length.intValue()];
  for( int i = 0; i < length.intValue(); i++ )
    arg[i] = b[currentOffset++];
  args.addElement( arg );

  if( currentOffset >= b.length )
    break;

  s = new String( b, 0, currentOffset, PREFIX_SIZE );
  currentOffset += PREFIX_SIZE;
```

```
        }
      System.out.println("Successfully parsed dispatch message");
      return( true );
      }


   }


   package agent.util;

   import java.util.*;
   import java.io.*;
   import java.net.*;
   import java.applet.*;
   import java.awt.*;
   import agent.util.*;
   import agent.Launcher.*;
   import agent.Agent.*;

   /** A message telling the recipient to terminate with extreme
   prejudice any instance of the named Agent that might be running
   on the server. Format:

   Message hdr Kill 4 bytes
   Length of length  4 bytes ASCII integer
   Length  length bytes, ASCII integer


            ID
   Field hdr ID__ 4 bytes
   length  4 bytes ASCII integer
   ID data   length bytes

   @version 1.0
   @author John Rodley 12/1/1995
   */
   public class KillMessage extends Message  {
   public static final String KILL_PREFIX = new String( "Kill" );
   public static final String ID_PREFIX = new String( "ID__" );
   public static int IDLEN_SIZE = 4;
   String s;
   String aid;
   byte baid[];

   /** Save the agent id for later use */
     public KillMessage( String AgentID ) {
       aid = new String( AgentID );
```

```
    }

/** Build a kill message in the byte array msg from the
previously constructed instance variables:
 aid
When this method is done, the byte array msg contains a valid
kill message that can be sent over the wire.
*/
  public void createMessage() {
    int totallength = 0;
    s = makePrefix( KILL_PREFIX, totallength, 10 );
    totallength = s.length();
    s = makePrefix( ID_PREFIX, aid.length(), IDLEN_SIZE );
    baid = new byte[s.length()+aid.length()];
    s.getBytes( 0, s.length(), baid, 0 );
    aid.getBytes( 0, aid.length(), baid, s.length());
    totallength += s.length();
    totallength += aid.length();
    s = makePrefix( KILL_PREFIX, totallength, 10 );
    command = new byte[s.length()];
    s.getBytes( 0, s.length(), command, 0 );
    msg = new byte[totallength];
    int currentOffset = 0;
    for( int i = 0; i < command.length; i++ )
      msg[currentOffset++] = command[i];
    for( int i = 0; i < baid.length; i++ )
      msg[currentOffset++] = baid[i];
    }

/** Parse a kill message.
@param b The byte array containing the kill message data
@param co The length of the message.
*/
  public String parse(byte b[], int co) {
    int currentOffset = co;

    System.out.println( "KillMessage.parse" );
    // We enter here with byte[currentOffset] at the byte
    // right after the length.
    byte prefix[] = new byte[4];
    for( int i = 0; i < 4; i++ )
      prefix[i] = b[currentOffset++];
    String sprefix = new String( prefix, 0 );
    System.out.println( "sprefix = "+sprefix );
    if( sprefix.compareTo( ID_PREFIX ) == 0 ) {
      byte bsize[] = new byte[IDLEN_SIZE];
```

```
      for( i = 0; i < IDLEN_SIZE; i++ ) {
        bsize[i] = b[currentOffset++];
        }
    String ssize = new String( bsize, 0 );
    Integer isize = new Integer( ssize );
    byte bid[] = new byte[isize.intValue()];
    for( i = 0; i < isize.intValue(); i++ ) {
      bid[i] = b[currentOffset++];
      }
    String sid = new String( bid, 0 );
    return( sid );
    }
  return( null );
  }


}

package agent.util;

import java.awt.*;
import java.lang.*;
import agent.util.*;
import java.util.*;
import java.net.*;
import java.io.*;

/** A message telling an AgentLauncher that the named Agent has
started work on the named server. This message will be
followed at some point by a ResultsMessage, telling the
AgentLauncher that the Agent has finished.  Format:

Message hdr Star 4 bytes
length of length  4 bytes ASCII integer
length    length bytes ASCII integer

        Agent ID
Field hdr ID__ 4 bytes
length  4 bytes ASCII integer
ID data   length bytes

        Name of Server
Field hdr Serv 4 bytes
length  4 bytes ASCII integer
Server data   length bytes

@see Message
*/
public class StartMessage extends Message{
```

```
    public static final int PREFIX_SIZE=4;
    public static final int LOADLEN_SIZE=10;
    public static final int IDLEN_SIZE = 4;
    public static final int SERVERLEN_SIZE = 4;

    public static final String START_PREFIX = new String( "Star" );
    public static final String ID_PREFIX = new String( "ID__" );
    public static final String SERVER_PREFIX = new String( "Serv" );

    public String sid;
    public String server;

    byte bsid[];
    byte bserver[];

    public StartMessage() { };
    public StartMessage(String AgentID, String srv){
      System.out.println( "startmsg "+AgentID+"  "+srv );
      sid = new String( AgentID );
      server = new String( srv );
      }


/** Parse the specified byte array as a Start message.  Fill in
the public instance variables:
  sid
  server
from the message data.
*/
public void parse(byte b[], int currentOffset) {
String command;
byte sig[];
byte clas[];
String s;


  // Followed by some number of byte array arguments
  s = new String( b, 0, currentOffset, PREFIX_SIZE );
  System.out.println( "next field "+s);
  currentOffset += PREFIX_SIZE;

  if( s.compareTo( ID_PREFIX ) == 0 )
    {
    String sl = new String( b, 0, currentOffset,IDLEN_SIZE );
    currentOffset += IDLEN_SIZE;
    Integer length = new Integer( sl );
    System.out.println( "got id of length "+length );
    bsid = new byte[length.intValue()];
```

```
      for( int i = 0; i < length.intValue(); i++ ) {
        bsid[i] = b[currentOffset++];
          }
      sid = new String( bsid, 0 );
        }
    else
      System.out.println( "out of sync at ID" );


    s = new String( b, 0, currentOffset, PREFIX_SIZE );
    currentOffset += PREFIX_SIZE;
    System.out.println( "next field "+s);

    if( s.compareTo( SERVER_PREFIX ) == 0 )
      {
      String sl = new String( b, 0, currentOffset,SERVERLEN_SIZE );
      currentOffset += SERVERLEN_SIZE;
      Integer length = new Integer( sl );
      System.out.println( "got server of length "+length );
      bserver = new byte[length.intValue()];
      for( int i = 0; i < length.intValue(); i++ ) {
        bserver[i] = b[currentOffset++];
          }
      server = new String( bserver, 0 );
        }
    else
      System.out.println( "out of sync at server" );
    }

/** Create a start message from the instance variables:
  sid
  server
which must have already been set via the constructor, or a call
to parse. When this method is done, the msg byte array
contains a valid start message that can be sent out over the
wire.
*/
public void createMessage() {
  String s;
  int totallength = 0;

// the load command
  totallength = PREFIX_SIZE+LOADLEN_SIZE;

// the AgentID
  s = makePrefix( ID_PREFIX, sid.length(), IDLEN_SIZE );
```

```
  bsid = new byte[s.length()+sid.length()];
  s.getBytes(0,s.length(),bsid, 0 );
  sid.getBytes(0,sid.length(), bsid, s.length());
  totallength += bsid.length;

// the server
  s = makePrefix(SERVER_PREFIX,server.length(),SERVERLEN_SIZE);
  bserver = new byte[s.length()+server.length()];
  s.getBytes(0,s.length(),bserver, 0 );
  server.getBytes(0,server.length(), bserver, s.length());
  totallength += bserver.length;

// the raw class data is already set via LoadClassFromFile

  s = makePrefix( START_PREFIX, totallength, 10 );
  command = new byte[s.length()];
  s.getBytes( 0, s.length(), command, 0 );

  msg = new byte[totallength];
  int currentOffset = 0;
  for( i = 0; i < command.length; i++ )
    msg[currentOffset++] = command[i];
  for( i = 0; i < bsid.length; i++ )
    msg[currentOffset++] = bsid[i];
  for( i = 0; i < bserver.length; i++ )
    msg[currentOffset++] = bserver[i];
  }
}
```

Most of the message bodies are fairly monotonous string and byte-array manipulations. When sending a message, the theory of message creation is that:

- The constructor stores the distinct fields.
- CreateMessage fills the byte array msg with the actual message text.
- GetMessageBytes returns the msg byte array, which can be sent over the Net.

On the parsing end, the steps are even simpler:

- The constructor does nothing.
- Parse takes the message as a byte array and reduces it to the constituent fields.
- The constituent fields, as public members, can now be used by whomever called **Message.parse**.

Writing the messages this way means that the receiver of a message only needs to read the first four bytes, instantiate the proper message class based on those four bytes, then call parse to break up the message properly. When the message is broken up by parse, the public instance variables then correspond to the constituent fields of the message

As written, the message classes are not particularly efficient, as they stage message data several times before getting it into, or out of, the actual msg byte array. This is a debugging tool that allows us to dump constituent parts at various stages of construction/parsing.

Conclusion

Java makes network communication easy, through a set of simple classes—**URL**, **ServerSocket**, **Socket**, and **InetAddress**—that abstract the important concepts in Internetworking. While URLs provide some high-level functionality through **getContent**, you can easily program right down to the lowest levels using the **Socket** class.

Using these basic tools, we've constructed a functional system of cooperating Java objects. While security restrictions force some inelegance in the design, our purpose has been achieved with a modular, portable, and fairly readable implementation.

Chapter **8**

Handling
Exceptions

Handling Exceptions

Unexpected events can short circuit any program. Java exceptions give you a way to handle them.

I like to think of programming as drawing a circle of solution around a problem. Each bit of code is another little arc in the circle. A bugless, deliverable program would be a complete circle around the problem; every aspect of the problem encompassed by the solution.

Unfortunately, there's no such thing as a bugless program. Parts of the problem always "seep" through the solution. How a program deals with errors often marks the difference between a usable, commercial program and an interesting-but-useless programming exercise.

In Java, the notion of programmatic error is encapsulated in *exceptions*. **Exception** is a Java class that embodies everything you need to pinpoint where (and often why) an exception occurred. In this chapter we'll first talk about what exceptions are, then we'll talk about how they're used and what effect they have on a program's flow of execution.

The Exception Class

The **Exception** class is a subclass of **Throwable**. Strictly speaking, it is not exceptions, but throwables that get thrown in a Java program. In normal use though, you will almost always throw and catch exceptions. Figure 8.1 shows the class hierarchy for the **Throwable** class and its descendants.

In the earlier test versions of Java, all of the functionality of exceptions resided solely in the **Exception** class. The release version, however, split **Exception** into

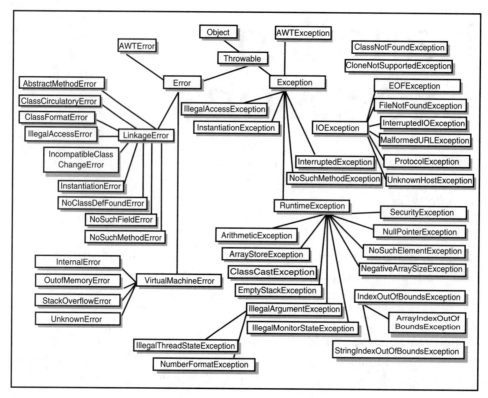

Figure 8.1

The Throwable class hierarchy.

two classes: the superclass **Throwable**, which contains the **toString** and **StackTrace** methods, and a subclass, **Exception**, which contains only the two constructors. This approach makes a lot of sense because, as we will see later, not all that is throwable is necessarily an exception.

What information does an exception really need to embody? Under Java, an exception stores two pieces of information: a *detail message* describing the problem and a *stack trace* that describes where in the program's source code the exception occurred. All the methods included in the **Exception, Error,** and **Throwable** classes are devoted to storing and displaying these two pieces of information.

The Error Class

Exception has a mirror image, an "evil twin," if you will: the **Error** class. Functionally, **Error** is identical to **Exception**. It exists mainly to provide exception throwers with a way around your exception-handling code. At first glance, this seems outrageous. You go to all the trouble of catching and dealing with exceptions, and somebody goes and throws an error just to get around you. In practice, it turns out that there are some problems from which you just can't recover. A classic example of this is when your program runs out of memory. Literally anything you do after running out of memory will only make the problem worse because you can't instantiate anything. You end up in a spiral of exception-handling code because your exception handler itself causes more exceptions. It's just not worth it.

As the Sun documentation for **Error** says: Only catch errors if you really know what you're doing. Error handling, as you might have guessed, is beyond the scope of this book. All you really have to remember about errors is that the base **Error** class is identical in function to the **Exception** class. It exists as a separate entity solely to get around statements like the one in the following code line:

```
catch( Exception e ) { ... }
```

Anything we say about exceptions applies equally to errors, unless otherwise noted.

Throwables In Detail

As you can see in Tables 8.1, 8.2, and 8.3, the line of inheritance for errors and exceptions goes **Object-Throwable-Error/Exception**. Thus, all the functionality of exceptions is embodied in the **Throwable** and **Exception** classes. Table 8.1 shows the methods and constructors for the **Throwable** class, while Tables 8.2 and 8.3 show the methods and constructors for **Throwable**'s two subclasses, **Error** and **Exception** (there are no public variables).

Table 8.1 The Throwable Class

Return Type	Method	Description
None	Throwable()	Constructs a Throwable with no detail message.
None	Throwable(String DetailMessage)	Constructs a Throwable with the specified detail message.
String	getMessage()	Returns the detail message.
String	toString()	Returns a description of the Throwable.
void	printStackTrace()	Prints the Throwable and its stack trace on standard output.
void	printStackTrace (PrintStream s)	Prints the Throwable and its stack trace on the specified. PrintStream.
Throwable	fillInStackTrace()	Fills in the stack trace; must be used whenever you rethrow a Throwable.

Table 8.2 The Exception Class	
Constructor	**Description**
Exception()	Constructs an exception with no detail message.
Exception(String DetailMessage)	Constructs an exception where the detail message is specified by the DetailMessage parameter.

Table 8.3 The Error Class	
Constructor	**Description**
Error()	Constructs an error with no detail message.
Error(String DetailMessage)	Constructs an error where the detail message is specified by the DetailMessage parameter.

Exceptions are designed to accomplish the following tasks:

- *Break the flow of execution.* The **throw** mechanism, which we'll discuss shortly, accomplishes this task.

- *Preserve and display the call stack at the exception point.* The **StackTrace** methods, **fillInStackTrace** and **printStackTrace,** deal with this task.

- *Preserve and display a "label" that names the exception and gives a description that would be meaningful to debuggers who don't have access to the source code.* The constructors store the label, while **toString** and **getMessage** return it.

As we said, **Error** and **Exception** contain only the two constructors—one that sets the detail message, and one that doesn't. Within the superclass **Throwable,** **getMessage** and **toString** both give you a **String** that describes the exception. This **String** is the detail message that the exception designer attached to this exception. **getMessage** returns only the detail message, while **toString** prepends the class name to the **detailMessage.**

FillInStackTrace loads the exception with a description of the call stack at the time the **fillInStackTrace** was called. The call stack is simply the list of method invocations that the applet took to get to a particular source line. If methodA calls methodB, and methodB calls methodC, which then calls **fillInStackTrace,** the call stack will contain methodA, methodB, and methodC. **fillInStackTrace** loads the exception with this information. **PrintStackTrace** prints it back out again.

Pre-Defined Exceptions and Errors

Java and its accompanying packages define a number of exceptions and errors, which are detailed in Tables 8.4 and 8.5.

Table 8.4 A Comprehensive List of Java Exceptions

Exception Name	Description
ArithmeticException	Divide by zero/mod by zero.
ArrayIndexOutOfBoundsException	Tried to access past current bounds of array.
ArrayStoreException	Tried to put the wrong class of Object into an array.
AWTException	Exception occurred somewhere in the window toolkit.
ClassCastException	Tried to cast between classes that are not related.
ClassNotFoundException	ClassLoader failed to load class (See Chapter 9).
CloneNotSupportedException	Tried to clone an Object that doesn't support it.
EmptyStackException	Tried to use an empty stack.
EOFException	File I/O reached end of file.
Exception	Base Exception class; never thrown.
FileNotFoundException	Tried to create a File object from a file that doesn't exist.
IllegalAccessException	Tried to invoke a method that couldn't be found.
IllegalArgumentException	Invoked method detected a bad argument.
IllegalMonitorStateException	Tried to notify a monitor that you don't own.
IllegalThreadStateException	Tried to set daemon status on a Thread that was already running.
IndexOutOfBoundsException	Generic bad index.
InstantiationException	Problem in new.
InterruptedException	The receiving thread has been interrupted by another thread.
InterruptedIOException	A blocking I/O operation has been interrupted.
IOException	I/O device (socket or file) broke while in use; often socket connection lost.
MalformedURLException	String URL passed to URL constructor was nonsense.
NegativeArraySizeException	Tried to create an array with negative size "int j[] = new int[-5]."
NoSuchElementException	Tried to access Vector element < 0 or beyond size() of Vector.
NoSuchMethodException	Method that existed during compile no longer exists.
NullPointerException	Tried to use an uninitialized object.
NumberFormatException	Tried to make a number from a non-numeric string.
ProtocolException	Problem in protocol handler.

Continued

Table 8.4 A Comprehensive List of Java Exceptions *(continued)*

Exception Name	Description
RuntimeException	Base class for exceptions generated by the interpreter; never thrown.
SecurityException	Operation failed security check.
SocketException	Generic socket use problem.
StringIndexOutOfBoundsException	Tried to access character at index < 0 or beyond length( )of String.
UnknownHostException	Host name couldn't be resolved to an IP address.
UnknownServiceException	There is no handler for the Stream type.
UTFDataFormatException	Malformed string encountered in a DataInputStream.

Table 8.5 A Comprehensive List of Java Errors

Error Name	Description
AbstractMethodError	Tried to invoke abstract method.
AWTError	Unexpected error in window toolkit.
ClassCircularityError	Circular dependence detected while loading class.
ClassFormatError	Bad file format detected by implicit class loader.
Error	Base Error class; never thrown.
IllegalAccessError	Non-permitted access.
IncompatibleClassChangeError	Bad type cast.
InstantiationError	Tried to instantiate abstract class or interface via new.
InternalError	Catch-all for interpreter problems.
LinkageError	Base class for indicating that interdependent classes have changed incompatiblly.
NoClassDefFoundError	Class that was available at compile-time is no longer available.
NoSuchFieldError	Field could not be found.
NoSuchMethodError	Invoked method that couldn't be found.
OutOfMemoryError	System is out of memory.
StackOverflowError	Ran out of stack; possibly unterminated recursion. See Listing 7.5.
UnknownError	Error of unknown nature.
UnsatisfiedLinkError	Unsatisfied link.
VerifyError	Class bytecode file failed security check during class load operation.
VirtualMachineError	The virtual machine has a problem.

Many of the exceptions and errors listed in the tables—especially **RunTimeExceptions**, such as **NullPointerException** and **IllegalAccessException**, and **VirtualMachineErrors**, like **OutOfMemoryError** and **StackOverflow Error**—should be familiar to C and C++ coders. Others, like **ArrayIndex OutOfBoundsException** and **NoSuchMethodError**, are designed specifically to implement new features of the Java language.

The thing to remember about all these exceptions and errors is that they usually differ *only* in the information contained in their detail message. Exceptions, in general, do not implement new methods or public variables. Given that any exception is going to go traveling up the call stack, and get caught who knows where, there is no additional functionality that it makes any sense for **Exception** to provide.

Exceptions and The Flow of Execution

The purpose of an exception is to break the normal flow of execution. To understand how a thrown exception affects the flow of execution, we have to think back to our discussion of threads. Everything that happens within a thread is within the scope of the **Thread** object's **run** method. At any point in the execution of the program, you'll be executing somewhere within a set of nested scopes with the **run** method being the outermost scope. When you throw an exception, Java stops execution of the current method. Then it checks the current scope to see if the object is caught there; that is, whether or not the current scope is bracketed by a **try-catch** block. If the throw occurs within a **try-catch** block, the **catch** clause is checked to see whether the exception thrown is the same class (or some subclass) as the exception being caught. If it is, the method continues execution at the start of the **catch** block. If there is no matching **catch** clause in this scope, Java exits that scope and runs the same check on the next scope. This process continues until the exception is caught. By traveling back through the call stack this way, an uncaught exception effectively terminates the thread.

There are two ends to any exception: the **throw** statement, which starts the exception traveling up through all the nested scopes, and the **try-catch** control structure, which stops this runaway object from traveling up through any more scopes. The general form is shown in the following code snippet:

```
try { set of expressions }
catch ( exception ) { expressions to run if we catch an exception. }
```

The syntax really describes the function. We "try" the block of code, and "catch" the named exception class if it occurs. In fact, the **try** block describes a scope of its own. In order for this pseudo-code to catch the exception, it must be thrown within the **try** block (set of curly braces following **try**). The **catch** clause is easiest to understand if you think of it as almost a sub-method that takes an argument. In the **catch** clause, you can name a single exception type, then follow it with a block of code to execute if that exception is caught. Listing 8.1 shows an actual exception-handling block.

Listing 8.1   An Exception Handling Block

```
public void readit( Socket s ) {
   int ret;
   try {
     ret = s.getInputStream().read(); }
   catch( IOException ourExc ) {
     System.out.println( "Socket error "+ourExc ); }
   }
```

In this example, if **s.getInputStream().read** throws an **IOException**, the variable **ourExc** is initialized with the specifics of the exception. Then, the block attached to the **catch** clause executes, printing a message to standard output. In order to throw this exception, somewhere in the source for **InputStream.read** must be a statement that reads something like:

```
throw( new IOException());
```

If an **IOException** is *not* thrown by **s.getInputStream().read**, the **catch** block never executes. This is a simple, but illustrative example. Let's take a look at a complete example, shown in Listing 8.2, that generates an exception two levels down the call stack. Listing 8.3 shows the output generated by running the applet in appletviewer.

Listing 8.2   Generating an Exception

```
package chap8;

import java.awt.Graphics;
import java.awt.*;
import java.applet.Applet;
import java.net.*;
import java.lang.*;
```

```
import java.io.*;
import java.util.*;


/** A class for demonstrating a thrown-exceptions effect on the
flow of execution.
*/
public class ch8_fig2 extends Applet implements Runnable {

public Thread myThread;

public void start() {
  if( myThread == null ) {
    myThread = new Thread( this );
    myThread.start();
    }
}

/** Override of Thread.run. */
public void run() {
  System.out.println( "run invoked" );
  try {
  while( true ) {
    System.out.println( "run-while-1" );
    myMethodA();
    myMethodB();
      System.out.println( "run-while-2" );
    }
  }
  catch( Exception e )
    { System.out.println( "run caught exception "+e ); }
  }

/** A method that gets called by run, which calls another
method that generates an exception.
*/
public void myMethodA() throws Exception {
  try {
    System.out.println( "\tmyMethodA invoked" );
    lastMethod();
    System.out.println( "\tmyMethodA-2" );
    }
  catch( Exception e ) {
    System.out.println( "\tmyMethodA caught Exception" );
    e.printStackTrace( System.out );
    throw (Exception)e.fillInStackTrace();
    }
```

```
    }
/** A method, called by myMethodA, that calls another method
that generates an exception.
*/
public void myMethodB() throws MalformedURLException {
  try {
    System.out.println( "\tmyMethodB invoked" );
    lastMethod();
    System.out.println( "\tmyMethodB-2" );
    }
  catch( Exception e ) {
    System.out.println( "\tmyMethodB caught Exception" );
    throw (MalformedURLException)e.fillInStackTrace();
    }
  finally { System.out.println( "\tmyMethodB finally" ); }
  }


/** A method that generates an MalformedURLException. */
public void lastMethod() throws MalformedURLException {
  int ret;
  int j = 0;
  System.out.println( "\t\tlastMethod invoked" );
  URL u = new URL( "JohnHost" );
  System.out.println( "\t\tlastMethod-2" );
  j++;
  }
}
```

Listing 8.3 The Call Stack Printout from Listing 8.2

```
thread applet-chap8/ch8_fig2.class find class chap8.ch8_fig2
Opening stream to: file:/C:/agent/classes/rel/chap8/ch8_fig2.class to get
chap8.ch8_fig2
run invoked
run-while-1
  myMethodA invoked
    lastMethod invoked
  myMethodA caught Exception
java.net.MalformedURLException: no protocol: JohnHost
  at java.net.URL.<init>(URL.java:157)
  at java.net.URL.<init>(URL.java:107)
  at chap8.ch8_fig2.lastMethod(ch8_fig2.java:78)
  at chap8.ch8_fig2.myMethodA(ch8_fig2.java:47)
  at chap8.ch8_fig2.run(ch8_fig2.java:32)
  at java.lang.Thread.run(Thread.java:289)
run caught exception java.net.MalformedURLException: no protocol: JohnHost
```

Here we've intentionally passed a bad string URL to the **URL** constructor in order to make it throw a **MalformedURLException**. We've also placed **println**'s throughout the code to show where the generated exception breaks the normal flow of execution. As you can see from Listing 8.2, the methods **run**, **myMethodA**, and **lastMethod** get invoked. Taking it from the bottom up, let's see what these methods do:

- **lastMethod**'s first **println** ("... invoked") executes, but then the invocation of the **URL** constructor throws an exception, so **lastMethod**'s second **println** never gets called.

- **myMethodA**'s initial **println** ("... invoked") gets executed, but then the invocation of **lastMethod** throws an exception, so the second **println** ("myMethodA-2") never gets called. The **catch** clause matches the exception, so our **catch** block gets executed, printing out the "caught exception" method, then generating the stack trace (via **printStackTrace**) that tells us which lines in the source code we were at when the exception blew through. **myMethodA** then rethrows the exception.

- **run**'s initial **println** ("... invoked") executes and we fall into the **while** loop and execute the second **println** ("run-while-1"). **myMethodA** is then invoked, which throws an exception. The exception bounces us straight out of the **while** loop without executing either **myMethodB** or the third **println** ("run-while-2"), then it matches the **catch** clause and executes the **println** there.

Using Finally

If you're only catching a single exception type, you'll probably end up writing a lot of code like this:

```
try { expressions }
catch( exception ) {
   Do cleanup;
   rethrow the Exception
   }
```

The fact is, most code can't really do anything with caught exceptions, but merely needs to do some housekeeping if an exception should break the method at an inconvenient spot. To deal with this situation, Java allows a shortcut using the

try-finally syntax. Using this technique, our pseudo-code **try-catch-rethrow** example then becomes:

```
try { expressions }
finally {
  Do cleanup;
  }
```

The effect is similar: Any caught throwable gets rethrown, but some unneccessary source code is eliminated. Where **try-finally** really differs from **try-catch** is that in **try-catch**, the **catch** block *only gets executed if a thrown object is caught, while a finally block is always executed whether or not a throw occurs.* To illustrate, consider the following blocks:

```
try{
  myMethod();
  }
catch( Exception e ) { System.out.println( "myMethod is done" );  }

try{
  myMethod();
  }
finally { System.out.println( "myMethod is done" );  }
```

The first block prints out "myMethod is done" only if **myMethod** throws an **Exception**, while the second block prints out "myMethod is done" whether or not **myMethod** throws an **Exception**. The **finally** block executes no matter what happens, whether or not any kind of object gets thrown.

Catching Multiple Exceptions

Each **catch** clause specifies a single class/interface to catch, but **catch** clauses can be cascaded as shown in Listing 8.4. The **catch** clauses are evaulated in order. When an object is thrown, it passes through each of the **catch** clauses and the first **catch** clause that it happens to match gets executed.

Listing 8.4 Cascaded catch Clauses

```
try {
  MyClass.doSomeFtpStuff();
}
catch( FtpLoginException fe ) { System.out.println( "FTP login exception" ); }
```

```
catch( FtpProtocolException fpe ) { System.out.println( "FTP protocol
  exception" ); }
```

Thus, you can write a **try-catch** block to do one thing for a particular exception and something else for all the other exceptions, as shown in Listing 8.5.

Listing 8.5   Sifting Exceptions Using Subclasses

```
try {
   MyClass.myMethod();
}
catch( ParticularException pe) { System.out.println("particular exception"
); }
catch( Exception e) { System.out.println( "Some other exception" ); }
finally { System.out.println( "The try block has finished." ); }
```

ParticularException is caught by the first clause, while all others fall through to the second clause. Note the **finally** clause cascaded with the **catch** clauses.

Exceptions and Scope

Java's object orientation not only encourages proper scoping of variables, but in some not-so-subtle ways, it actually enforces proper scoping. One of the places where you see this most clearly is in the development of exception-handling code. The code in Listing 8.6 attempts to connect to a URL and get the contents of the file located there.

Listing 8.6   Connecting to a URL

```
public void start() {
URL u = new URL("http://www.myhouse.com/images/image.gif" );
Object o = u.getContent();
System.out.println( "connected to "+u+" and got object "+o);
}
```

If you compile this code, it bombs with two messages saying you need to catch **MalformedURLException** and **IOException**. So you rewrite the code as in Listing 8.7.

Listing 8.7   Connecting to a URL, Take 2

```
public void start() {
try {
   URL u = new URL("http://www.myhouse.com/images/image.gif" );
```

```
} catch( MalformedURLException e ){ System.out.println( "url exception "+e
); }
try {
   Object o = u.getContent();
} catch( IOException e ) { System.out.println( "io exception "+e ); }

System.out.println( "connected to "+u+" and got object "+o);
}
```

When you recompile this code, it bombs again, complaining that the identifiers **u** and **o** are undefined. You berate yourself for being so stupid and rewrite it, taking the declaration of *u* and *o* out to the next scope as in Listing 8.8.

Listing 8.8   Connecting to a URL, Take 3

```
public void start() {
URL u;
Object o;
try {
   u = new URL("http://www.myhouse.com/images/image.gif" );
} catch( MalformedURLException e ){ System.out.println( "url exception "+e
); }
try {
    o = u.getContent();
} catch( IOException e ) { System.out.println( "io exception "+e ); }

System.out.println( "connected to "+u+" and got object "+o);
}
```

When you compile this one, Java complains that **u** and **o** are uninitialized when they get printed. At this point, you could just set **u** and **o** to something such as **null**: The applet would compile, and in the best case, it would run okay. But all you've really accomplished is to work around the compiler's best efforts to guide you in the right direction. What you really want to end up with is the code shown in Listing 8.9.

Listing 8.9   Connecting to a URL, The Final Chapter

```
public void start() {
try {
   URL u = new URL("http://www.myhouse.com/images/image.gif" );
   try {
     Object o = u.getContent();
     System.out.println( "connected to "+u+" and got object "+o);
   } catch( IOException e ) { System.out.println( "io exception "+e ); }
```

```
} catch( MalformedURLException e ){ System.out.println( "url exception "+e
); }


}
```

As you can see, Java strives mightily to encourage and enforce good coding prac-
tices, but our first instincts and old habits of mind can often lead us astray.

When to Catch Exceptions

Exceptions are like grenades: Don't catch one unless you know what to do with
it. Fortunately, we don't have to catch every exception, or keep every exception
we catch. The trick is knowing which ones to ignore, which to catch and keep,
and which to pass through.

What often makes exceptions/errors confusing to Java novices is that some of
them can be ignored, and others can't. If a method declares itself as throwing a
particular exception, any method that calls that method must either catch, or
declare itself as throwing that exception. For example, consider the method shown
in the following code snippet:

```
void myRead( InputStream is ) {
   int myInt = is.read();
   }
```

This method will not compile because we haven't accounted for the **IOException**
that **InputStream.read** throws. We have only two options for dealing with this.
The first option is to catch the exception ourselves, as in Listing 8.10. The second is to pass the exception through, as shown in Listing 8.11.

Listing 8.10   Catching the Exception

```
void myRead( InputStream is ) {
   try {
      int myInt = is.read();
   } catch( IOException e )
      { System.out.println( "bad read "+e ); }
   }
```

Listing 8.11   Passing the Exception Through

```
void myRead( InputStream is ) throws IOException {
   int myInt = is.read();
   }
```

This situation arises only because **InputStream.read** contains a **throw** statement like:

```
throw (new IOException());.
```

and declares itself as throwing **IOException** as in:

```
public int read() throws Exception { ...
```

Within an applet, if you call a method that declares itself as throwing an exception, that exception *must* eventually be caught within your code. This step is not so obvious, unless you think about it a while. Any method that calls an exception-throwing method must either catch the exception or pass it through. So assume that all of our methods pass the exception through. Thus, all these methods will be declared as **throws Exception**. Eventually, there will be an applet override that has to call a method that throws an exception. That applet override either has to catch the exception or pass it through. But it can't pass the exception through because none of the applet's methods are declared as throwing an exception. Thus, any exceptions must be caught at least at the applet level.

Runtime Exceptions

It should be clear that if exceptions are thrown by a method that declares itself as throwing an exception, they are part of a closed loop, and they must eventually be caught. However, there is another type of exception that occurs outside this closed loop: This type of exception doesn't necessarily have to be caught. These are the exceptions/errors that emanate from the interpreter itself. In the class hierarchy diagram shown earlier in the chapter in Figure 8.1, three huge branches—**LinkageError**, **VirtualMachineError**, and **RuntimeException** (as well as a few other exceptions)—fall into this category. These exceptions/errors can be thrown by such innocuous statements as:

```
Integer I = new Integer(1) or Integer I = (Integer)j.
```

In fact, almost any statement can result in one of these exceptions. Java does not expect us to catch or deal with interpreter-generated exceptions/errors. In general, you should not try to catch errors at all, and the only exceptions you should try to catch are those that you are forced to catch because they're declared as being thrown by a method you've called.

For example, take a look at the following listings. In the **addAgentDisplay** method where a new agent reports its existence, we try to find an unused member of the **agentFaces** array that has a hard limit of **agentFaces.length** members. The original implementation, shown in Listing 8.12, checks the member index. If it overruns the array, an error message is displayed. Listing 8.13 shows how this works when we use an **ArrayOutOfBoundsException**.

Listing 8.12   addAgentDisplay Using a Traditional Loop

```
/** The original addAgentDisplay method. Runs through array looking for
a spot to place the new AgentFace.
@param server  The name of the server that's running this agent.
*/
public void addAgentDisplay(String server) {
  int i;
  System.out.println( "addAgentDisplay("+server+")" );
  for( int i = 0; i < agentFaces.length; i++ )
    {
    if( agentFaces[i] != null && agentFaces[i] == true )
      continue;
    agentFaces[i] = new AgentFace( server );
    return;
    }
  // We made it here, so we've gotten an error
  MessageBox( "Too many agents, can't display "+server );
  }
```

Listing 8.13   addAgentDisplay Using ArrayIndexOutOfBoundsException

```
/** The new addAgentDisplay method. Runs through array
looking for a spot to place the new AgentFace, letting us
throw exception if we overrun array.
@param server  The name of the server that's running this agent.
*/
public void addAgentDisplay1(String server) {
  int i = 0;
  System.out.println( "addAgentDisplay("+server+")" );
  while( true )
    {
    try {
      if( agentFaces[i] != null && agentFaces[i] == true)
        {
        i++;
        continue;
        }
```

```
            agentFaces[i] = new AgentFace( server );
            return;
         }
      catch( ArrayIndexOutOfBoundsException e ) {
         MessageBox( "Too many agents, can't display "+server );
         }
      }
   }
}
```

In the normal course of events, we blithely add members to the array. When the index overruns the array, we execute the **catch** block, which puts up a message.

Another **RunTimeException** you can use in the same way is **NumberFormatException**. In the parse method of the **ResultMessage** class, we take a byte array from the **price** field of the message and turn it into a number representing the value of the results. In C or C++, we'd have scanned the string for illegal characters, flagging an error if we found one. To do the same thing in Java, you'd write something like Listing 8.14.

Listing 8.14   Number from Dubious String, the Hard Way

```
if( s.compareTo( PRICE_PREFIX ) == 0 )
   {
   String s1 = new String( b, 0, currentOffset,PRICELEN_SIZE);
   currentOffset += PRICELEN_SIZE;
   Integer length = new Integer( s1 );
   System.out.println( "got price of length "+length );
   bprice = new byte[length.intValue()];

   boolean bError = false;
   for( int i = 0; i < length.intValue(); i++ ) {
     bprice[i] = b[currentOffset++];
     if( bprice[i] < '0' || bprice[i] > '9' )
    bError = true;
     }
   String sprice = new String( bprice, 0 );
   if( bError == true )
     System.out.println( "price number format error" );
   else {
     Integer J = new Integer( sprice );
     price = J.intValue();
     }
   }
 else
   System.out.println( "out of sync at price" );
```

See the grief we go through to check each member of the byte array? Listing 8.15 does it the Java way, simply passing the **String** to the **Number** constructor and catching the **NumberFormatException** the constructor throws if there is any problem converting the **String**.

Listing 8.15   Number from Dubious String, the Java Way

```
if( s.compareTo( PRICE_PREFIX ) == 0 )
  {
  String s1 = new String( b, 0, currentOffset,PRICELEN_SIZE);
  currentOffset += PRICELEN_SIZE;
  Integer length = new Integer( s1 );
  System.out.println( "got price of length "+length );
  bprice = new byte[length.intValue()];
  for( int i = 0; i < length.intValue(); i++ ) {
    bprice[i] = b[currentOffset++];
    }
  String sprice = new String( bprice, 0 );
  try {
    Integer J = new Integer( sprice );
    price = J.intValue();
    }
  catch( NumberFormatException e ) {
    System.out.println( "price number format error" );
    }
  }
else
  System.out.println( "out of sync at price" );
```

Essentially, the format checking we did in Listing 8.14 to see whether each byte was a valid number, was redundant. The **Integer** constructor already does this checking. All we need to do is catch the exception.

When to Throw Exceptions

Never, never, never use method return values to pass errors back up the call stack. If you find yourself thinking of implementing a return value for an error condition, this is where you need to throw an exception.

When throwing exceptions there are three rules by which you need to abide:

1. If a method throws an exception, it must declare it in the method declaration.

2. If a method overrides a method in a superclass or interface, it can only throw exceptions that the overridden method has declared.

    This rule is very restrictive, but there is good reason for it. Java is a language for distributed computing, where there are millions of programmers writing large numbers of small-ish objects that interact via interfaces. The percentage of reused code in the Java environment is some large multiple of that experienced with C and C++. In order to make code reuse a viable option, the published APIs (including thrown exceptions) for public methods must be reliable, and immutable. If you were to override a public method, and then go throwing exceptions that users of your method weren't prepared for (because it wasn't part of the published API), you'd end up breaking perfectly good code, and the writers of that perfectly good code would have much less confidence in that published API. It is for this reason that the compiler enforces this rule. Remember, your applets are traveling over the network and executing within applications you could never have envisioned.

3. If a method overrides a method in a superclass or interface, it must catch any exception that the overridden method doesn't throw, if that exception is thrown by a method that it calls. In other words, the method can't allow any disallowed exception from proceeding up the call stack through it. As an example, the **run** method from the **Runnable** interface declares no exceptions, but **Thread.sleep** throws the **InterruptedException**. So if we call **Thread.sleep**, we must catch **InterruptedException**.

These three rules help close a large hole in our coding methodology. The fact that interface declarations specify the exceptions that emanate from implementations will limit the actual number of exceptions that coders can throw (and define). Forcing coders to catch any disallowed exceptions limits the propagation of exceptions through the call stack, and declaring thrown exceptions in the method declaration guarantees that there will never be undocumented exceptions. The hope is that Java applets will be "closed" systems where problems that arise within the system are handled gracefully within the system.

Catching a Dying Thread

We saw earlier how a thrown exception, traveling back up through the call stack, eventually terminates a thread. This is, in fact, how **Thread.stop** works—by throwing a **ThreadDeath** object. The **ThreadDeath** class is defined expressly for this purpose. It has no variables or methods other than the constructor. It was designed as a subclass of **Throwable**, rather than **Exception**, for the same reason **Error** was: so that it would not be caught by exception-handling code.

In Listing 8.16, we catch **ThreadDeath** in order to implement a bit of debugging code. What we want is a runtime switch that allows us to report the appearance and disappearance of **AgentConnectionHandler** threads. These threads are very short-lived, but crucial to the correct operation of the system.

The modification to the **run** method is fairly simple, bracketing the **run** loop in a **try-catch** block. Notice, however, that having caught **ThreadDeath**, we rethrow it. This is not strictly neccessary in this case, since our thread would die when we returned from **run** anyway. It is, however, recommended practice, and there is no guarantee that Java itself might not catch **ThreadDeath** for its own purposes, so we toe the line and rethrow it.

Listing 8.16 Catching ThreadDeath in the AgentConnectionHandler

```
/** The main run loop for the socket handler, reads the socket
until the client disconnects.
*/
  public void run() {
    byte buffer[] = new byte[8192];
    boolean bContinue = true;
    try {
      while( bContinue == true ) {
        int ret;
        if(( ret = as.read( buffer, buffer.length )) != 0 )
          {
          if( ret < 0 )
            {
            if( bDispatcher )
              AgentServer.currentAgentServer.deleteDispatchedAgent(this);
            System.out.println( "connection lost");
            break;
            }
          bContinue = ClientProcess( buffer, ret );
          }
        }
    } catch( ThreadDeath td ) {
        System.out.println( "Caught ThreadDeath "+td );
        as.close();
        throw( td );
        }
```

```
as.close();
}
```

This catch-rethrow sequence is useful to us in debugging the effect of exceptions.

Throwing has a side effect that's useful all by itself, but that has nothing to do with error conditions. Throwing an object at a thread breaks that thread out of any blocking I/O in which it might be stuck. In this way, throwing is similar to sending a signal in Unix. In fact, some Java implementations use signals to implement throw. If you think about what object-throwing has to accomplish, it's easy to see why **throw** must break out of any blocking I/O. If a thread continued to block on I/O after an exception was thrown, the exception might never actually happen, which would, of course, defeat the purpose.

In the example in Listing 8.16, the thread spends the vast majority of its time sitting blocked in the call to **Socket.read** (as.read). Calling **Thread.stop**, which throws an exception within the thread, breaks us out of that call to **Socket.read**.

Native Exceptions

Generating exceptions within native methods is easy and good practice. The mechanism you use is signals. In Solaris, for example, you use the **SignalError** system call to send a signal as in Listing 8.17.

Listing 8.17   Using the Solaris SignalError System Call to Throw a Java Exception

```
SignalError( int x, char *ExceptionName, int y );
int x;
// what is X?
char *ExceptionName;
// This is the string name of the Java class of the object you want to
throw. It must be a
// fully qualified class name.
int y;
// What is Y???

Solaris Example:
SignalError( 0, "myPackage/myException", 0 );
```

In this example, **myPackage** is an actual Java package (with its attendant directory structure), and **myException** is a class all its own, defined in a file called myException.class.

Calling **SignalError** does not actually throw the exception. What happens is that the exception is "recorded" when **SignalError** is called, but doesn't get thrown until your native method returns to the interpreter. After the native method returns, the native method invoker simply checks whether or not an exception has been recorded, and, if it has, throws it. This has one important side effect. If you throw two exceptions within a single native method (probably bad practice in any case), the second exception will overwrite the first and upon return to the interpreter only the second exception will be thrown. Thus, any native method can throw only one exception per invocation.

Conclusion

We've spent a lot of time talking about how to use throwable objects in general and exceptions in particular. I've focused on this aspect of Java because proper use of exceptions (and other thrown objects) allows us to write more efficient and readable Java code. Learning to work within the bounds imposed by Java exception handling will also make our applets better and more respected citizens of the global applet society Java has spawned.

Chapter 9

Downloadable Classes

Downloadable Classes

The fun part of Java is that browsers can load applets over the network. Here's how they do it.

The crux of our Agent system is the ability of agents to find agent servers, load themselves across the network, and run on the agent server machine with a fair degree of freedom. So far, we've talked about standalone Java apps, network connections, user interfaces ... all the pieces we need but one: the ability to turn an indistinct lump of bytes into a runnable Java class.

In order to understand what class loading involves, we have to take a little closer look inside the Java interpreter. What happens when, for example, the interpreter runs across the following statement:

```
Car car = new Car();
```

If this is the first time the interpreter has run across the class called **Car**, it initially has no idea how to make this thing. It has no internal representation of the **Car** class. It has to build that internal representation, which in Java is a class called **Class**. Table 9.1 shows the methods for the **Class** class.

Why Doesn't Java Know about the Car Class?

Java doesn't resolve all links at compile time. When it runs across the first reference to the **Car** class, it tells its class loader to resolve that class reference. The class loader goes out and looks in the classpath for a file named Car.class. The class loader loads that file, and builds an object of type **Class** that represents the **Car**.

Java Note

You cannot compile a program using the **Car** class unless you have declared that class. However, once the compilation has been completed, Java doesn't keep the information about the Car class, and so it has to re-learn about the **Car** class at runtime by loading the file Car.class into an object of type **Class**.

The **Class** class is entirely devoted to what in C++ would be called run-time type information (RTTI) in C++. What this mostly amounts to is the information contained in the first line of the class declaration. For instance, consider the class **Convertible**, declared as follows:

```
public class Convertible extends Object implements Car {
```

In the **Convertible** class, the **Class** methods are implemented as follows. **getInterfaces** returns an array of Classes with one member, the **interface** Car. **getName** returns the **String** "Convertible." **getSuperClass** returns the **Class** object. **isInterface** returns false. **toString** returns the **String** "class Convertible."

Table 9.1	The Java Class Class		
Return	**Method Name**	**Argument**	**Description**
static Class	forName	String className	Returns the Java class associated with the specified name..
ClassLoader	getClassLoader		Returns the ClassLoader that was used to create this class.
Class[]	getInterfaces		Returns the interfaces that this class implements.
String	getName		Returns the String name of this class.
Class	getSuperclass		Returns the class that this class "extends".
boolean	isInterface		Returns true if this class is an interface.
Object	newInstance		Returns an Object that is a new instance of this class.
String	toString		Returns the name of the object with either "class" or "interface" prepended.

This leaves us with the more interesting methods: **forName**, **newInstance**, and **getClassLoader** (which we'll talk about later).

forName is used to get the **Class** object associated with a particular class. If, for instance, we wanted to know whether Convertible was a class or interface, we might write the code shown in the following snippet:

```
Class c = Class.forName("Convertible);
if( c.isInterface() == true )
   System.out.println( "Convertible is an interface" );
else
   System.out.println( "Convertible is a class" );
```

This code only works because **forName** is a static method. Feed it a class or interface name and it returns the class that has that name.

Like **forName**, **newInstance** is another key piece of the internal workings of the Java interpreter. It creates a new instance of the class. Consider the following code:

```
Convertible conv = new Convertible();
```

Using **forName** and **newInstance** we could re-write this as:

```
Class c = Class.forName( "Convertible" );
Object o = c.newInstance();
Convertible conv = (Convertible)o;
```

That's all the **new** operator really is: a combination of **forName**, **newInstance**, and a typecast.

newInstance brings us to an interesting question. Why does Java use the **Class** class to represent interfaces as well as classes? You'll remember from Chapters 1 and 2 that Java thinks of classes as having two distinct pieces: interface and implementation. A Java interface is just that, the class's interface, while a Java class is both, interface and implementation. If you look at the methods in Class, you can see that with the exception of for **newInstance**, these methods all deal with the definition of the class (its interface) rather than its implementation.

Thus, for every class, or interface that a Java applet (or application) uses, there is a corresponding **Class** object that exists within the Java interpreter. The interpreter uses the object to instantiate the class (whenever we use **new**), and which we can get access to via **Class.forName**. This discussion points us toward one of the key steps in our Agent system. Say, for example, we write an **Agent** declared as follows:

```
public class FileFinder extends Agent implements Runnable {
```

In order to instantiate and run a **FileFinder** on our AgentServer, within the AgentServer we have to first create an object of type **Class** that represents the run time type information for the **FileFinder** class. For this, we need to write a new type of object: a **ClassLoader**.

The ClassLoader Class

The **ClassLoader** class is designed specifically to allow applications, or applets, to obtain raw class data —, a lump of bytes —, from some unknown source and turn it into a Java **Class** object. It is one of the things that makes Java absolutely unique among today's development tools.

To understand just what this means, consider the analogous case in, for example, Borland C++. In BC++ you compile a class in a "cpp" source file into a binary ."obj" file. In order to duplicate the functionality of Java's **ClassLoader**, BC++ would have to provide a class that allowed you to read an "obj" file from disk, and instantiate an object from it. No C++ class library currently provides this, in large part because the "obj" files have a huge amount of application and operating-system-specific information in them. Writing such a class for a C++ class library would require replicating a large part of the compiler's object file linker and the operating system's executable file loader.

ClassLoader is an abstract class whose methods are detailed in Table 9.2.

Loading classes splits pretty neatly into three steps:

- Get a lump of bytes that contains the class data into a byte array
- Create a Java class from the lump of bytes (**defineClass**)
- Resolve all the references within the new class (**resolveClass**)

Once the class has been created, and resolved, we can instantiate it, and then use it as we would any other class. As you can see, the heavy lifting in this exercise

Table 9.2 The ClassLoader Class

Return	Method	Argument	Description
	constructor		Creates a new ClassLoader.
abstract Class	loadClass	String name, boolean resolve	Gets the named class.
Class	defineClass	byte data[], int offset, int length	Converts the byte array into an unresolved class.
void	resolveClass	Class c	Resolves all the references in the specified class.
Class	findSystemClass	String name	Loads the specified class via the primordial class loader.

is done by **defineClass** and **resolveClass**, which Java already provides for us. Where we are left to our own devices is in getting the class data into a byte array. This is by design. Java leaves the door open for this class data to spring from *any* source. The obvious sources for class data are the local file system and the network, but the truth is that, if we were clever enough, we could just build a byte array from thin air and make a class from it via **ClassLoader**. The class data source is not important.

So **ClassLoader** leaves us on our own when it comes to making the byte array that contains the class data we're trying to load. This is the functionality that we have to write into our **loadClass** method. **loadClass** is the heart of any new **ClassLoader**. *Because it is declared as abstract, this method must be implemented by any class that subclasses ClassLoader.* It is responsible not only for getting the lump of raw class data, but also (via **defineClass** and **resolveClass**) for creating the **Class** object that represents all the run time type information for the new class.

The Primordial Class Loader

There are two types of class loading, primordial and **ClassLoader**. The primordial class loader handles the loading of classes that are local to the workstation, and living somewhere along the classpath. Thus, if you have Java installed on your workstation and you run the HotJava browser, all the classes used by HotJava will be loaded via the primordial class loader. If, on the other hand, while using HotJava, you connect to a page that contains an applet, that applet will be loaded using a network **ClassLoader** that HotJava has implemented. The primordial class loader is *not* an instance of **ClassLoader**.

A File-Based ClassLoader

Now that we have the neccessary background, let's write our own file-based **ClassLoader**. What we'll do is take it in three steps. First, we'll write a **ClassLoader** that reads a single .class file from disk, and creates one instance of the class contained in that file. Next, we'll check this single class to see if it's runnable (implements **Runnable** or extends **Thread**), and set it running if it is. Finally, we'll modify our **ClassLoader** to deal with a whole set of class files rather than just the single class. When we're done, we'll have all the tools neccessary to write the **ClassLoader** for the Agent system. Listing 9.1 shows the standalone Java application that uses our **ClassLoaders**.

Listing 9.1   A Standalone Application That Creates ClassLoaders

```
package chap9;

import java.awt.*;
import java.lang.*;
import agent.util.*;
import java.util.*;
import java.net.*;
import java.io.*;

/** A standalone application for testing class loading
functions.
@author John Rodley
@version 1.0 12/1/1995
*/
public class ch9_fig1 extends Thread {
public static ServerFrame f;
static Panel p;
MenuBar m;
public static boolean bRun = true;
static List li;

/** The main method for this standalone application. Creates
one of our ch9_fig1 classes, then sets it running via Thread.start.
@see Thread
*/
public static void main(String argv[] ) {
  ch9_fig1 as = new ch9_fig1();
  as.start();
```

```
  }

/** Cause the main thread to exit by setting static variable bRun to
false.
*/
public static void quit() {
  bRun = false;
  }

/** Constructor creates a frame window (the window the user
sees) and adds a menubar and loadtest menuitems to it.
@see ServerFrame
@see List
@see Frame
@see Panel
@see MenuBar
@see MenuItem
*/
public ch9_fig1() {
  f = new ServerFrame();
  f.resize(450, 300);
  f.setTitle( "Chapter 9, Listing 9.1 - A file-based ClassLoader" );
  li = new List(10, false);
  li.show();
  f.add( "Center", li );
  f.show();
  m = new MenuBar();
  f.setMenuBar( m );
  Menu m1 = new Menu("File");
  m.add(m1);
  MenuItem m2 = new MenuItem( "Load test 1" );
  m1.add( m2 );
  m2 = new MenuItem( "Load test 2" );
  m1.add( m2 );
  m2 = new MenuItem( "Load test 3" );
  m1.add( m2 );
  m2 = new MenuItem( "Exit" );
  m1.add( m2 );
  }

/** Add a String to our debugging list box.
@param  str The string we want to appear in the list box.
*/
public static void show( String str ) {
  System.out.println( "show "+str );
  li.addItem( str );
  f.repaint();
  }

/** The main loop for the AgentServer. Sits in a loop,
sleeping for 1 second, then waking up to check whether the user
interface has been terminated.
```

```
@see Thread.sleep
*/
public void run() {
  while( bRun == true ) {
    try {
    Thread.sleep( 1000 );
      } catch( Exception e ) { }
    }
  System.out.println( "out of run loop" );
  f.dispose();
  System.exit(0);
  }


/** Test the loading of classes at this site by allowing the
user to choose a class file to load, then creating/parsing a
LoadMessage from that class file. DEBUGGING method.
@see ch9_fig1_FileLoader
@see FileDialog
*/
public static void LoadTest1() {
  System.out.println( "Load test" );

  FileDialog fd = new FileDialog(f, "LoadTest");
  fd.setFile( "*.class" );
  fd.setDirectory( "/agent/classes/beta/agent" );
  fd.show();
  if( fd.getFile() != null ) {
    System.out.println( "Load test - "+fd.getFile() );
    if( fd.getFile() == null )
      return;
    ch9_fig1_FileLoader fl = new ch9_fig1_FileLoader(
                            fd.getFile() );
    Class c = fl.getTheClass();
    try {
      Object o = c.newInstance();
      ch9_fig1.show("Successfully created new instance of "+c);
      }
    catch( Exception e ) {
      ch9_fig1.show( "Failed to create object from class file "
                    +fd.getFile() );
    }
  }
  else
    System.out.println( "getFile == null" );
  }

/** Test the loading of classes at this site by allowing the
user to choose a class file to load, then creating an object
from that class file. If the new object is an instance of
either Runnable or Thread, we start it running in its own
thread.
```

```
@see ch9_fig1_FileLoader
@see FileDialog
*/
public static void LoadTest2() {
  System.out.println( "Load test" );

  FileDialog fd = new FileDialog(f, "LoadTest");
  fd.setDirectory( "/agent/classes/beta/agent" );
  fd.setFile( "*.class" );
  fd.show();
  if( fd.getFile() != null ) {
    System.out.println( "Load test - "+fd.getFile() );
    if( fd.getFile() == null )
      return;
    ch9_fig1_FileLoader fl = new ch9_fig1_FileLoader(
                    fd.getFile() );
    Class c = fl.getTheClass();
    try {
      Object o = c.newInstance();
      ch9_fig1.show("Successfully created new instance of "+c);
      if( o instanceof Thread ) {
        Thread t = (Thread)o;
        t.start();
        ch9_fig1.show("Successfully started Thread");
        }
      else
        {
        if( o instanceof Runnable ) {
          Thread t = new Thread( (Runnable)o );
          t.start();
          ch9_fig1.show("Successfully started Runnable");
          }
        }
      }
    catch( Exception e ) {
      ch9_fig1.show( "Failed to create object from class file "+fd.getFile() );
      }
    }
  else
    System.out.println( "getFile == null" );
  }


/** Test the loading of classes at this site by allowing the
user to choose a class file to load, then creating an object
from it. If the new object is an instance of either Runnable
or Thread, we set it running in its own thread.
@see ch9_fig3_FileLoader
@see FileDialog
*/
public static void LoadTest3() {
  System.out.println( "Load test" );
```

```
      FileDialog fd = new FileDialog(f, "LoadTest");
      fd.setDirectory( "\temp" );
      fd.setFile( "*.class" );
      fd.show();
      if( fd.getFile() != null ) {
        System.out.println( "Load test - "+fd.getFile() );
        if( fd.getFile() == null )
          return;
        ch9_fig3_FileLoader fl = new ch9_fig3_FileLoader(
                          fd.getDirectory(), fd.getFile() );
        Class c = fl.getLeadClass();
        try {
          Object o = c.newInstance();
          ch9_fig1.show("Successfully created new instance of "+c);
          if( o instanceof Thread ) {
            Thread t = (Thread)o;
            t.start();
            ch9_fig1.show("Successfully started Thread");
            }
          else
            {
            if( o instanceof Runnable ) {
              Thread t = new Thread( (Runnable)o );
              t.start();
              ch9_fig1.show("Successfully started Runnable");
              }
            }
          }
        catch( Exception e ) {
          ch9_fig1.show( "Failed to create object from class file "+fd.getFile() );
          }
        }
      else
        System.out.println( "getFile == null" );
    }
}


/** The main window functionality - window creation/refresh
handling, application exit handling ...
@see Frame
*/
class ServerFrame extends Frame {

/** Handle any events that might come up. Right now, only
deals with WINDOW_DESTROY, which is what happens when the user
tries to close the application via the system menu.
*/
  public synchronized boolean handleEvent(Event evt) {
    if( evt.id == Event.MOUSE_UP ) {
      return( true );
      }
    else
```

```
      {
    if( evt.target instanceof Frame ) {
      if( evt.id == Event.WINDOW_DESTROY ) {
        ch9_fig1.quit();
        System.out.println( "window destroy "+evt );
        return( true );
        }
      else
        return super.handleEvent(evt);
      }
    else
      return super.handleEvent(evt);
    }
  }


/** Handle any menu item picks. Right now, only has, Exit
and Load Test 1, 2, and 3. Exit sets the agentServers bRun
flag to false, causing the AgentServer.run to fall out of the
endless while loop. Load Test 1, 2, and 3 call (in that order),
ch9_fig1.LoadTest1, 2 and 3.
@see ch9_fig1
@see ch9_fig1.LoadTest1
@see ch9_fig1.LoadTest2
@see ch9_fig1.LoadTest3
*/
public boolean action( Event evt, Object o ) {
  if( evt.target instanceof MenuItem )
    {
    if( evt.arg.toString().compareTo( "Exit" ) == 0 )
      {
      ch9_fig1.quit();
      System.out.println( "action event "+evt );
      }
    else
      {
      if(evt.arg.toString().compareTo( "Load test 1" ) == 0 )
        {
        ch9_fig1.LoadTest1();
        }
      else {
        if(evt.arg.toString().compareTo( "Load test 2" ) == 0 )
          {
          ch9_fig1.LoadTest2();
          }
        else {
          if(evt.arg.toString().compareTo( "Load test 3" )==0)
            {
            ch9_fig1.LoadTest3();
            }
          }
        }
      }
```

```
        }
      }
    return( true );
    }


    }


/** A ClassLoader that serves to load a SINGLE class from a
class file. This class may ONLY reference classes that can be
loaded through the primordial class loader. Thus, this class
can have only a single public class and NO private classes,
because this ClassLoader doesn't know how to load private
classes.
@version 1.0 1/1/1996
@author John Rodley
*/
class ch9_fig1_FileLoader extends ClassLoader {
  Class ourClass;
  String fileName;

  public ch9_fig1_FileLoader(String file) {
    super();
    fileName = new String( file );
    byte classBytes[] = LoadFileBytes();
    ourClass = loadFromByteLump(classBytes,true);
    }

/** This ClassLoader only serves a single class, returned by
this method.
@return Class The Class object that this ClassLoader created.
*/
  public Class getTheClass() {
    return( ourClass );
    }


/** Load the specified class file into a byte array and return
that byte array. All class files are read into the load
message via this method.
@return byte[]  The array of bytes that this class file is made
up of.
*/
  public byte[] LoadFileBytes() {
    byte bret[] = null;
    System.out.println( "Loading class from file "+fileName );
    try {
      FileInputStream fi = new FileInputStream( fileName );
      int filesize = fi.available();
      bret = new byte[filesize];
      fi.read( bret );
      } catch( IOException e ) {
        System.out.println("LoadClass "+fileName+" ex "+e );}
```

```
      return( bret );
    }

/** Create a Class from an array of bytes. Define the class,
and resolve references if specified.
@param  lump  An array of bytes that represent the class file
data.
@param  resolve A boolean, if true we try to resolve all
references within this class file, otherwise, we don't.
@return Class The Class object that we created from the lump of
bytes.
*/
  public synchronized Class loadFromByteLump( byte[] lump,
                                       boolean resolve ) {
    Class c;
    c = defineClass(lump, 0, lump.length);
    if( resolve )
      resolveClass( c );
    return( c );
    }

/** Load the named class and resolve references if the caller
specifies.
@param  name  The name of the class, as in "java.lang.String".
@param  resolve If true, we try to resolve all references in
this class.
@return Class The Class object that we created from this class
file.
*/
  public synchronized Class loadClass(String name,
                                  boolean resolve) {
    Class c = null;

    System.out.println( "loadClass("+name+")");
    try {
      c = findSystemClass( name );
      System.out.println( "Resolved "+name+" locally" );
      }
    catch( ClassNotFoundException e ) {
      System.out.println( "Resolving "+name+" remotely" );
      if( name.compareTo( ourClass.getName() ) == 0 ) {
        c = ourClass;
        resolveClass(c);
        }
      }
    return c;
    }
  }

/** A ClassLoader that can load an entire package (subdirectory
of classes) given the filename of a single class file in that
```

package. Keeps a Hashtable of class names, and tries to load
any unresolved references as class files from the same
directory as the one that the original class file came from.
@version 1.0 1/1/1996
@author John Rodley
*/

```
class ch9_fig3_FileLoader extends ClassLoader {
  Class ourClass;
  Hashtable cache;
  String directory;

/** Constructor saves the directory dir for use in finding new
classes supplied to loadClass by the interpreter. Loads file
immediately so that the caller can instantiate it and get the
whole loading thing going. file is considered the "lead" class
in this operation.
@param  dir A String directory name gotten from the FileDialog.
@param  file  The fully qualified filename of the lead class.
*/
  public ch9_fig3_FileLoader(String dir, String file) {
    super();
    directory = new String( dir );
    cache = new Hashtable();
    byte classBytes[] = LoadFileBytes(file);
    ourClass = loadFromByteLump(classBytes,true);
    }

/** Return the lead class.
@return Class A Class object created from the class file
supplied to the constructor.
*/
  public Class getLeadClass() {
    return( ourClass );
    }

/** Load the specified class file into a byte array and return
that byte array. All class files are read into the load
message via this method.
*/
  public byte[] LoadFileBytes(String fileName) {
    byte bret[] = null;
    System.out.println( "Loading class from file "+fileName );
    try {
      FileInputStream fi = new FileInputStream( fileName );
      int filesize = fi.available();
      bret = new byte[filesize];
      fi.read( bret );
      } catch( IOException e ) {
        System.out.println("LoadClass "+fileName+" ex "+e );}
    return( bret );
    }

/** Return the byte lump that corresponds to the CLASS NAME
```

```
supplied.
@param  name   The CLASS name of the class we want to load. We
create the fully-qualified filename by appending the class name
and ".class" to the directory we saved in the constructor.
@return the byte array we created from this class file.
*/
  private byte loadClassData(String name)[] {
    System.out.println( "loading secondary class "+name );
    String filename = new String( directory+name+".class" );
    System.out.println( "loading secondary class filename "+filename );
    return( LoadFileBytes(filename));
    }


/** Create a Class from an array of bytes. Defines the class,
adds the class name to the Hashtable so that we only load it
once, and resolve references if specified.
@param lump The byte array that contains the class data read
from the .class file.
@param  resolve A flag telling us whether to try to resolve
this Class now.
@return Class A Class object created from the byte lump.
*/
  public synchronized Class loadFromByteLump( byte[] lump,
                                    boolean resolve ) {

    Class c;
    c = defineClass(lump, 0, lump.length);
    if( resolve )
      resolveClass( c );
    return( c );
    }


/** Load the named class. This method is called by the
interpreter whenever it runs into a class name it needs to
resolve. Checks with the primordial class loader first via
findSystemClass, then checks our Hashtable to see if we've
loaded the desired class already, then calls loadClassData to
actually load the thing from disk.
@param  name   The class name (NOT THE FILE NAME).
@param  resolve A flag telling us whether to resolve this class
or not.
@return A Class representing the class named in name.
*/
  public synchronized Class loadClass(String name,
                                    boolean resolve) {

    Class c = null;

    System.out.println( "loadClass("+name+")");
    try {
      c = findSystemClass( name );
      System.out.println( "Resolved "+name+" locally" );
      }
    catch( ClassNotFoundException e ) {
      if(( c = (Class)cache.get(name)) == null ) {
```

```
    System.out.println( "Resolving "+name+" remotely" );
    byte[] b = loadClassData( name );
    c = loadFromByteLump( b, true );
    }
  }
 return c;
 }
}
```

We use a standalone application rather than an applet because, again, security restrictions make it nearly impossible for applets to create their own **ClassLoaders**. The purpose of this standalone application is to allow the user to choose a class file from all the files on the system, load it, and instantiate it. The basic skeleton for our standalone application should look familiar.

A single public class, ch9_fig1, with a public static **main** method gets the whole thing going. The **run** method for the class contains a simple loop that sleeps and checks the state of the **Run** boolean variable. When the **run** method returns, the application exits. The ch9_fig1 constructor builds the user interface. The user interface consists of the following elements.

- A menubar, containing one item.
- The File menu containing four items: Load Test 1, which calls **LoadTest1**, the single-class, non-threaded class-load; Load Test 2, which calls **LoadTest2**, the single-class, threaded class-load; Load Test 3, which calls **LoadTest3**, the multi-class, threaded class-load; and Exit, which causes the application to exit.
- A list box containing our debugging output via ch9_fig1.show.

The **ServerFrame** class contains our user interface and the entry point to our three styles of class loading. The Load Test menu choices are linked to the LoadTest methods in **ServerFrame.action**, where we check the **String** value of the selected item and call the selected method.

ServerFrame.action calls either **ch9_fig1.LoadTest1**, **ch9_fig1.LoadTest2**, or **ch9_fig1.LoadTest3** when the user selects one of the Load Test menu items. Within ch9_fig1, the three LoadTest methods are very similar, so let's look at **LoadTest1** first. **LoadTest1** puts up a FileDialog, that shows all the .class files in a particular directory. Figure 9.1 shows the FileDialog in action.

Most GUIs provide a file dialog as a standard, high-level element that can be instantiated with a single call. Java's FileDialog will use this standard element,

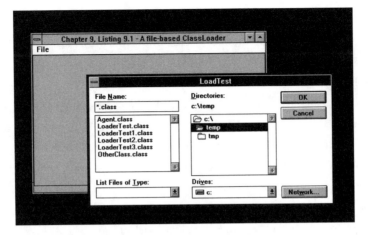

Figure 9.1
The class loader FileDialog in action.

the same way it uses the supplied buttons and check boxes. We instantiate this FileDialog, give it a title, a starting directory and a filespec to list, in this case *.class. The FileDialog does not appear until we call **FileDialog.show**. This simply displays the dialog box, allowing the user to make a choice. **FileDialog.show** does not return until the user has pressed either OK or Cancel. Thus, when we reach the call **fd.getFile**, there should be a .class file selected. If the user hit Cancel, **fd.getFile** will return null, and we simply exit the method.

If the user actually selects a file, we instantiate our new **ClassLoader**, passing it the name of the file. The constructor actually creates the **Class** object, which we can then retrieve by calling our own method, **ch9_fig1_FileLoader.getTheClass**. We then try to instantiate this class. If the instantiation works, we display one message in the list box. If it fails, we display another.

So much for the preliminaries. The heart of this application is our implementation of **ClassLoader**, ch9_fig1_FileLoader. This particular **ClassLoader** crams all the functionality into the constructor. Our constructor takes the name of the .class file and loads that file into a byte array (via **LoadFileBytes**), then creates a **Class** object from that byte array (via **loadFromByteLump**). We store the new **Class** object in **ourClass**, to be returned whenever **getTheClass** is called.

LoadFileBytes is a simple method. It instantiates a **File**, using the name of the .class file that was supplied to our constructor. It creates a byte array big enough to hold the file, then reads the file into that array, and returns the array.

loadFromByteLump is an equally simple method, but it contains the key method in this whole classloading sequence: **ClassLoader.defineClass**. **defineClass** takes a byte array (presumably containing class data) and turns it into a Java **Class** object. Simple as that: Byte array in, **Class** object out.

The **Class** that exists after the call to **defineClass** is not quite complete though, because it contains a zillion references to other classes, some of which may also need to be loaded. The **Class** cannot be instantiated until these references are all resolved. We can do this by calling **resolveClass**.

resolveClass goes through the whole **Class**, calling **ClassLoader.loadClass** for each **Class** that gets referenced. This is why we need to check if the **Class** has already been loaded by the primordial class loader. Figure 9.2 shows the debugging output for a single run of our **ClassLoader** run against our **LoaderTest** class. Notice that **ClassLoader.loadClass** gets called not only for **LoaderTest**, but also for **Object** (**LoaderTest**'s superclass), **System** (because of our static call to **System.out.println**), and **PrintStream** (because **System.out** is an instance of **PrintStream**).

We now have a **Class**. That is, we have the run time-type information neccessary to make objects of type **LoaderTest**. All that's left is to actually make one. In our response to the OK button in our file dialog, we call **loadClass**, which returns an instance of the class **Class**. We instantiate our new **Class** by calling **Class.newInstance** (), which gives us back an instance of **Object**, the base Java class.

Now that we have a way of loading a class, all we need is a class to load. Listing 9.2 shows a simple, standalone class, **LoaderTest**, that is suitable for loading via our new **ClassLoader**.

Listing 9.2   LoaderTest.java, a Simple Non-Threaded Class

```
/** A class that merely reports, to standard output whenever it
gets instantiated. Used to test our ClassLoader.
*/
public class LoaderTest {
   public LoaderTest() {
     System.out.println( "loadertest constructor" );
     }
   }
```

We place the .class file we get when we compile this class into a directory, \temp, that is purposely outside our classpath. If this were within our classpath, we

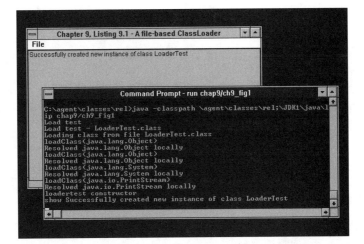

Figure 9.2

The class loader application window and the standard output of the application having loaded LoaderTest.class.

might be able to load it with the primordial class loader, which we don't want. Figure 9.2 shows one run of our application and its standard output loading LoaderTest.class from the \temp directory via the the "Load Test 1" menu choice.

Notice that the message in our constructor prints out. Our class has been successfully instantiated. Listing 9.3 shows the **LoadTest2** method, which is a version of **LoadTest1** modified slightly to give our newly loaded classes a little bit of freedom.

Listing 9.3   The LoadTest2 Method

```
/** Test the loading of classes at this site by allowing the
user to choose a class file to load, then creating an object
from that class file. If the new object is an instance of
either Runnable or Thread, we start it running in its own
thread.
@see ch9_fig1_FileLoader
@see FileDialog
*/
public static void LoadTest2() {
  System.out.println( "Load test" );

  FileDialog fd = new FileDialog(f, "LoadTest");
  fd.setDirectory( "/agent/classes/beta/agent" );
  fd.setFile( "*.class" );
  fd.show();
  if( fd.getFile() != null ) {
```

```
    System.out.println( "Load test - "+fd.getFile() );
    if( fd.getFile() == null )
      return;
    ch9_fig1_FileLoader fl = new ch9_fig1_FileLoader(
                        fd.getFile() );
    Class c = fl.getTheClass();
    try {
      Object o = c.newInstance();
      ch9_fig1.show("Successfully created new instance of "+c);
      if( o instanceof Thread ) {
        Thread t = (Thread)o;
        t.start();
        ch9_fig1.show("Successfully started Thread");
        }
      else
        {
        if( o instanceof Runnable ) {
          Thread t = new Thread( (Runnable)o );
          t.start();
          ch9_fig1.show("Successfully started Runnable");
          }
        }
      }
    catch( Exception e ) {
      ch9_fig1.show( "Failed to create object from class file "+fd.getFile() );
      }
    }
  else
    System.out.println( "getFile == null" );
  }
```

In **LoadTest2**, we test the object that comes back from **Class.newInstance** to see whether it's an instance of **Thread**, or if it implements the **Runnable** interface. If the object is an instance of **Thread**, we start it running by invoking **Thread.start**. If the object implements **Runnable**, we start it up by creating a **Thread** object with our new **Object** as its argument, and then calling **Thread.start**. In order to test this method, we need to write two new test classes: **LoaderTest1**,: shown in Listing 9.4, and **LoaderTest2**, shown in Listing 9.5.

Listing 9.4 LoaderTest1.java, a Simple Threaded Class That Prints a Message to Standard Out

```
/** A simple, threaded class that reports its instantiation to
standard out. When it gets run via Thread.start, it sits in a
loop, sleeping for 1 second then reporting to standard out.
*/
public class LoaderTest1 extends Thread {
  public LoaderTest1() {
```

```
        System.out.println( "loadertest (subclasses Thread) constructor" );
      }
   public void run() {
      while( true ) {
        System.out.println( "Thread Subclass running" );
        try {
          Thread.sleep( 1000 );
          } catch( InterruptedException e ) {}
        }
      }
   }
```

Listing 9.5   LoaderTest2.java, a Simple Runnable Class That Prints a Message to Standard Out

```
/** A simple, Runnable class that reports its instantiation to
standard out. When it gets run via Thread.start, it sits in a
loop, sleeping for 700 milliseconds then reporting to standard
out.
*/
public class LoaderTest2 implements Runnable {
   public LoaderTest2() {
      System.out.println(
      "loadertest2 (implements Runnable) constructor" );
      }
   public void run() {
      while( true ) {
        System.out.println( "Runnable interface running" );
        try {
          Thread.sleep( 700 );
          } catch( InterruptedException e ) {}
        }
      }
   }
```

LoaderTest1 merely extends **Thread**. Once started, via **Thread.start**, **LoaderTest1**'sits **run** method sits in a loop printing a message to standard output every second, so that we know that it instantiated and was able to run in its own thread. Figure 9.3 shows the application window and the standard output after LoaderTest1.class has been loaded via the "Load Test 2" menu choice.

LoaderTest2 is virtually the same code as **LoaderTest1** with the class implementing **Runnable** rather than extending **Thread**. Figure 9.4 shows the application window and the standard output after LoaderTest2.class has been loaded via the Load Test 3 menu choice.

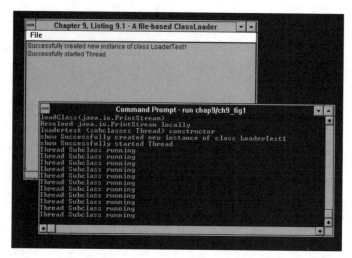

Figure 9.3

The class loader application window and standard out having loaded the Thread subclass LoaderTest1.class.

The three examples we've seen so far have all loaded and run a single, self-contained class: a class with no references to any class that is not available via the primordial class loader. But what if our class wants to load a private class? In Listing 9.6, **LoaderTest3** modifies our previous **LoaderTest** class to reference a new private class, **OtherClass**, which ends up in its own .class file.

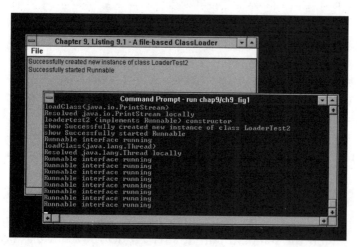

Figure 9.4

The class loader application window and standard out having loaded the Runnable class LoaderTest2.class.

Listing 9.6   LoaderTest3 References OtherClass

```
/** A simple, Runnable class that reports its instantiation to
standard out. When it gets run via Thread.start, it sits in a
loop, sleeping for 700 milliseconds then reporting to standard
out. It also references OtherClass, so that our ClassLoader
has to load multiple class files; that is,it has to respond to
loadClass when called by the interpreter.
*/
public class LoaderTest3 implements Runnable {
   public LoaderTest3() {
      System.out.println( "loadertest3 (implements Runnable) constructor" );
      }
   public void run() {
    OtherClass oc = new OtherClass();
      while( true ) {
         System.out.println( "Runnable interface running" );
         try {
         oc.Ping();
            Thread.sleep( 700 );
            } catch( InterruptedException e ) {}
         }
      }
   }

/** Our other class, simply reports every invocation of Ping to
standard out.
*/
class OtherClass {
  int iteration = 0;
  public void Ping() {
     System.out.println( "OtherClass iteration "+iteration);
     iteration++;
     }
  }
```

Figure 9.5 shows what happens when we try to load the new LoaderTest3 class file using the old, single-class, **ClassLoader**, ch9_fig1_FileLoader.

What happens is that when, within **LoaderTest3.run**, we tried to instantiate **OtherClass** from within **LoaderTest3.run**, the Java interpreter called **ch9_fig1_FileLoader.loadClass** (our implementation of **ClassLoader.loadClass**), passing the **String** "OtherClass" as the argument. The interpreter expects our **ClassLoader** to load this class. But ch9_fig1_FileLoader can only load one class. When **loadClass** is called, we compare the class name ("OtherClass") to the name of the class we've loaded ("LoaderTest3"). That isn't it, so we return null. The interpreter fails to find the class, and throws a **NoClassDefFoundError**. All very simple.

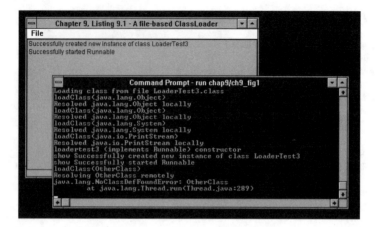

Figure 9.5

Trying to load Runnable class LoaderTest3.class.

What we need to do is to write a new **ClassLoader** that can load the other classes (such as **OtherClass**) that our original class (LoaderTest3) might need. Listing 9.7 shows our new **ClassLoader**, ch9_fig3_FileLoader, and Listing 9.8 shows the new method, **LoadTest3** that invokes this new **ClassLoader**.

Listing 9.7   The New, Multi-Class ClassLoader

```
/** A ClassLoader that can load an entire package (subdirectory
of classes) given the file name of a single class file in that
package. Keeps a Hashtable of class names, and try to load
any unresolved references as class files from the same
directory as the one that the original class file came from.
@version 1.0 1/1/1996
@author John Rodley
*/
class ch9_fig3_FileLoader extends ClassLoader {
  Class ourClass;
  Hashtable cache;
  String directory;

/** Constructor saves the directory dir for use in finding new
classes supplied to loadClass by the interpreter. Loads file
immediately so that the caller can instantiate it and get the
whole loading thing going. file is considered the "lead" class
in this operation.
@param  dir A String directory name gotten from the FileDialog.
@param  file  The fully qualified file name of the lead class.
*/
  public ch9_fig3_FileLoader(String dir, String file) {
    super();
```

```
      directory = new String( dir );
      cache = new Hashtable();
      byte classBytes[] = LoadFileBytes(file);
      ourClass = loadFromByteLump(classBytes,true);
      }

/** Return the lead class.
@return Class A Class object created from the class file
supplied to the constructor.
*/
  public Class getLeadClass() {
    return( ourClass );
    }

/** Load the specified class file into a byte array and return
that byte array. All class files are read into the load
message via this method.
*/
  public byte[] LoadFileBytes(String fileName) {
    byte bret[] = null;
    System.out.println( "Loading class from file "+fileName );
    try {
      FileInputStream fi = new FileInputStream( fileName );
      int filesize = fi.available();
      bret = new byte[filesize];
      fi.read( bret );
      } catch( IOException e ) {
        System.out.println("LoadClass "+fileName+" ex "+e );}
    return( bret );
    }

/** Return the byte lump that corresponds to the CLASS NAME
supplied.
@param  name  The CLASS name of the class we want to load. We
create the fully -qualified file name by appending the class name
and ".class" to the directory we saved in the constructor.
@return the byte array we created from this class file.
*/
  private byte loadClassData(String name)[] {
    System.out.println( "loading secondary class "+name );
    String filename = new String( directory+name+".class" );
    System.out.println( "loading secondary class filename "+filename );
    return( LoadFileBytes(filename));
    }

/** Create a Class from an array of bytes. Defines the class,
adds the class name to the Hashtable so that we only load it
once, and resolve references if specified.
@param lump The byte array that contains the class data read
from the .class file.
@param  resolve A flag telling us whether to try to resolve
this Class now.
@return Class A Class object created from the byte lump.
```

```
*/
  public synchronized Class loadFromByteLump( byte[] lump,
                                             boolean resolve ) {
    Class c;
    c = defineClass(lump, 0, lump.length);
    if( resolve )
      resolveClass( c );
    return( c );
    }
```

```
/** Load the named class. This method is called by the
interpreter whenever it runs into a class name it needs to
resolve. Checks with the primordial class loader first via
findSystemClass, then checks our Hashtable to see if we've
loaded the desired class already, then calls loadClassData to
actually load the thing from disk.
@param  name  The class name (NOT THE FILE NAME).
@param  resolve A flag telling us whether to resolve this class
or not.
@return A Class representing the class named in name.
*/
  public synchronized Class loadClass(String name,
                                      boolean resolve) {
    Class c = null;

    System.out.println( "loadClass("+name+")");
    try {
      c = findSystemClass( name );
      System.out.println( "Resolved "+name+" locally" );
      }
    catch( ClassNotFoundException e ) {
      if(( c = (Class)cache.get(name)) == null ) {
        System.out.println( "Resolving "+name+" remotely" );
        byte[] b = loadClassData( name );
        c = loadFromByteLump( b, true );
        }
      }
    return c;
    }
  }
```

Listing 9.8   The Method That Invokes Our New ClassLoader

```
/** Test the loading of classes at this site by allowing the
user to choose a class file to load, then creating an object
from it. If the new object is an instance of either Runnable
or Threadwe set it running in its own thread.
@see ch9_fig3_FileLoader
@see FileDialog
*/
public static void LoadTest3() {
  System.out.println( "Load test" );
```

```
FileDialog fd = new FileDialog(f, "LoadTest");
fd.setDirectory( "\temp" );
fd.setFile( "*.class" );
fd.show();
if( fd.getFile() != null ) {
  System.out.println( "Load test - "+fd.getFile() );
  if( fd.getFile() == null )
    return;
  ch9_fig3_FileLoader fl = new ch9_fig3_FileLoader(
                  fd.getDirectory(), fd.getFile() );
  Class c = fl.getLeadClass();
  try {
    Object o = c.newInstance();
    ch9_fig1.show("Successfully created new instance of "+c);
    if( o instanceof Thread ) {
      Thread t = (Thread)o;
      t.start();
      ch9_fig1.show("Successfully started Thread");
      }
    else
      {
      if( o instanceof Runnable ) {
        Thread t = new Thread( (Runnable)o );
        t.start();
        ch9_fig1.show("Successfully started Runnable");
        }
      }
    }
  catch( Exception e ) {
    ch9_fig1.show( "Failed to create object from class file "+fd.getFile() );
    }
  }
else
  System.out.println( "getFile == null" );
}
}
```

The key elements of this new setup are the directory supplied to the **ClassLoader** constructor, the **loadClass** method and the Hashtable **cache**. The one thing we absolutely need to know when loading 'secondary' classes like **OtherClass** is what directory they're in. The file name of the file we need to load, by definition, must be *<directory>/<classname>*.class. So when we invoke the **ClassLoader** from **LoadTest3**, we pass in the directory name, which we obtain from **FileDialog.getDirectory**. Then, when the interpreter invokes **ch9_fig3_FileLoader.loadClass** with **OtherClass** as the argument, we simply append OtherClass.class to the directory and we have the name of the file that needs to be loaded. Figure 9.6 shows the application window and standard output when we load LoaderTest3.class via the "Load Test 3" menu choice.

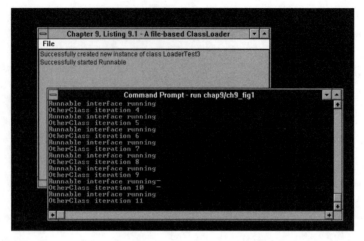

Figure 9.6
Loading the Runnable class LoaderTest3.class.

The one thing we haven't talked about is the Hashtable **cache**. The Hashtable is simply there to prevent us from loading classes over and over again. Once a class is loaded, we add it to the Hashtable, and then, whenever the **Class** is requested in the future, we simply retrieve the stored **Class** from the Hashtable rather than loading it from disk, or over the network again.

This ability to load and run classes is the heart of any browser's Java-bility. Browsers provide a lot more service to the classes they load than our AgentServers do. Browsers also make a few more assumptions about the classes that they load, specifically that each sub-classes **Applet**, but the basic theory is no different: Load a class, find out what it is, and set it running if possible.

Loading Agents

So now we know how to take a lump of bytes and instantiate a Java class from it. We're still one short step away from having a useful agent, primarily because our loaded class is isolated. It's loaded, and possibly running in its own thread, but it has no connection to the AgentServer: no way to request the kind of services that an AgentServer might reasonably be expected to supply. This is painfully obvious from the examples inof Listing 9.5 and 9.6 in which the loaded class reports its instantiation and every pass through its run loop. Ideally, we'd have it report to the list box on the application's frame window, but the loaded class has no connection to that list box. It doesn't know anything about the ch9_fig1 class. It needs an interface to that class. For applets, that interface is the **AppletContext** interface. In our AgentServer application, that interface is the **AgentContext** interface.

In Chapter 4 we talked about how applets communicate with their browser via the **AppletContext** interface. Essentially, the **AppletContext** is the environment in which the an applet executes. All the services the applet can get from a browser are provided through the **AppletContext**. In the AgentServer, we'll implement something very similar to the **AppletContext**, the **AgentContext** interface. The **AgentContext** interface is simply a way for the AgentServer to help the agent do its job. The **AgentContext** source is listed back in Chapter 3, Listing 3.1. Its methods are summarized again here in Table 9.3.

For security reasons, we've designed our **AgentContext** to supply a very high level of service to the agent. For instance, the fact that the agent doesn't doesn't directly create, or write to, the results file means that we can completely eliminate file I/O for agents, the same way Netscape does for applet. The same applies to network access. The agent dispatches, and reports back not directly via **Socket**, but via methods in the **AgentContext** interface (not directly via **Socket**), so we could reasonably eliminate network I/O from the services available to agents.

The Base Agent Class

All agents must subclass the base class **Agent**, shown in Chapter 3, Listing 3.2. **Agent** is almost purely abstract. The only bit of implementation written into it merely sets an **AgentContext** for the agent to use. Realistically, **Agent** could as

Table 9.3 The AgentContext Interface Methods	
Method	**Description**
dispatch	Tells the AgentServer to re-dispatch this Agent to all the AgentServers in its list. This is how the Agent multiplies across the network.
writeOutput	Writes a line of HTML output to the output file the AgentServer has opened for us. The Agent has *no* other access to the opened file.
getResultsURL	Gets a String URL of the output file. The agent sends this back to the AgentLauncher via reportFinish.
reportStart	Tells the AgentLauncher that this agent is running.
reportFinish	Tells the AgentLauncher that this Agent has finished, and gives the output file URL if any.

easily have been written as an interface. In fact, you should think of the **Agent** class and the **AgentContext** interface as two ends of the same conversation. The agent "sees" the AgentServer through the **AgentContext** interface, and the AgentServer "sees" the agent through the abstract **Agent** base class.

It's important to realize that an agent has to be able to run in two very different environments: within an applet at the AgentLauncher, and within its own thread at the AgentServer. Thus, you have two sets of methods, one to be used by the AgentLauncher, and one by the AgentServer.

From these methods, we can now see the series of interactions an agent has with its hosts, AgentLauncher and AgentServer:

- AgentLauncher calls **Agent.configure**, which gets the arguments from the user.

- AgentLauncher calls **getArguments**, which packages the arguments the user set as a Vector of Strings.

- At this point, the AgentLauncher dispatches the agent. It arrives on an AgentServer where it gets instantiated. At that point, there is an Object of type **Agent** on the AgentServer. It has not been set running yet.

- AgentServer calls **setArguments** to give the **Agent** the arguments it needs to perform its task.

- AgentServer calls **setAgentContext** to give the **Agent** a way to talk to the AgentServer.

- At this point, the AgentServer can set the **Agent** running in its own thread because the **Agent** now has a way to report its existence back to the AgentLauncher—via **AgentContext.reportStart** and **reportFinish**.

The driving design ideal behind the **Agent** is that Agents are entirely self-contained. Neither the AgentServer nor the AgentLauncher knows anything more about the **Agent** than it absolutely has to. Thus, the **Agent** is required to obtain its own arguments from the user on the AgentLauncher. This is pure object orientation(O-O), and pretty neat, but it does have one unpleasant implication: When the **Agent** gets transmitted across the network, it drags this configuration code with it despite the fact that it will probably never be run out on the AgentServer.

An Sample Agent: FileFinder

Well, we've talked around the issue long enough. It's time to write a real, live agent and see what it looks like, and how it works. Listing 9.9? shows our **FileFinder** class, a relatively simple agent that merely tries to match the files it finds out on an AgentServer against any of a series of file specifications the user on the AgentLauncher provides.

Listing 9.9 The FileFinder Agent

```
package agent.FileFinder;

import java.lang.*;
import java.util.*;
import java.awt.*;
import java.io.*;
import agent.Agent.*;
import agent.FileFinder.*;
// To catch the definition of AgentContext
import agent.Server.AgentContext;

/** An Agent subclass for finding files that match a particular
set of file name filters.
@version 1.1
@author John Rodley
*/
public class FileFinder extends Agent {
   ConfigurationDialog cfd;
   Vector args;

/** Constructor - does nothing by design, but it's useful to
leave the println in there just to convince yourself that the
Agent has been instantiated on the AgentServer.
*/
   public FileFinder() {
      System.out.println( "FileFinder constructor" );
      }

/** Put up a ConfigurationDialog that gets the arguments this
Agent needs to run on an AgentServer.
@param  frame The frame window of the browser, needed for the
dialog constructor.
*/
   public void configure( Frame frame ) {
      cfd = new ConfigurationDialog( frame );
      cfd.show();
      }

/** Return whatever arguments the configure method got from the
user as a Vector of Strings.
```

```
@return A Vector of Strings that are only meaningful to the
Agent itself, not to either the AgentLauncher or AgentServer.
*/
   public Vector getArguments() {
      return( cfd.args );
      }

/** Configure the Agent with the specified Vector of Strings as
"'arguments'." Called by the AgentLauncher, passing the arguments
it pried out of the LoadMessage.
@param  ar  A Vector of Strings identical to the one returned
to the AgentLauncher by getArguments.
*/
   public void setArguments( Vector ar ) {
      args = ar;
      }

/** The run loop for this Agent. Gets the top-level directory
that this Agent is allowed to read from the properties file
via the key acl.read, and checks all the files in that
directory against the filenamefilter specified by the user back
on the AgentLauncher.
*/
   public void run() {
      String topDirectory = System.getProperty( "acl.read" );
      if( topDirectory == null ) {
        System.out.println( "can't read this machine" );
        return;
        }
      System.out.println( "got value "+topDirectory
                    +" for property acl.read" );
      boolean keepGoing = true;
      String currentDirectory = new String(topDirectory);
      ac.reportStart( "" );
      while( keepGoing ) {
        System.out.println( "currentDirectory = "+currentDirectory );
        File f = new File(currentDirectory);
        AgainstArgs aa = new AgainstArgs( args );
        String filelist[] = f.list( aa );
        System.out.println( "filelist = "+filelist );
        keepGoing =false;
        if( filelist.length == 0 ) {
          ac.reportFinish( "XXXXX", null, 0, "no results, sorry" );
          }
        else {
          // Start the HTML file
          ac.writeOutput(
  "<HTML><HEAD><TITLE>FileFinderOutput</TITLE></HEAD><BODY>" );
          // Start an unordered list
          ac.writeOutput( "<UL>" );
          for( int i = 0; i < filelist.length; i++ ) {
            System.out.println( "filelist["+i+"] = "+filelist[i] );
            String s = new String("<LI>"+filelist[i]+"</LI>" );
```

```
               ac.writeOutput( s );
               }
           // End the unordered list
           ac.writeOutput( "</UL>" );
           // End the HTML file
           String s = new String( "</BODY></HTML>" );
           ac.writeOutput( s );
           try {
               Thread.sleep( 10000 );
           } catch( InterruptedException e ){System.out.println("ex "+e); }
           keepGoing =false;
           ac.reportFinish( "XXXXX", ac.getResultsURL(""), 100,
            "This is the comment" );
           }
       }
     ac.dispatch();
     }
  }

/** A dialog box for configuring a FileFinder Agent. Allows
the user to enter up to seven file names to search for.
@see Dialog
*/
class ConfigurationDialog extends Dialog {
  Label theLabel;
  Button theButton;
  TextField tf[] = new TextField[7];
  Panel ButtonPanel;
  Panel TextFieldPanel;
  public Vector args;

/** Constructor create a dialog with a certain title, lay it
out border style, add a prompt, seven TextFields for entering the
file specs and OK and Cancel buttons.
@param  parent  The Frame that is the parent of this dialog box.
*/
  public ConfigurationDialog(Frame parent) {
   super(parent, "Configure File Finder", true);
     setLayout(new BorderLayout());
   theLabel = new Label( "Enter up to 7 file specifications:" );
     add("North",theLabel);
   TextFieldPanel = new Panel();
     TextFieldPanel.setLayout( new GridLayout(7, 1 ));
   add("Center", TextFieldPanel );
     for( int i = 0; i < 7; i++ ) {
        tf[i] = new TextField( "", 25 );
      TextFieldPanel.add( tf[i] );
      }
   Dimension d = tf[0].preferredSize();
   ButtonPanel = new Panel();
     add( "South", ButtonPanel );
   theButton = new Button( "Ok" );
     ButtonPanel.add( theButton );
```

```
    setResizable(false);
    }

/** Deal with the user hitting either OK or Cancel. In either
case, fill the argument Vector with whatever's in the
TextFields and dispose of the dialog box.
*/
  public boolean action(Event e, Object o) {
    if( e.target instanceof Button )
      {
      args = new Vector(1);
      for( int i = 0; i < 7; i++ ) {
          if( tf[i].getText().length() > 0 &&
                  (tf[i].getText().compareTo("") != 0 ))
            {
            byte b[] = new byte[tf[i].getText().length()];
            tf[i].getText().getBytes( 0, b.length, b, 0 );
            args.addElement( b );
            }
        }
      }
  dispose();
    return true;
  }
  }


/** A FilenameFilter to use to screen files against the file
specs the user has configured this FileFinder Agent with.
Accepts the file if it's in the list, rejects it otherwise.
*/
class AgainstArgs implements FilenameFilter {
  Vector args;

/** constructor, stores the filename list Vector for later use
by accept.
@param  arglist The Vector of filenames.
*/
  public AgainstArgs( Vector arglist ) {
    args = arglist;
    }

/** Return true if the file name supplied matches one of the
files named in the Vector of file names the user configured this
Agent with.
@param  f The file as a File object.
@param  filename  The name of the file.
*/
  public boolean accept( File f, String filename ) {
    for( int i = 0; i < args.size(); i++ ) {
      String s = new String( (byte [])args.elementAt(i), 0);
      if( filename.compareTo(s) == 0 ){
        return( true );
        }
```

```
        }
    return( false );
    }
}
```

Our Agent consists of three classes: **FileFinder**, **ConfigurationDialog**, and **AgainstArgs**.

We've already talked about the configuration process back in Chapter 3 and dialog boxes in general in Chapter 5, so we won't waste a lot of time talking about the **ConfigurationDialog** class here. All you should probably note there is that in the **action** method we save the contents of the **TextFields** so that the **FileFinder.getArguments** method can get them later.

The **AgainstArgs** class is an implementation of the **FilenameFilter** interface. What the **FilenameFilter** interface provides is a way of plucking just the files you want out of an arbitrarily large directory of files. The **FilenameFilter** interface has only one method, **accept**. **accept** takes a file name as an argument and returns true if the file should be part of the list, false otherwise. Our implementation of **accept** simply does a **String.compareTo** of the supplied file name against each of the (up to seven) file names the user supplied to the configuration dialog.

With those two classes out of the way, it's time to look at the **FileFinder** itself. As a subclass of **Agent**, **FileFinder** has to implement all of **Agent**'s methods except **setAgentContext**. **configure** (called on the AgentLauncher) merely runs the **ConfigurationDialog**. **getArguments** (also called on the AgentLauncher) merely returns the Vector of String file names the user entered in the configuration dialog. **setArguments** (called on the AgentServer) is a little trickier.

In order to explain the **setArguments** method, we have to backtrack a bit, and look at the **LoadMessage** class. In Chapter 7, we talked about the messages that AgentServers exchange and listed them in dreary detail. The one message we didn't talk about was the **LoadMessage**, shown in Listing 9.10.

Listing 9.10   The LoadMessage

```
package agent.util;

import java.awt.*;
import java.lang.*;
import agent.util.*;
import java.util.*;
import java.net.*;
import java.io.*;
```

```
/** A message that tells the receiver to load, instantiate, and
run the class that is supplied in the message. Message
format:

 The command  Load  4 bytes
 The length    10 bytes ASCII int


        The dispatching agent server
Field hdr    Dsrv  4 bytes
length             4 bytes
server-name:port   length bytes

        The arguments (unlimited repetitions)
Field hdr Arg_     4 bytes
length             4 bytes ASCII int
Argument data      length bytes

        The signature
Field hdr Sig_     4 bytes
The length         4 bytes
The sig data       length bytes

        The run id
Field hdr ID__     4 bytes
The length         4 bytes
The run id         length bytes

        The class data (unlimited repetitions)
Field hdr Clas     4 bytes
length             10 bytes ASCII int
the class data     length bytes

Class contains both message construction and message parsing
methods. Also contains some message processing in the form of
class loading. Essentially, the receiver of a load message is
looking to receive a Java class, so the parse method
implements this.

@version 1.0 1/1/1996
@author John Rodley
@see DispatchMessage
@see Message
*/
public class LoadMessage extends Message{
  byte args[][];
  public Vector vargs;
  byte sig[];
  byte leadclas[];
  Vector otherclasses = new Vector(1);
  byte id[];
  byte bdsrv[];
```

```
      String ssig;
      public String sid;
      String sname;
      public String dispatching_server_name;
      public int dispatching_server_port;

      int i, j;
      public static final int PREFIX_SIZE=4;
      public static final String LOAD_PREFIX = new String("Load");
      public static final String ARG_PREFIX = new String("Arg_");
      public static final String CLASS_PREFIX = new String("Clas");
      public static final String SIG_PREFIX = new String("Sig_");
      public static final String ID_PREFIX = new String("ID__");
      public static final String DSRV_PREFIX = new String("DSrv");

      public static final int LOADLEN_SIZE=10;
      public static final int ARGLEN_SIZE=4;
      public static final int CLASSLEN_SIZE=10;
      public static final int SIGLEN_SIZE=4;
      public static final int IDLEN_SIZE = 4;
      public static final int DSRVLEN_SIZE = 4;
      public static final String ClassPath =
          new String( "/agent/classes/rel/" );

/** The do-nothing constructor. Called when parsing a Load
Message */
  public LoadMessage() { };

/** This is the constructor used by an AgentServer that wishes
to SEND a load message. Supply the name of the lead class,
the ID, the signature, arguments, dispatching server, and port.
*/
  public LoadMessage( String name, String ID, String thesig,
      Vector args, String dispatchServer, int dispatchPort )
    {
    StringTokenizer st = new StringTokenizer( name, "." );
    Vector v = new Vector(1);
    while( st.hasMoreElements())
      v.addElement( st.nextElement());
    String filename = new String("");
    for( int i = 0; i < v.size(); i++ ) {
      filename = new String(filename+(String)v.elementAt(i));
      if( i < (v.size()-1))
        filename = filename+"/";
      System.out.println( "filename = "+filename );
      }
    // file name is the name of the root class of this agent
    // the class that needs to be instantiated on the AgentServer
    filename = filename+".class";
    leadclas = LoadClassFromFile( ClassPath+filename );
    LoadClassesFromDirectory( filename );
    vargs = new Vector(1);
```

```
    for( int i = 0; i < args.size(); i++ )
      vargs.addElement( args.elementAt(i) );
    sid = new String( ID );
    ssig = new String( thesig );
    dispatching_server_name = dispatchServer;
    dispatching_server_port = dispatchPort;
    }


/** Parse the supplied byte array as if it were a load
message. Start parsing at the supplied current Offset.
currentOffset should point to the FIRST byte of the SECOND
field in a load message; that is,, i.e. to the first character in the
word "DSrv.". Fills the instance variables:
  dispatching_server_name
  dispatching_server_port
  vargs
  leadclass
  otherclasses
  ssig
  sid
with data from the message. Instantiates the lead class if
the message is OK, but does not call the run method.
*/
public Object parse(byte b[], int currentOffset) {
String command;
byte sig[];
String s;
Class leadC = null;


  // Followed by some number of byte array arguments
  s = new String( b, 0, currentOffset, PREFIX_SIZE );
  currentOffset += PREFIX_SIZE;

  if( s.compareTo( DSRV_PREFIX ) == 0 )
    {
    // the next thing is ASCII 4 bytes of length
    String sl = new String( b, 0, currentOffset, DSRVLEN_SIZE);
    currentOffset+=DSRVLEN_SIZE;
    Integer length = new Integer( sl );
    bdsrv = new byte[length.intValue()];
    for( int i = 0; i < length.intValue(); i++ )
      bdsrv[i] = b[currentOffset++];
    StringTokenizer st =
          new StringTokenizer( new String(bdsrv,0), ":" );
    dispatching_server_name =
          new String( (String)st.nextElement());
    Integer iport = new Integer( (String)st.nextElement());
    dispatching_server_port = iport.intValue();

    s = new String( b, 0, currentOffset, PREFIX_SIZE );
    currentOffset += PREFIX_SIZE;
    }
```

```
  else {
    System.out.println( "out of sync at DSRV" );
    return( null );
    }

vargs = new Vector(1);
int numargs = 0;
while( s.compareTo( ARG_PREFIX ) == 0 )
    {
    // the next thing is ASCII 4 bytes of length
    String sl =
        new String( b, 0, currentOffset, ARGLEN_SIZE);
    currentOffset+=ARGLEN_SIZE;
    Integer length = new Integer( sl );
    byte arg[] = new byte[length.intValue()];
    for( int i = 0; i < length.intValue(); i++ )
      arg[i] = b[currentOffset++];
    vargs.addElement( arg );

    s = new String( b, 0, currentOffset, PREFIX_SIZE );
    currentOffset += PREFIX_SIZE;
    }

// s is already set to the command name
  if( s.compareTo( SIG_PREFIX ) == 0 ) {
    // the next thing is ASCII 4 bytes of length
    String sl = new String( b, 0, currentOffset, SIGLEN_SIZE );
    currentOffset+=SIGLEN_SIZE;
    Integer length = new Integer( sl );
    sig = new byte[length.intValue()];
    for( int i = 0; i < length.intValue(); i++ )
      sig[i] = b[currentOffset++];
    ssig = new String( sig, 0 );
    }
  else {
    System.out.println( "out of sync at sig" );
    return( null );
    }

  s = new String( b, 0, currentOffset, PREFIX_SIZE );
  currentOffset += PREFIX_SIZE;
  if( s.compareTo( ID_PREFIX ) == 0 )
    {
    String sl = new String( b, 0, currentOffset,IDLEN_SIZE );
    currentOffset += IDLEN_SIZE;
    Integer length = new Integer( sl );
    id = new byte[length.intValue()];
    for( int i = 0; i < length.intValue(); i++ ) {
      id[i] = b[currentOffset++];
      }
    sid = new String( id, 0 );
    }
  else {
```

```
        System.out.println( "out of sync at ID" );
        return( null );
        }

    s = new String( b, 0, currentOffset, PREFIX_SIZE );
    currentOffset += PREFIX_SIZE;
    int classnum = 0;
    otherclasses = new Vector(1);
    while( s.compareTo( CLASS_PREFIX ) == 0 )
        {
        // the next thing is ASCII 10 bytes of length
        String s1 = new String( b, 0, currentOffset,CLASSLEN_SIZE);
        currentOffset += CLASSLEN_SIZE;
        Integer length = new Integer( s1 );
        byte bclas[] = new byte[length.intValue()];
        for( int i = 0; i < length.intValue(); i++ ) {
          bclas[i] = b[currentOffset++];
          }
        // Only instantiate the first class in the message
        if( classnum == 0 )
          leadclas = bclas;
          else {
          otherclasses.addElement(bclas);
          }
        s = new String( b, 0, currentOffset, PREFIX_SIZE );
        currentOffset += PREFIX_SIZE;
        classnum++;
        }
    if( classnum == 0 )
      System.out.println( "out of sync at class" );
    else {
      AgentLoader al = new AgentLoader(otherclasses);
      leadC = al.loadFromByteLump(leadclas, true);
      try {
        Object o = leadC.newInstance();
        return( o );
        } catch( Exception e1 )
          { System.out.println( "new instance exception" ); }
      }
    return( null );
    }

/** Load the instance variable classes with byte arrays
that are filled from ALL the class files (except the lead
class) in the directory embedded in the supplied class name.
*/
public void LoadClassesFromDirectory( String leadclass ) {
  System.out.println( "LoadClassesFromDir "+leadclass);

  int j = leadclass.lastIndexOf('/');
  String absoluteDir = leadclass.substring(0,j);
  System.out.println( "absoluteDir = "+absoluteDir );
  File f = new File( absoluteDir );
```

```
   if( f.isDirectory() != true ) {
     System.out.println( absoluteDir+" not a directory" );
     return;
     }
  ExtensionFilter ef = new ExtensionFilter( ".class" );
  String sa[] = f.list( ef );
  for( int i = 0; i < sa.length; i++ ) {
    if( leadclass.compareTo(absoluteDir+"/"+sa[i]) == 0 )
      // lead class is already loaded
      {
      System.out.println( "Skipping leadclass "+sa[i] );
      continue;
      }
    otherclasses.addElement(
        LoadClassFromFile( absoluteDir+"/"+sa[i] ));
    }
  }

/** Load the specified class file into a byte array and return
that byte array. All class files are read into the load
message via this method.
*/
public byte[] LoadClassFromFile( String name ) {
  byte bret[] = null;
  System.out.println( "Loading class from file "+name );
  try {
    FileInputStream fi = new FileInputStream( name );
    int filesize = fi.available();
    byte[] lump = new byte[filesize];
    fi.read( lump );
    String prefix = makePrefix( CLASS_PREFIX,
                               filesize, CLASSLEN_SIZE );
    bret = new byte[prefix.length()+lump.length];
    prefix.getBytes( 0, prefix.length(), bret, 0 );
    for( i = 0; i < lump.length; i++ )
      bret[prefix.length()+i] = lump[i];
    } catch( IOException e ) {
      System.out.println("LoadClass "+name+" ex "+e );}
  return( bret );
  }

/** Actually fill the byte array "'msg"' with ALL the bytes that
make up this load message. Expects the instance variables:
  dispatching_server_name
  dispatching_server_port
  vargs
  leadclass
  otherclasses
  ssig
  sid
to already be filled with valid data.
*/
public void createMessage() {
```

```
  String s;
  int totallength = 0;

  if( leadclas == null )
    System.out.println( "No lead class loaded" );

// the load command
  totallength = PREFIX_SIZE+LOADLEN_SIZE;

// the dispatching server
  String srv = new String( dispatching_server_name+":"+
                           dispatching_server_port );
  s = makePrefix( DSRV_PREFIX, srv.length(), DSRVLEN_SIZE );
  bdsrv = new byte[s.length()+srv.length()];
  s.getBytes(0,s.length(),bdsrv, 0 );
  srv.getBytes(0,srv.length(), bdsrv, s.length());
  totallength += bdsrv.length;

// the arguments
  args = new byte[vargs.size()][];
  for( i = 0; i < vargs.size(); i++ ) {
    byte ba[] = (byte [])vargs.elementAt(i);
    s = makePrefix( ARG_PREFIX, ba.length, ARGLEN_SIZE );
    args[i] = new byte[s.length()+ba.length];
    s.getBytes( 0, s.length(), args[i], 0 );
    for( int k = 0; k < ba.length; k++ )
      args[i][k+s.length()] = ba[k];
    totallength += args[i].length;
    }

// the signature
  s = makePrefix( SIG_PREFIX, 40, SIGLEN_SIZE );
  sig = new byte[s.length()+40];
  s.getBytes( 0, s.length(), sig, 0 );
  totallength += sig.length;

// the ID
  s = makePrefix( ID_PREFIX, sid.length(), IDLEN_SIZE );
  id = new byte[s.length()+sid.length()];
  s.getBytes( 0, s.length(), id, 0 );
  sid.getBytes( 0, sid.length(), id, s.length());
  totallength += id.length;

// the raw class data is already set via LoadClassFromFile
  totallength += leadclas.length;
  for( i = 0; i < otherclasses.size(); i++ ) {
    byte ba[] = (byte [])otherclasses.elementAt(i);
    totallength += ba.length;
    }

  s = makePrefix( LOAD_PREFIX, totallength, 10 );
  command = new byte[s.length()];
  s.getBytes( 0, s.length(), command, 0 );
```

```
  msg = new byte[totallength];
  int currentOffset = 0;
  for( i = 0; i < command.length; i++ )
    msg[currentOffset++] = command[i];
  for( i = 0; i < bdsrv.length; i++ )
    msg[currentOffset++] = bdsrv[i];
  for( j = 0; j < args.length; j++ ) {
    for( i = 0; i < args[j].length; i++ )
      msg[currentOffset++] = args[j][i];
    }
  for( i = 0; i < sig.length; i++ )
    msg[currentOffset++] = sig[i];
  for( i = 0; i < id.length; i++ )
    msg[currentOffset++] = id[i];
  for( i = 0; i < leadclas.length; i++ )
    msg[currentOffset++] = leadclas[i];
  for( i = 0; i < otherclasses.size(); i++ ) {
    byte ba[] = (byte [])otherclasses.elementAt(i);
    for( j = 0; j < ba.length; j++ )
      msg[currentOffset++] = ba[j];
    }


  }
}

/** A class to implement a class loader for loading agents on
an AgentServer. The AgentServer uses this class loader to
resolve references that occur when it loads an agent from a
load message.
@see LoadMessage
@version 1.0 1/1/1996
@author John Rodley
*/
class AgentLoader extends ClassLoader {
        static Hashtable cache = new Hashtable();
  Vector otherclasses;
  Vector classes = new Vector(1);

/** Take a vector of byte arrays filled with all the classes
UNIQUE TO THIS AGENT (except the lead class) and create a
class for each one, without resolving the references in those
classes. Reference resolution is only done when the lead
class is instantiated.
*/
  public AgentLoader(Vector oc) {
    super();
    otherclasses = oc;
    for( int i = 0; i < otherclasses.size(); i++ ) {
      Class c = loadFromByteLump(
          (byte[])otherclasses.elementAt(i), false );
      classes.addElement(c);
      }
```

```
    }
```

/** Load the specified class into the Java system. This
should only happen ONCE for any class. Ideally, we shouldn't
be loading all the classes every time this gets called, but
we're boxed into this by the fact that the message design
doesn't "'label"' the class bytecodes with the class name. Thus,
we can't pick an individual byte lump to load. Message
structure should be revisited in light of this.

Resolves references for the named class, but not for other
classes. Any other classes referenced by the named class will
have their references resolved automatically by the single
call to resolveClass.
*/

```
  private byte loadClassData(String name)[] {
    for( int i = 0; i < otherclasses.size(); i++ )
      {
      Class c = loadFromByteLump(
                (byte[])otherclasses.elementAt(i), false );
      System.out.println( "loaded "+c );
      if( c.getName().compareTo(name) == 0 )
        {
        System.out.println( "match "+c );
        resolveClass(c);
        return( (byte[])otherclasses.elementAt(i) );
        }
      else
        System.out.println( "no match "+c );
      }
    return( null );
    }
```

/** Create a Class from an array of bytes. Defines the class,
adds the class name to the hashtable so that we only load it
once, and resolves references if specified.
*/

```
  public synchronized Class loadFromByteLump( byte[] lump,
                                    boolean resolve ) {
    Class c;
    c = defineClass(lump, 0, lump.length);
    cache.put(c.getName(), c );
    if( resolve )
      resolveClass( c );
    return( c );
    }
```

/** Top-level method called by Java when classes within an
Agent need to be loaded. We call it once for the lead class,
any other calls are generated internally by Java via the call
we make to resolveClass when loading the lead class. The
return value is a fully resolved Class that can be instantiated.
This is the implementation of a ClassLoader method.
*/

```
    public synchronized Class loadClass(String name,
                                boolean resolve) {
    Class c;

    System.out.println( "loadClass("+name+")");
    try {
      c = findSystemClass( name );
      System.out.println( "Resolved "+name+" locally" );
    } catch( ClassNotFoundException e ) {
      System.out.println( "Resolving "+name+" remotely" );
                c = (Class)cache.get(name);
                if (c == null) {
        byte data[] = loadClassData(name);
        c = loadFromByteLump( data, resolve );
        }
      resolveClass(c);
      }
                return c;
    }
  }


/** A file name filter that simply looks for file names with a
particular extension. If the extension of the file name
supplied  to accept matches the extension supplied to the
constructor, the file is accepted.

@version 1.0
@author John Rodley
*/
class ExtensionFilter implements FilenameFilter {
  String soughtExtension;
  public ExtensionFilter(String ext) {
    soughtExtension = new String(ext);
    }

/** If the extension of the file name supplied
to accept matches soughtExtension the file is
accepted -- accept returns true.
*/
  public boolean accept( File f, String name ) {
    int i = name.lastIndexOf( '.' );
    if( i > 0 ) {
      String extension = name.substring(i);
      if( extension.compareTo(soughtExtension) == 0 ) {
        System.out.println( "accepting "+name);
        return( true );
        }
      }
    System.out.println( "rejecting "+name );
    return( false );
    }
  }
```

The **LoadMessage** carries the actual **Agent** class data from one AgentServer to another. Thus, when an AgentServer receives a LoadMessage, it knows to pull the class data out of that message, instantiate it, and start it running as an **Agent**. Like all messages, **LoadMessage** has two ends: creation and parsing. A **LoadMessage** is created on the dispatching AgentServer and parsed on another AgentServer. We have gone over the basics of message creation in Chapter 7. The unique twists **LoadMessage** adds are the two methods, **LoadClassFromFile** and **LoadClassesFromDirectory**. **LoadMessage** has two types of classes:, the lead class, of which there can only be one, and all the other classes. This is just like back in Listing 9.7 where our multi-class, **ClassLoader** instantiated needed one "lead class" to start the whole process, then it loaded all the other classes from the same directory. Same theory here, only in the **LoadMessage** constructor we're not trying to load the classes into a **Class** object: We're trying to put them into a message to transmit over the Net. So the constructor calls **LoadClassFromFile** for the lead class, then **LoadClassesFromDirectory** for all the other classes. This puts all the class data into byte array Vector, which **createMessage** uses to fill up the actual Net-transmittable message.

The arguments are passed in as a Vector of byte arrays, so **createMessage** has a simple, if tedious job to do, running through the byte arrays containing the message data, attaching a field header to each, and copying the fields into the final message byte array. And that takes care of **LoadMessage** creation.

On the other end, in order to start up the **Agent**, the AgentServer which receives the **LoadMessage**, has to parse it. If you look closely at **LoadMessage.parse**, you'll see that it takes each field preceded by an ARG_PREFIX, and turns it into an array of bytes that it adds to the **vargs** Vector. It takes the first CLAS field it finds and puts that into the **leadclas** byte array, then puts all the other class fields into the **otherclasses** byte array Vector. When we have the lead class stored in the **leadclas** byte array, and all the other classes stored in the byte arrays of **otherclasses**, we have everything we need to successfully instantiate our new **Agent**, which we do at the bottom of parse.

There is, however, one crucial difference between the classes we've pried out of the **LoadMessage** and the classes we load from files in Listing 9.7. Remember that in order to use a class, all the references must be resolved. This call to **resolveClass** will cause the interpreter to call **ClassLoader.loadClass** for each class that needs to be loaded. In Listing 9.7, we know which file to load when the interpreter asks us to load a class (via **ClassLoader.loadClass**) because the file name is the class name. In our Vector of class data files, we do not know the names of the classes. In fact, we must instantiate the classes in order to find out their names. This leads to the unorthodox design of the **AgentLoader**, also shown in Listing 9.10.

LoadMessage.parse creates an instance of **AgentLoader** in order to instantiate the **Agent**. The constructor to **AgentLoader** takes the Vector of "other" classes as its only argument. It then runs through that array instantiating each class *without resolving that class*. Thus, when the constructor is finished, it has a Vector of unresolved classes stored in the Hashtable **cache**. Notice, we haven't tried to instantiate the lead class yet. **When LoadMessage.parse** invokes **loadFromByteLump** with the lead class as its argument, it also tells **loadFromByteLump** to resolve the lead class.

The call to **resolveClass** within **loadFromByteLump** causes a chain reaction of calls to **loadClass**. The interpreter will call **loadClass** for each of the "other" classes with the resolve flag set to true. Each of the other classes is already loaded and, they, in turn just need only to be resolved. And so, by a most complicated route, our **Agent** is finally instantiated.

Listing 9.11 shows the section of code in the AgentServer where we turn a LoadMessage into a running **Agent**.

Listing 9.11 Turning a LoadMessage into a Running Agent

```
/** Parse and process a message from the client. Follows the
basic system of: read 4 bytes and figure out the message type,
instantiate a message class appropriate to the type, then tell
that new instance to parse the lump. Deal with the parsed
message by looking at public members of the new class and
acting appropriately.
@param b An array of bytes read over the socket.
@param numbytes The number of read-bytes in b.

*/
public boolean ClientProcess( byte b[], int numbytes ) {

String command;
int currentOffset = 0;
String s;
int messageStart;
boolean bret = false;

while( currentOffset != numbytes ) {
  messageStart = currentOffset;
```

```
System.out.println( "currentOffset "+currentOffset+
    " numbytes "+numbytes );
// Every message starts with 4 bytes of command
command = new String( b, 0, currentOffset, 4 );
currentOffset += LoadMessage.PREFIX_SIZE;

// Followed by 10 bytes ASCII length - length of the whole message
// including command
String sLength = new String( b, 0, currentOffset, 10 );
currentOffset += LoadMessage.LOADLEN_SIZE;
System.out.println( "got "+command+" of length "+sLength );

if( command.compareTo( LoadMessage.LOAD_PREFIX ) == 0 ) {
  LoadMessage lm = new LoadMessage();
  Object o = lm.parse( b, currentOffset );
  if( o instanceof Agent ) {
    Agent a = (Agent)o;
    AgentServer.currentAgentServer.addRunningAgent(lm.sid);
    a.setAgentContext( new SepContext( lm.sid,
      lm.dispatching_server_name,
        lm.dispatching_server_port ));
    a.setArguments( lm.vargs );
    a.start();
    }
```

Notice that **LoadMessage.parse** does not start the **Agent** running in its own thread. Why not? Because the Agent hasn't been configured yet. Our instantiated FileFinder has no idea which files to find. It needs that list of files that the user entered into the configuration dialog and which the AgentServer who created the **LoadMessage** stuffed into the **LoadMessage. parse** pulls these file names out into a Vector of byte arrays, instantiates the **FileFinder**, and returns the instantiated **FileFinder** to **ClientProcess**. **ClientProcess** then gives the file names to the new **FileFinder** via **setArguments** and starts the **FileFinder** running in its own thread via **Thread.start**.

Having finished our long digression into **LoadMessages** and **SocketHandlers**, we can now polish off the **FileFinder** class with a short discussion of its key method: **run**. **run** contains the guts of the **FileFinder**, the part that does the actual work the user wants done out on the AgentServer. When **SocketHandler.ClientProcess** calls **Thread.start**, our **FileFinder.run** method starts running in its own thread. We want to start our file find at a particular sub-directory that the AgentServer can set, so we get the value for acl.read from the System properties file. We report back to the AgentLauncher (via **AgentContext.reportStart**) that we've started work. At that point, the AgentLauncher should start running the digging animation. Then we create a **File** object from the starting directory, and run **File.list** against it using our

AgainstArgs FilenameFilter to actually decide which files remain in the list. The String array **filelist** that **File.list** returns contains only those files that match the users criteria. If there are no files in the list, we report "no -results" back to the AgentLauncher. If there are files in the list, we write each file name out to the results file, then report the results file URL back to the AgentLauncher via **AgentContext.reportFinish**. And finally, we re-dispatch ourselves to the rest of the network.

Conclusion

If you've made it this far without tearing your hair out, congratulate yourself. Class loading is undoubtedly one of the most difficult topics in all of Java. In this chapter we've seen how Java encapsulates runtime type information in the class **Class**. We've also seen how Java provides an easy way to instantiate classes from arbitrary sources via the **ClassLoader** class. Along the way we've implemented both file-based and network-based **ClassLoaders** and seen how the lack of file name-to-class-name linkage in the network based Class Loader forced an unorthodox sequence of class instantiation and reference resolution.

In fact, we now have a functional Agent system. Our Agents can be picked, configured, and dispatched. Once dispatched, they can traverse the Net, instantiating on each AgentServer they encounter and re-dispatching to points further out on the Net. While running, they can report back whatever results they might have produced.

Chapter 10

Security in Detail

Security
in Detail

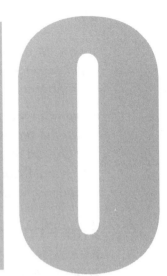

*Java gives browsers a sophisticated set of
tools for protecting us all from applets. Let's
see how they work.*

Security was one of the hardest topics to deal with in this book because Sun
and the browser designers are still wrestling with the issue themselves. Within
Java itself, security is pretty much a settled issue. The mechanism for implementing security (the **SecurityManager** class) is in place. What is unsettled is
how browsers will use this mechanism to protect their users.

The question is one of risk reward. How much risk are users willing to risk to
enjoy the, as yet undetermined, benefit of running Java applets?

Netscape has taken a very cautious approach to the subject, with the result that
applets under Netscape are severely restricted. The security rules that Netscape
applies to applets are:

- Applets cannot read or write files on the local file system.
- Applets can only open network connections to the host from which they
  were loaded.
- When an applet opens a pop-up window (such as a dialog box), Netscape
  will warn the user that it's an applet window.

Properties

Java supports the concept of a *"property."* A property is essentially a global variable that Java programs (applet or application) can read or write via the
System.getProperty and **System.setProperty** methods. A group of "system" prop-

erties exist that have a value in every situation, whether standalone, Netscape, appletviewer, or HotJava. Table 10.1 shows the system properties and describes their purpose.

As you can see, most of the system properties deal with the environment in which the browser operates—current directory, user name, operating system version, and so on. There can also be any number of "user" properties, which are essentially private properties that are meaningful only to specific applications or applets.

The Properties File

For HotJava and appletviewer, you can set properties for your computer via the ~/.hotjava/properties file, where ~ stands for your home directory. For reasons of its own, Netscape does not use the properties file. All properties must be set using dialog boxes within Netscape.

Table 10.1   The System Properties

Property	Description
java.class.path	Value of "classpath:" the toplevel directory under which all classes to be loaded via the primordial class loader will be found.
java.class.version	Version of the Java packages.
java.home	Directory where the Java executables live.
java.vendor	Name of the vendor of this Java interpreter.
java.vendor.url	URL of the vendor's home page.
java.version	Version of Java in use.
file.separator	Character that separates files in a multi-file string.
line.separator	Character sequence that indicates the end of a line in this operating system.
path.separator	Character that separates directories in this operating system.
os.arch	"Architecture" of this machine;. for Intel Pentium and 486 this will be "x86."
os.name	Name of the operating system;. for Windows NT, this will be "Windows NT."
os.version	Version of the operating system.
user.dir	Current directory.
user.home	Name of the user's home directory.
user.name	User's login name.

All Windows programmers are familiar with the idea of initialization files such as WIN.INI. These files usually contain a series of statements of the form:

```
key=value
```

where *key* is the name of something, and *value* is the value we want to initialize this something to. Java supports the same concept in the properties file. Listing 10.1 shows the properties file I use locally for applet development.

Listing 10.1   My Properties File

```
#AppletViewer
#Fri Feb 09 12:04:35  1996
firewallSet=false
appletviewer.version=1.0
package.restrict.access.netscape=false
proxySet=false
firewallHost=
package.restrict.access.sun=false
acl.read.applet=true
acl.write.applet=true
acl.read=/temp/
firewallPort=80
appletviewer.security.mode=unrestricted
acl.write=/temp/
```

As you can see, I've defined thirteen variables, and set each to some string value. All of these variables are meaningful to appletviewer, though I could have easily defined my own variables and set them here manually. Table 10.2 shows some of the properties that are unique to appletviewer and HotJava.

The most interesting of these, and the most important from a security stand-point, are the **acl.read** and **acl.write** properties. acl stands for Access Control List, and that's just what these properties are—lists of directories that an applet can access. Let's take a look at an example. What if our properties file contained the following lines:

```
acl.read=/home/johnr;/temp;/usr/ajr
acl.write=/temp;/usr/ajr
```

Applets loaded on a computer that had this properties file would be allowed to read the directories /home/johnr, /temp, and /usr/ajr directories, *and* all the subdirectories beneath them. They would be able to write to /temp and /usr/ajr, *and* all the subdirectories beneath them. It's as easy as that.

Table 10.2	appletviewer and HotJava Properties
Property	**Description**
awt.toolkit	Package name of the AWT package in use.
acl.read	Directory that applets are allowed to read; all subdirectories of this directory are readable too.
acl.write	Directory that applets are allowed to write; all subdirectories are writeable too.
appletviewer.version	Version of the appletviewer.
firewallSet	Set to "true" if we're behind a firewall.
firewallProxyPort	Set to the http port number of the firewall proxy.
firewallProxyHost	Set to the hos tname of the firewall proxy.
firewallPort	Set to the http port number of the firewall.
firewallHost	Set to the host name of the firewall.
proxySet	Set to true if we're using a proxy.
cachingProxyPort	Set to the port number of the caching proxy.
cachingProxyHost	Set to the host name of the caching proxy.
appletviewer.security.mode	Set to the security mode of the appletviewer; appletviewer supports restricted and unrestricted class loading.

Querying Properties

Having persistent properties is a wonderful thing, but how do we get at these properties from within an applet? Listing 10.2 shows a simple applet that tries to get the value of each of these properties.

Listing 10.2   A Property-Reading Applet

```
package chap10;

import java.awt.*;
import java.applet.Applet;
import java.lang.*;
import java.util.*;

/** An applet that tries to read and display various
properties. Displays the properties in a list.
@author John Rodley
@version 1.0
*/
public class ch10_fig1 extends Applet {

  Vector props = new Vector(1);
```

```
/** Set the screen in border layout, put a list in the center,
and then display all the properties in the list.
*/
  public void init() {
    setLayout( new BorderLayout());
    List l = new List();
    add( "Center", l );
    props.addElement( new String( "firewallSet" ));
    props.addElement( new String( "appletviewer.version" ));
    props.addElement(
        new String("package.restrict.access.netscape"));
    props.addElement( new String( "proxySet" ));
    props.addElement( new String( "firewallHost" ));
    props.addElement(
        new String("package.restrict.access.sun"));
    props.addElement( new String( "acl.read.applet" ));
    props.addElement( new String( "acl.write.applet" ));
    props.addElement( new String( "acl.read" ));
    props.addElement( new String( "firewallPort" ));
    props.addElement(new String("appletviewer.security.mode"));
    props.addElement( new String( "acl.write" ));
    props.addElement( new String( "xyzabc" ));

    for( int i = 0; i < props.size(); i++ ) {
      try {
        l.addItem((String)props.elementAt(i)+
          "="+System.getProperty((String)props.elementAt(i)));
        System.out.println( (String)props.elementAt(i)+
          "="+System.getProperty((String)props.elementAt(i)));
      }
      catch( Exception e ) {
          l.addItem( "Unable to read property "+
              (String)props.elementAt(i));
          System.out.println("Unable to read property "+
              (String)props.elementAt(i));
      }
    }
  }
}
```

In the **init** method we build a Vector of Strings containing all the variable names we expect to find in the properties file. Then we run through this Vector calling **System.getProperty** for each variable name. If the **getProperty** call throws an exception, we catch it and print a message declaring that the property is somehow inaccessible.

If we run this applet against this properties file in appletviewer, we get the application window and standard output shown in Figure 10.1.

What happened? appletviewer's **SecurityManager** goes by the rule that, by default, all properties should be inaccessible to applets. Thus, our call to **getProperty**

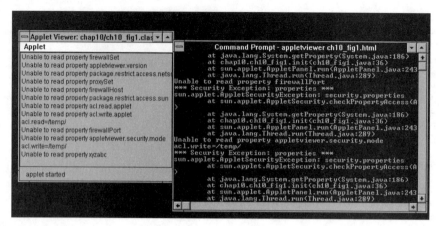

Figure 10.1

Output of the property reading applet.

bombs for almost every property in the file. Notice that even for properties that don't exist, like the **xyzabc** property, we get the same reaction from Java, a thrown **AppletSecurityException**. This measure protects the system from applets ferreting out properties by testing the system's reaction to various words.

Strangely enough, our **getProperty** call succeeds for **acl.read** and **acl.write**. Why? Because of the two statements:

```
acl.write.applet=true
acl.read.applet=true
```

These two statements tell the appletviewer **SecurityManager** that the values of **acl.read** and **acl.write** can be returned to applets via **getProperty**. You can do this with any property simply by appending ".applet" to the property name. For instance, to make the property **firewallSet** visible to applets, we'd add the following line to our properties file:

```
firewallSet.applet=true
```

Another thing to note about Figure 10.1 is that the exception prints to standard output despite the fact that we catch, and purposely ignore it. Security exceptions will always print at the lowest levels, for reasons that will be obvious if you think about the purpose of security. A **SecurityException** is meant to indicate that an applet tried something that wasn't allowed. If Java allowed applets to "hide" the occurrence of a **SecurityException**, it would defeat the purpose. Thus, although we can catch and ignore security exceptions, we can't prevent them from generating a notice of their occurrence.

The SecurityManager Class

A standalone Java executable, such as HotJava, implements security by subclassing **SecurityManager** and attaching an instance of the new class to the **System** via **System.setSecurityManager**. **setSecurityManager** can only be called once in the life of the JVM, so that once a browser sets the **SecurityManager**, a rogue applet cannot reset it. By the time an applet executes, the browser will already have set the **SecurityManager**. Table 10.3 shows the **SecurityManager** class.

As you can see, there are protective methods guarding each of the resources that is vulnerable to abuse by misbehaved applets—properties, class loading, windows, network I/O, file I/O, and thread processes. Let's look at how the protective methods of **SecurityManager** guard these resources.

Table 10.3 The Methods of the SecurityManager Class

Method Name	Arguments	Description
Helper Methods		
classDepth	String	Returns the index into the current class stack where the specified class is located; 0 is top of stack.
currentClassLoader		Returns the class loader or null if the primordial class loader is current.
getClassContext		Returns an array of classes that is the list of classes on the stack.
inClass	String	Returns true if the String argument is in the class.
inClassLoader		Returns true if there is a ClassLoader, false if the primordial class loader in use.
The Network		
CheckAccept	String, int	Can we accept connections on a socket?
CheckConnect	String, int	Can we connect to the specified network socket?
CheckListen	int	Can we listen to the specified local socket?

Continued

Table 10.3 The Methods of the SecurityManager Class (Continued)

Method Name	Arguments	Description
Threads and Processes		
checkAccess	Thread or ThreadGroup	Can the specified Thread/ThreadGroup modify *this* ThreadGroup?
checkExec	String	Can we execute the specified system command?
checkExit	int	Has the system exited the virtual machine?
checkLink	String	Can we use the specified linked library?
The File		
SystemcheckRead	int or String	Can we read from the specified file name or file descriptor?
checkWrite	int or String	Can we write to the specified file name or file descriptor?
Top-Level Windows		
checkTopLevelWindow		Can we create a window with no warning on it?
Classes and Class Loading		
checkCreateClassLoade		Can we create a ClassLoader?
checkPackageAccess	String	Can we use classes from the specified package?
checkPackage	Definition	Can we define a new package?
Properties		
checkProperties	Access	Can we read the list of properties?
checkPropertyAccess	String	Can we read the value of the specified property?

SecurityManager is an abstract class. An application that implements security, such as a browser, must define its own subclass of **SecurityManager**. We can divide the **SecurityManager** into two big sections: check methods and helper methods. The helper methods are utilities that security managers will find useful. and which we'll talk more about later. As for the check methods, Java puts all the sensitive resources in the system (file I/O, network I/O and so on) behind a lockable security door. The **SecurityManager's** check methods are the deadbolt lock of Java security.

Whenever the interpreter runs into an instruction that accesses a protected resource, it turns that instruction into two distinct operations:

- Check if the access in the instruction is allowed
- Execute the instruction

To check if the access is allowed, the interpreter calls the check method that protects that resource. If the check method returns, the access is allowed. If the check method throws a **SecurityException**, the next operation (execute the instruction) doesn't happen because (harking back to Chapter 6) the thrown exception has broken the flow of execution. By design, there is nothing we (or any hacker) can do to get around this restriction.

Writing a SecurityManager

So much for the theory of **SecurityManagers**. What does a real **SecurityManager** look like? In Listing 10.3, we add a configurable **SecurityManager** to the AgentServer that predicates access to resources on the state of a simple boolean.

Listing 10.3   The AgentServer's SecurityManager

```
/** A class that implements security for the AgentServer.
Brute-force strategy that simply uses a flag for each of the
methods in SecurityManager. Can configure itself using a
SecurityDialog. Initializes with ALL ACCESS ALLOWED.
*/
class AgentServerSecurityManager extends SecurityManager {
  public static Vector v = new Vector(1);

/** Build a vector of SecurityItems, one for each of the check
methods in SecurityManager. Initialize each SecurityItem to
true (access allowed). Can be changed later using configure.
*/
  public AgentServerSecurityManager() {
    v.addElement( new SecurityItem( "Accept", true ));
    v.addElement( new SecurityItem( "AccessThread", true ));
    v.addElement( new SecurityItem( "AccessThreadGroup", true ));
    v.addElement( new SecurityItem( "Connect", true ));
    v.addElement( new SecurityItem( "ConnectBoth", true ));
    v.addElement( new SecurityItem( "CreateClassLoader", true ));
    v.addElement( new SecurityItem( "Delete", true ));
    v.addElement( new SecurityItem( "Exec", true ));
    v.addElement( new SecurityItem( "Exit", true ));
    v.addElement( new SecurityItem( "Link", true ));
    v.addElement( new SecurityItem( "Listen", true ));
    v.addElement( new SecurityItem( "PackageAccess", true ));
```

```
    v.addElement( new SecurityItem( "PackageDefinition", true ));
    v.addElement( new SecurityItem( "PropertiesAccess", true ));
    v.addElement( new SecurityItem( "PropertyAccess", true ));
    v.addElement( new SecurityItem( "ReadFD", true ));
    v.addElement( new SecurityItem( "ReadName", true ));
    v.addElement( new SecurityItem( "ReadBoth", true ));
    v.addElement( new SecurityItem( "SetFactory", true ));
    v.addElement( new SecurityItem( "Window", true ));
    v.addElement( new SecurityItem( "WriteFD", true ));
    v.addElement( new SecurityItem( "WriteName", true ));
    }

/** Change the state of a SecurityItem based on the name of the
item. This is called for each SecurityItem by the
SecurityDialog when the the OK button is hit.
@param  name  The name of the SecurityItem.
@param  state The state true/false we want to set the
SecurityItem to.
*/
  public void setFlagState( String name, boolean state ) {
    for( int i = 0; i < v.size(); i++ ) {
      SecurityItem si = (SecurityItem)v.elementAt(i);
      if( si.name.compareTo(name) == 0 ) {
        si.state = state;
        break;
        }
      }
    }
/** Return the true/false state of the named SecurityItem.
@param  name  The name of the item we want to query.
*/
  boolean isSet( String name ) {
    for( int i = 0; i < v.size(); i++ ) {
      SecurityItem si = (SecurityItem)v.elementAt(i);
      if( si.name.compareTo(name) == 0 )
        return si.state;
      }
    return( false );
    }

/** Allow the user to configure this security manager by
filling out a SecurityDialog.
*/
  public void configure() {
    dumpContext();
    SecurityDialog sd = new SecurityDialog(AgentServer.f);
    sd.ShowAndLayout();
    }


/**  Checks to see if a socket connection to the specified
port on the specified host has been accepted.
*/
```

```
    public void checkAccept(String host, int port) {
      if( isSet( "Accept" ))
         return;
      throw new AgentServerSecurityException( );
      }

/** Checks to see if the specified thread is allowed to
modify the thread group.
*/
    public void checkAccess(Thread t) {
      if( isSet( "AccessThread" ))
         return;
      throw new AgentServerSecurityException( );
      }

/**     Checks to see if the specified thread group is allowed
to modify this group.
*/
    public void checkAccess(ThreadGroup tg) {
      if( isSet( "AccessThreadGroup" ))
         return;
      throw new AgentServerSecurityException( );
      }

/**     Checks to see if a socket has connected to the specified
port on the the specified host.
*/
    public void checkConnect(String host, int port) {
      if( isSet( "Connect" ))
         return;
      throw new AgentServerSecurityException( );
      }

/**     Checks to see if the current execution context and the
indicated execution context are both allowed to connect to the
     indicated host and port.
*/
    public void checkConnect(String host, int port, Object o) {
      if( isSet( "ConnectBoth" ))
         return;
      throw new AgentServerSecurityException( );
      }

/**     Checks to see if the ClassLoader has been created.
*/
    public void checkCreateClassLoader() {
      if( isSet( "CreateClassLoader" ))
         return;
      throw new AgentServerSecurityException( );
      }

/**     Checks to see if a file with the specified system
dependent file name can be deleted.
```

```
*/
  public void checkDelete(String filename) {
    if( isSet( "Delete" ))
       return;
    throw new AgentServerSecurityException();
    }

/**     Checks to see if the system command is executed by
trusted code.
*/
  public void checkExec(String cmdname) {
    if( isSet( "Exec" ))
       return;
    throw new AgentServerSecurityException();
    }

/**     Checks to see if the system has exited the virtual
machine with an exit code.
*/
  public void checkExit(int i) {
    if( isSet( "Exit" ))
       return;
    throw new AgentServerSecurityException();
    }

/**     Checks to see if the specified linked library exists.
*/
  public void  checkLink(String libname) {
    if( isSet( "Link" ))
       return;
    throw new AgentServerSecurityException();
    }

/**     Checks to see if a server socket is listening to the
specified local port that it is bounded to.
*/
  public void  checkListen(int port) {
    if( isSet( "Listen" ))
       return;
    throw new AgentServerSecurityException();
    }

/**     Checks to see if an applet can access a package.
*/
  public void  checkPackageAccess(String pkgname) {
    if( isSet( "PackageAccess" ))
       return;
    throw new AgentServerSecurityException();
    }

/**     Checks to see if an applet can define classes in a
package.
*/
```

```
    public void  checkPackageDefinition(String pkgname)  {
      if( isSet( "PackageDefinition" ))
          return;
      throw new AgentServerSecurityException();
      }

/**     Checks to see who has access to the system properties.
*/
  public void  checkPropertiesAccess() {
    if( isSet( "PropertiesAccess" ))
        return;
    throw new AgentServerSecurityException();
      }

/**     Checks to see who has access to the system property
named by key.
*/
  public void  checkPropertyAccess(String property) {
    if( isSet( "PropertyAccess" ))
        return;
    throw new AgentServerSecurityException();
    . }

/**     Checks to see who has access to the system property
named by key and def.
*/
  public void  checkPropertyAccess(String property, String s) {
    if( isSet( "PropertyAccess" ))
        return;
    throw new AgentServerSecurityException();
      }

/**     Checks to see if an input file with the specified file
descriptor object gets created.
*/
  public void  checkRead(FileDescriptor fd) {
    if( isSet( "ReadFD" ))
        return;
    throw new AgentServerSecurityException();
      }

/**     Checks to see if an input file with the specified
system dependent file name gets created.
*/
  public void  checkRead(String filename) {
    if( isSet( "ReadName" ))
        return;
    throw new AgentServerSecurityException();
      }

/**     Checks to see if the current context or the indicated
context are both allowed to read the given file name.
*/
```

```
   public void  checkRead(String filename, Object o) {
     if( isSet( "ReadBoth" ))
         return;
     throw new AgentServerSecurityException();
     }

/**      Checks to see if an applet can set a
networking-related object factory.
*/
   public void  checkSetFactory() {
     if( isSet( "SetFactory" ))
         return;
     throw new AgentServerSecurityException();
     }

/**      Checks to see if top-level windows can be created by
the caller.
*/
   public boolean  checkTopLevelWindow(Object o) {
     if( isSet( "Window" ))
         return true;
     throw new AgentServerSecurityException();
     }

/**      Checks to see if an output file with the specified
file descriptor object gets created.
*/
   public void  checkWrite(FileDescriptor fd)  {
     if( isSet( "WriteFD" ))
         return;
     throw new AgentServerSecurityException();
     }

/**      Checks to see if an output file with the specified
system- dependent file name gets created.
*/
public void  checkWrite(String filename)  {
   if( isSet( "Write" ))
       return;
   throw new AgentServerSecurityException();
   }

   }

/** A class representing a violation of the AgentServer's
security strategy.
*/
class AgentServerSecurityException
                   extends SecurityException {
  public AgentServerSecurityException() {
    super( "AgentServerSecurityException" );
    }
  }
```

```
/** A class for holding the name and current state of a
security property.
*/
class SecurityItem {
/** The name of the resource this security item is protecting. */
  public String name;
/** Set to true if the access to this resource is ALLOWED. */
  public boolean state;

/** Constructor - force the user to initialize the name and
state of this property.
@param  label The name of this property.
@param  initState The initial state of this property.
*/
  public SecurityItem( String label, boolean initState ) {
    name = new String( label );
    state = initState;
    }
  }

/** A modal dialog box that allows the user to set the security
strategy for the AgentServer.
@version 1.0 1/4/1996
@author John Rodley
*/
class SecurityDialog extends Dialog {
  int selectIndex = -1;
  Frame parent;
  Panel ButtonPanel;
  public boolean bFinished = false;
  Vector cbV = new Vector(1);

/** Constructor.
*/
  public SecurityDialog(Frame p) {
  super(p, "Setup AgentServer Security", true);
    parent = p;

    // Set up all the graphical elements
    // Split the dialog main panel into three elements, top,
    // bottom, and middle, via the BorderLayout. The top and
    // bottom size themselves according to the preferred sizes
    // of the text on the top and the buttons on the bottom.
    // The Center panel, which the list fills, uses all the
    // space left in the middle.
     setLayout(new BorderLayout());
     ButtonPanel = new Panel();
    add( "South", ButtonPanel );

    Panel checkPanel = new Panel();
    checkPanel.setLayout( new GridLayout( 8, 3 ));
```

```
      Vector v = AgentServerSecurityManager.v;
      for( int i = 0; i < v.size(); i++ ) {
        Checkbox cb = new Checkbox(
          ((SecurityItem)v.elementAt(i)).name,
          null, ((SecurityItem)v.elementAt(i)).state);
        checkPanel.add( cb );
        cbV.addElement(cb );
        }

    add( "Center", checkPanel );

      Button okbutton = new Button("OK");
    ButtonPanel.add( okbutton );
    Button cancelbutton = new Button( "Cancel" );
    ButtonPanel.add( cancelbutton );
      }


/** Size the dialog to something appropriate, then make it
non-resizeable so that users don't go resizing it themselves.
*/
  public void ShowAndLayout() {
    show();
    resize( 600, 300 );
    layout();
    setResizable(false);
      }

/** Process the OK and Cancel buttons. This also gets called
every time the user changes the state of one of our check boxes
so we explicitly ignore that case. When OK is hit, roll
through the SecurityItem Vector setting the state of each of
the items based on the check box state.
*/
public boolean action(Event e, Object o) {

  if( e.target instanceof Checkbox ) {
    return false;
    }
  if( e.target instanceof Button ) {
    if( ((Button)e.target).getLabel().compareTo("OK") == 0 ) {
      for( int i = 0; i < cbV.size(); i++ ) {
        AgentServer.assm.setFlagState(
          ((Checkbox)cbV.elementAt(i)).getLabel(),
            ((Checkbox)cbV.elementAt(i)).getState());
        }
      }
    }
  bFinished = true;
  dispose();
  return true;
  }
}
```

In Listing 10.3, we define a class, **SecurityItem**, that holds the name of the resource, and a **boolean**, state, that tells whether or not access to the resource is allowed. In the **AgentServerSecurityManager** constructor, we build a **Vector** of these **SecurityItem**s, one for each resource, and set its initial state. Each check method merely reads the current state of "its" **SecurityItem**, returning if the access is allowed, or throwing an exception if the access is not allowed. To facilitate our use of **SecurityItem**s, we define two of our own methods, **isSet** and **setFlagState**, which allow us to set and check the state of a **SecurityItem** based on its name.

All these "locks" would be useless without some way to turn them on and off. Thus, we define a dialog box, SecurityDialog, that simply allows us to set or clear each of the **SecurityItem.state** booleans.

Now we have all the pieces of a brute-force security solution. We need to link them into the AgentServer. Listing 10.4 shows the AgentServer modifications we make to set up our **SecurityManager**, as well as to call our SecurityDialog.

Listing 10.4 AgentServer with SecurityManager and SecurityDialog

```
public AgentServer() {
    ...
  m = new MenuBar();
  f.setMenuBar( m );
  Menu m1 = new Menu("File");
  m.add(m1);
  MenuItem m2 = new MenuItem( "Load test" );
  m1.add( m2 );
  m2 = new MenuItem( "Exit" );
  m1.add( m2 );
  m1 = new Menu("Options");
  m.add(m1);
  m2 = new MenuItem( "Configure" );
  m1.add( m2 );
    ...
  }


/** Handle any menu item picks. Right now, it only has two, Exit
and Load Test. Exit sets the agentServers bRun flag to false,
causing the AgentServer.run to fall out of the endless while
loop.
@see AgentServer
*/
public boolean action( Event evt, Object o ) {
```

```
if( evt.target instanceof MenuItem )
  {
  if( evt.arg.toString().compareTo( "Exit" ) == 0 )
    {
    AgentServer.currentAgentServer.bRun = false;
    System.out.println( "action event "+evt );
    }
  else
    {
    if(evt.arg.toString().compareTo( "Load test" ) == 0 )
      {
      AgentServer.currentAgentServer.LoadTest();
      System.out.println( "action event "+evt );
      }
    else
      {
      if(evt.arg.toString().compareTo( "Configure" ) == 0 )
        {
        AgentServer.assm.configure();
        System.out.println( "action event "+evt );
        }
      }
    }
  }
return( true );
}
```

Up in AgentServer's static **main** method, we instantiate our **SecurityManager**, then call **System.setSecurityManager** to make our **SecurityManager** the one, and only one, that Java will use for this application. *Once invoked, setSecurityManager can never be called again for the life of the application.* Once we've set our **SecurityManager**, Java will begin automatically calling its check methods whenever any security issues arise.

Down in the AgentServer constructor we add a new menu, Options, and a menu item, Configure. When Configure is selected, **action** will call **AgentServerSecurityManager.configure** ,which displays our dialog box.

If you look at our check methods, they're all fairly monotonous, simply throwing an exception if the flag they depend on is clear. This is simple and effective, but it's also far too broad to be useful to the AgentServer, or any browser for that matter.

Say you want to restrict agents from making their own network connections. In our current security setup, you'd open the security dialog and clear the "Connect" check box. All well and good, so far. The problem arises when you try to run our **FileFinder** agent with this flag cleared. Figure 10.2 shows the AgentServer's standard output when we run a **FileFinder** agent with connect restrictions "disallowed."

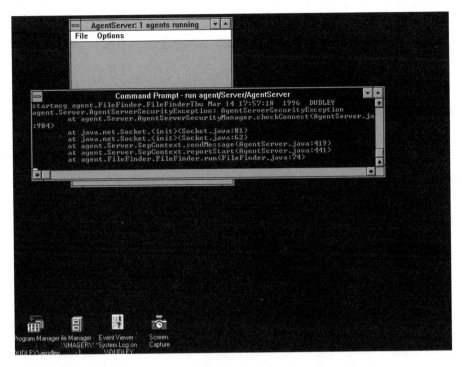

Figure 10.2

FileFinder running with connect restrictions disallowed.

As you might remember from Chapter 9, the **FileFinder** doesn't do any direct network communication. The problem is that our **checkConnect** method doesn't distinguish the AgentServer itself making connections (which is allowed) from the agent making connections (which is not allowed).

Selective Access Restriction

Another security issue along the same lines is file I/O. Way back in Chapter 3, we indicated that we might want to restrict disallow agents from doing direct file I/O. Let's give it a try. In Listing 10.5, we implement **checkWrite** methods that distinguish between the AgentServer and the agent, restricting direct agent writes, but allowing AgentServer writes, and agent writes via the **AgentContext** interface.

Listing 10.5   The checkWrite Methods, and Their Helper Methods

```
/**     Checks to see if an output file with the specified
file descriptor object gets created.
*/
```

```
     public void  checkWrite(FileDescriptor fd)  {
 if( isAgent()) {
        if( isAgentGoingThroughAgentContext())
          return;
        }
      else
        return;
//    if( isSet( "WriteFD" ))
//        return;
     throw new AgentServerSecurityException();
      }


/**      Checks to see if an output file with the specified
system dependent file name gets created.
*/
   public void  checkWrite(String filename)  {
     if( isAgent()) {
       if( isAgentGoingThroughAgentContext())
         return;
       }
     else
       return;
     throw new AgentServerSecurityException();
      }


    }
/** Return true if Agent is on the stack. This means we were
called from somewhere within an Agent.
@return true if an instance of Agent is somewhere on the stack.
*/
boolean isAgent() {
  Class c[] = getClassContext();
  for( int i = 0; i < c.length; i++ ) {
    if( subclassesAgent( c[i] )) {
      int AgentIndex = classDepth( c[i].getName() );
      if( AgentIndex >= 0 )
        return( true );
      }
    }
  return( false );
  }


/** Return true if the specified class subclasses
agent.Agent.Agent. All agents run over the Net should subclass
Agent. Runs through all the superclasses of c checking their
name against agent.Agent.Agent.
@param  c The class we're inquiring about.
@return true if c is a subclass of Agent, false otherwise.
*/
boolean subclassesAgent( Class c ) {
  Class cNext = c;
  while( true ) {
    Class c1 = cNext.getSuperclass();
```

```
   if( c1 == null )
     break;
   if( c1.getName().compareTo( "agent.Agent.Agent" ) == 0 )
     return( true );
   cNext = c1;
   }
 return( false );
 }

/** Return true if the Agent is calling us through the
AgentContext, false otherwise. Accomplish this by looking at
the stack. If the "classDepth" of the Agent is lower than that
of the AgentContext, or if the AgentContext isn't on the stack,
then the Agent is trying to go around us.
*/
boolean isAgentGoingThroughAgentContext() {
  Class c[] = getClassContext();
  for( int i = 0; i < c.length; i++ ) {
    if( subclassesAgent( c[i] )) {
      int AContextIndex = classDepth( "agent.Server.SepContext" );
      int AgentIndex = classDepth( c[i].getName() );
      // This is where we should catch an agent calling
      // File.write directly.
      if( AContextIndex < 0 )
        return( false );

      // This should never happen. Indicates SepContext
      // calling back to Agent!!
      if( AgentIndex < AContextIndex )
        return( false );
      else
        return( true );
      }
    }
  System.out.println( "NO AGENT!!" );
  return( true );
  }
```

The **checkWrite** methods are fairly simple, in themselves. First, we call **isAgent**, which tells us whether this call emanates from an instance of **Agent**. If the call doesn't come from an **Agent**, we allow it. If the call does come from an **Agent**, we call **isAgentGoingThroughAgentContext**, to see if the call goes through the **AgentContext**. If it does, we allow the call. If not, we throw an exception. Pretty easy, huh?

The real work here is done by the two methods: **isAgent** and **isAgentGoing ThroughAgentContext**. **isAgent** gets the list of classes on the stack by calling **SecurityManager.getClassContext**. This gives us an array of classes. We go through these classes one by one, checking to see if they subclass **Agent**. If any subclass of **Agent** is on the stack, we were called, somehow, by **Agent** and we return true.

At this point, we know that an instance of **Agent** caused this call to **checkWrite**. That's all we know. It could have been caused by a direct call to **FileOutputStream.write**, or it could have been some more convoluted invocation chain. What we need to know now is whether the **AgentContext** was between the invocation by **Agent** and the call to **writeCheck**. This is where **isAgentGoingThroughAgentContext** comes in. Like **isAgent**, we get the list of classes on the stack from **getClassContext**. Then we run through the array looking for the class that subclasses **Agent**. When we find it, we call **SecurityManager.classDepth** to find out where on the stack the **AgentContext** and the **Agent** reside. As methods call each other, Java builds a stack of classes. At the top of the stack (index 0) is the class you're in when you look at the stack. At index 1 is the class whose method called the current class, and so on .... So, when we call **classDepth**, at the top of the stack (index 0), **AgentServerSecurityManager** is at the top of the stack (index 0). Somewhere further down (index 6 in the upcoming example) is our subclass of **Agent**. All we need to know now is whether there's an **AgentContext** on the stack between our **Agent** and our **SecurityManager**. So, we compare the **classDepth** of our **Agent** against the **classDepth** of our **AgentContext** (**SepContext**). If there is no **AgentContext** (**AContextIndex** < 0) or its **classDepth** is greater than the **Agent**'s, we return false (operation disallowed).

The only method we haven't talked about is **subclassesAgent**. This method takes a class and determines whether that class subclasses **agent.Agent.Agent**. We do this by repeatedly calling **getSuperclass** until we reach the base class and **getSuperclass** returns null. We compare each superclass name to **agent.Agent.Agent**.

A Rogue Agent

Now we have a super-duper **SecurityManager** that implements fairly sophisticated security. How do we test it? We need a new agent, one that doesn't play by the rules. Listing 10.6 shows EvilAgent, a modification of Chapter 9's **FileFinder** agent, designed specifically to provoke our new security mechanism.

Listing 10.6   The EvilAgent

```
package agent.EvilAgent;
```

```
import java.lang.*;
import java.util.*;
import java.awt.*;
import java.io.*;
import agent.Agent.*;
import agent.EvilAgent.*;
// To catch the definition of AgentContext
import agent.Server.AgentContext;

/** An Agent designed to provoke the SecurityManager on the
AgentServer by trying to write directly to a file rather than
through the AgentContext. A demonstration of the capabilities
of the SecurityManager class.
@version 1.1
@author John Rodley
*/
public class EvilAgent extends Agent {
    ConfigurationDialog cfd;
    Vector args;

/** Constructor - does nothing by design, but it's useful to
leave the println in there just to convince yourself that the
Agent has been instantiated on the AgentServer.
*/
    public EvilAgent() {
        System.out.println( "EvilAgent constructor" );
        }

/** Put up a ConfigurationDialog that gets the arguments this
Agent needs to run on an AgentServer.
@param  frame The frame window of the browser, needed for the
dialog constructor.
*/
    public void configure( Frame frame ) {
        cfd = new ConfigurationDialog( frame );
        cfd.show();
        }

/** Return whatever arguments the configure method got from the
user as a Vector of Strings.
@return A Vector of Strings that are only meaningful to the
Agent itself, not to either the AgentLauncher or AgentServer.
*/
    public Vector getArguments() {
        return( cfd.args );
        }

/** Configure the Agent with the specified Vector of Strings as
'arguments'. Called by the AgentLauncher, passing the arguments
it pried out of the LoadMessage.
@param  ar  A Vector of Strings identical to the one returned
to the AgentLauncher by getArguments.
*/
```

```
    public void setArguments( Vector ar ) {
       args = ar;
       }
```

```
/** The run loop for this Agent. Gets the top-level directory
which this Agent is allowed to read from the properties file
via the key acl.read, and checks all the files in that
directory against the filenamefilter specified by the user back
on the AgentLauncher.
*/
    public void run() {
        String topDirectory = System.getProperty( "acl.read" );
        if( topDirectory == null ) {
           System.out.println( "can't read this machine" );
           return;
           }
        System.out.println( "got value "+topDirectory
                         +" for property acl.read" );
        boolean keepGoing = true;
        String currentDirectory = new String(topDirectory);
        ac.reportStart( "" );
        ac.writeOutput(
   "<HTML><HEAD><TITLE>FileFinderOutput</TITLE></HEAD><BODY>" );
        String writeDirectory = System.getProperty( "acl.write" );
        if( writeDirectory == null ) {
           System.out.println( "can't write this machine" );
          return;
           }

       // Here is where we stop acting like the FileFinder agent
       // and start misbehaving.
       System.out.println( "Creating "+
                 writeDirectory+"EvilFile.txt" );
       try {
         // This is the call that provokes the
         // AgentServerSecurityManager into excepting
         FileOutputStream fos =
             new FileOutputStream(writeDirectory+"/EvilFile.txt");
         byte b[] = new byte[20];
         fos.write( b );
         }
       catch( IOException e )
         { System.out.println( "Bad file io "+e ); }
         }
    }
```

```
/** A dialog box for configuring a FileFinder Agent. Allows
the user to enter up to seven file names to search for.
@see Dialog
*/
class ConfigurationDialog extends Dialog {
  Label theLabel;
  Button theButton;
```

```
    TextField tf[] = new TextField[7];
    Panel ButtonPanel;
    Panel TextFieldPanel;
    public Vector args;

/** constructor creates a dialog box with a certain title, lays it
out border style, adds a prompt, seven TextFields for entering the
file specs, and OK and Cancel buttons.
@param  parent  The Frame that is the parent of this dialog.
*/
    public ConfigurationDialog(Frame parent) {
     super(parent, "Configure File Finder", true);
       setLayout(new BorderLayout());
     theLabel = new Label( "Enter up to 7 file specifications:" );
       add("North",theLabel);
     TextFieldPanel = new Panel();
       TextFieldPanel.setLayout( new GridLayout(7, 1 ));
     add("Center", TextFieldPanel );
       for( int i = 0; i < 7; i++ ) {
          tf[i] = new TextField( "", 25 );
        TextFieldPanel.add( tf[i] );
        }
     Dimension d = tf[0].preferredSize();
     ButtonPanel = new Panel();
       add( "South", ButtonPanel );
     theButton = new Button( "Ok" );
       ButtonPanel.add( theButton );
     setResizable(false);
       }

/** Deal with the user hitting either OK or Cancel. In either
case, fill the argument Vector with whatever's in the
TextFields and dispose of the dialog box.
*/
    public boolean action(Event e, Object o) {
     if( e.target instanceof Button )
        {
        args = new Vector(1);
        for( int i = 0; i < 7; i++ ) {
            if( tf[i].getText().length() > 0 &&
                  (tf[i].getText().compareTo("") != 0 ))
              {
              byte b[] = new byte[tf[i].getText().length()];
              tf[i].getText().getBytes( 0, b.length, b, 0 );
              args.addElement( b );
              }
          }
          }
     dispose();
       return true;
     }
     }
```

FileFinder's well-behaved **run** method has been replaced by a **run** method that tries to open a file and write directly to it. The **run** method starts out well-behaved, reporting its startup via **reportStart**, and writing output to the results file via **writeOutput**. This write works because it goes through the **AgentContext**. Then EvilAgent gets into trouble. He reads the **acl.write** property just to get a good directory to write into. Then he tries to open a **FileOutputStream** in that directory. This action causes a call to **writeCheck**. **writeCheck** discovers that there's no **AgentContext** on the stack (**classDepth** returns -1) and throws an exception. Figure 10.3 shows the screen and standard output when our EvilAgent tries to run on an AgentServer.

As you can see from the debugging output, the **FileOutputStream** constructor in **EvilAgent.run** called **checkWrite**, which threw an **AgentServerSecurityException**. The illegal output file was never opened, and the **run** method terminated.

Notice that the EvilAgent's call to **AgentContext.writeOutput** did not throw an exception even though it caused a call to the same **FileOutputStream** constructor (via **AgentContext**)! The **SecurityManager** detected the **AgentContext** interface and allowed the file write on that call, but noticed the lack of an **AgentContext** in the misbehaved write call and threw an exception.

This file-write prohibition is a good start for a security strategy. A full-featured version would at least put a leash on network I/O and local program execution.

Figure 10.3

The EvilAgent meets his match.

However, using the techniques we've developed here, we can quickly add any other bits of security we might need.

Conclusion

Java applet security is a work-in-progress. In many cases, applet security restrictions are so severe that applets need to connect to a server daemon to get any useful work done at all. In this chapter, we've seen how applets are restricted, and how they can tell what those restrictions are by querying the system properties.

We've seen the mechanism, the **SecurityManager** class, that browsers use to protect the system against rogue applets. We've implemented our own **SecurityManager** to protect the AgentServer from rogue agents in the same way that browsers protect themselves from rogue applets. And within that **SecurityManager**, we've implemented one piece of a more sophisticated security strategy that rivals some of the mechanisms that browsers themselves implement.

Java Keywords

Keyword	Description
Abstract	Class modifier
boolean	Used to Defines a boolean data type.
break	Used to Breaks out of loops
byte	Used to Defines a byte data type.
byvalue	Not implemented yet
cast	Used to Translates from type to type
catch	Used with error handling
char	Used to Defines a character data type (16-bit).
Class	Used to Defines a class structure.
const	Not implemented yet
continue	Used to Continues an operation
default	Used with the switch statement
do	Used to Creates a do loop control structure.
Double	Used to Defines a floating-point data type (64-bit)
else	Used to Creates an else clause for an if statement
extends	Used to subclass
final	Used to Tells Java that this class can not be subclassed
finally	Used with exception to determine last option before exiting
float	Used to Defines a floating-point data type (32-bit)
for	Used to Creates a for loop control structure.
future	Not implemented yet
generic	Not implemented yet
goto	Not implemented yet
if	Used to Creates an if-then decision-making control structure
implements	Used to Defines which interfaces to use
import	Used to References external Java packages
inner	Used to Creates control blocks
instanceof	Used to Determines if an object is of a certain type
int	Used to Defines an integer data type (32-bit)

Keyword	Description
interface	Used to Tell Java that the following code is an interface
long	Used to Defines an integer data type (64-bit)
native	Used when Callsing external code
new	Operator used when Createsing an instance of a class (an object)
null	References to a non-existent value
operator	Not implemented yet
outer	Used to Creates control blocks
package	Used to Tells Java what package the following code belongs to
private	Modifier for classes, methods, and variables
protected	Modifier for classes, methods, and variables
public	Modifier for classes, methods, and variables
rest	Not implemented yet
return	Used to Sets the return value of a class or method
short	Used to Defines an integer data type (16-bit)
static	Modifier for classes, methods, and variables
super	Used to References the current class' parent class
switch	Block statement used to pick from a group of choices
synchronized	Modifier that Tells Java that only one instance of this method can be run at one time
this	Used to References the current object
throw	Statement that Tells Java what exception to pass on an error
transient	Modifier that can Accesses future Java code
try	Operator that is used to Tests for exceptions in code
var	Not implemented yet
void	Modifier for Setsting the return value of a class or method to nothing
volatile	Variable modifier
while	Used to Creates a while loop control structure.

What's on the CD-ROM?

- Web hyperlinks to the author and The Coriolis Group for getting technical support/addenda.
- Source code for all the example applets.
- HTML-hyperlinked guide to the example applets in each chapter. You can run the sample applets from within the guide.
- Exercises (with answers) to test your knowledge of each chapter's material.
- Hyperlinked documentation for the example applets.
- Documentation for running the standalone applications.
- The complete *Agent System,* source code and documentation.
- Dozens of applets not discussed in the book including:
  - The nuclear plant.
  - Missile command.
  - The game of life.
  - The Battle of the Java Sea.
  - … and many others.

All the material on the CD-ROM is linked together within a master HTML document. You can run the applets, view the applet source code, and view the documentation of that source code—all from within your Web browser.

Index

B

BackPanel class, **167**
Bartlett, Neil, 5
bind, 245
block
   synchronized, **196**-197
Boolean (composite type), 36
BorderLayout class, 123
   example (**Dialog**), 143
browser
   applet context, 96
   applet execution, 85
   applets, access to list of, 108
   behavior expected of, 86
   document, formatting, 79
   on applet resize, 82
   environment and system properties, 390
   file I/O restrictions, 56
   security, 248, 389
   SecurityManager class and, 14
   setSecurityManager, 395
   system resource access and, 14
   threaded applet and, 86
   threads belonging to, 199
Button class
   action, 133
buttons, 132–138
   event, catching, 133
bytecode file, 10
   vs. traditional executable, 11

C

C / C++
   vs. Java
   arrays, 38
   arrays, multi-dimensional, 39
   casting, 37
   delete, 108
   event handling, 145
   goto, 34
   inter-process communication, 199
   object of unknown type, 17
   pointers, 46
   socket I/O, 72
   variable, size of, 36
   void *, 18

Java equivalents
   #include directive, 27
   char*, 46
   runtime library, 36
   run-time type information, 338
   compatibility with Java, 34–40
   incompatibility with Java, 44–46
call stack, 314
CardLayout class, 123
cast, 37
   illegal, 18
   nextElement, return value, 101
catch block
   execution of, 318
   vs.**finally** block, 322
catch clause, 318
   cascaded, 322–323
   cascaded with **finally** clause, 323
Character (composite type), 36
checkWrite Methods, and Helper
   Methods, **407**
class
   attached to package, 27
   data, 340-341, 354, 382
   declared as **final**, 34
   file, equivalent to, 26
   implementing an interface, 41
   importing, 27
   instantiating, 354
   instantiation, 16, 340
   vs. interface, 18
   lead, 382
   loaded, and AgentServer, 364
   loading, 28, 341
   browsers, 364
   multiple, 360–364
   security, 395
   local, 342
   multiple inheritance, 46
   namespace, 26
   not attached to package, 27
   vs. object, 72–73
   private, loading, 358–364
   public, 27
   public vs. **private**, 29
   resolving references, 354, 383
   subclassing, 18
   restricted by **final**, 34
   superclass and, 19